Voices of
Revolutionary
America

Voices of Revolutionary America

Contemporary Accounts of Daily Life

Carol Sue Humphrey, Editor

Voices of an Era

AN IMPRINT OF ABC-CLIO, LLC
Santa Barbara, California • Denver, Colorado • Oxford, England

Library of Congress Cataloging-in-Publication Data

Humphrey, Carol Sue, 1956–
    Voices of revolutionary America : contemporary accounts of daily life /
Carol Sue Humphrey, editor.
        p. cm. — (Voices of an era)
    Includes bibliographical references and index.
        ISBN 978-0-313-37732-7 (hard copy : alk. paper) — ISBN 978-0-313-37733-4 (ebook)
    1. United States—History—Revolution, 1775–1783—Sources.   2. United States—Social life
and customs—1775–1783—Sources.   3. United States—History—Revolution, 1775–1783—Social
aspects—Sources.   I. Title.
    E203.H89   2011
    973.3—dc22   2010047815

ISBN: 978-0-313-37732-7
EISBN: 978-0-313-37733-4

15   14   13   12   11   1   2   3   4   5

This book is also available on the World Wide Web as an eBook.
Visit www.abc-clio.com for details.

Greenwood
An Imprint of ABC-CLIO, LLC

ABC-CLIO, LLC
130 Cremona Drive, P.O. Box 1911
Santa Barbara, California 93116-1911

This book is printed on acid-free paper ∞

Manufactured in the United States of America

CONTENTS

Contents

PREFACE

PRIMARY DOCUMENTS

The American Revolution constituted a pivotal event because it resulted in the creation of the United States. Historians have focused much of their attention on the battles and the important political events related to the war as well as the major leaders involved in the Revolution. They have paid less attention to the daily lives of people living at the time. The documents included in this volume are intended to provide insight into people's daily lives and how those lives were affected by the war. Some of the documents included are by famous and influential people such as Thomas Jefferson and Benjamin Franklin. Other documents discuss the experiences of lesser-known people such as Moses Hall and Temperance Smith. Although the details of their experiences are different, each person saw his or her life change in dramatic ways because of the conflict with Great Britain and the fighting resulting from the war. The original spelling and punctuation have been preserved in each document in order to provide a more realistic view of the lives of the people who lived through the Revolution and all the changes it produced.

ORGANIZATION OF SECTIONS AND SPECIAL FEATURES

The documents included in this book are divided into 46 sections that deal with various aspects of daily life during the American Revolution. Each section also includes other materials that will help the reader better understand the documents. Each section begins with an "Introduction" that sets the historical context for the documents. Also included is a list of items to "Keep in Mind While You Read" intended to help the reader evaluate the documents in each section. Following the documents, each section concludes with an "Aftermath" essay discussing the results and aftermath of the documents and a set of questions to "Ask Yourself" about the documents. Each section ends with "Topics and Activities to Consider" that provide ideas for papers or projects related to the material discussed in the documents as well as lists of further reading, television and films, and Web sites for additional research. Many of the sections also include "Definition Fact Boxes" that explain terms used in the documents and sidebars to further clarify some topic related to the document. Also included in the book are an overview "Introduction" that summarizes key events of the American Revolution and describes its impact on people, a chronology of the main events during the American Revolution, a biographical appendix that identifies people referred to in the sections, and a glossary of key terms used in the sections. All these materials are included in order to aid the reader in understanding the documents and how they reflect the lives of Americans during the turmoil of the Revolutionary War era. These documents and their supporting materials will be useful for anyone interested in learning more about what it was like to live during the American Revolution, whether for a class assignment or just from personal interest.

INTRODUCTION

CAUSES OF THE AMERICAN REVOLUTION

The American Revolution developed out of an argument between Great Britain and its American colonies over taxes. When the French and Indian War ended in 1763, Great Britain had successfully defeated the French and had driven them from the continent of North America. But the British had also amassed a large national debt because of the cost of fighting the war. British leaders sought ways to raise additional funds without raising taxes at home. The logical source for such funds appeared to be the colonies in North America. Arguing that the war had been fought primarily to protect the British colonies from French incursions, British officials suggested a number of different taxes to be applied to the colonies in an effort to raise money to pay off the war debt. These taxes included the Sugar Act of 1764, the Stamp Act of 1765, and the Townshend Duties of 1767.

From the initial effort at taxation by the British, colonists complained that the taxes were not fair. They argued that they were not represented in the British Parliament that had passed the taxes, and this fact made the taxes illegal. Colonists believed that only people they could vote for could represent them, while the British believed that every member of Parliament represented every citizen of the Empire, and thus the colonists were adequately represented. Because these differing definitions of representation were not fully clear at the time, each side accused the other of lying and misleading the public because each side talked about representation while meaning very different realities.

ESCALATION OF EVENTS AND AMERICAN VICTORY

The growing disputes over taxes slowly degenerated into a situation that could not be settled peacefully. Riots occurred in a number of colonies in the late 1760s, resulting primarily in property destruction (including the home of the royal governor of Massachusetts, Thomas Hutchinson, which was destroyed in a riot against the Stamp Act in 1765). In Boston in March 1770, a group of British troops fired into a crowd because they feared for their safety. This event became known as the Boston Massacre and further rallied many Americans in opposition to British rule. In December 1773, a group of men in Boston threw 342 chests of tea into the harbor to protest the Tea Act, a piece of British legislation passed earlier in the year to save the East India Company from financial ruin. The British reacted to the Boston Tea Party with the Coercive Acts, legislation intended to rein in the growing conflict between the mother country and her colonies. The result was the exact opposite: the colonies rallied around Massachusetts, the primary focus of the legislation, and began moving toward independence.

The actual fighting in the American Revolution began at Lexington and Concord, Massachusetts, on April 19, 1775. Fifteen months later, in July 1776, the colonies declared their independence. Fighting continued throughout the former colonies. In the early months of the war, the fighting was centered in New England. Beginning in the middle of 1776, the focus shifted to the middle states of Pennsylvania, New York, and New Jersey. In 1777 American forces under the command of Horatio Gates defeated a British army in such a spectacular fashion at Saratoga, New York, that the French began to openly support the Americans. In 1778 the British moved their focus south by conquering Georgia. They hoped to retake their former colonies one at a time, but that effort failed. In October 1781 American and French forces under the command of General George Washington defeated the British army under Lord Charles Cornwallis at Yorktown, Virginia. This victory marked the end of the fighting in the American Revolution. The American Revolution officially ended in 1783 with the signing of the Treaty of Paris, and the United States officially became independent.

EFFECTS ON DAILY LIFE

Throughout these years of arguing and fighting, people saw their daily lives greatly affected by the events surrounding the Revolution. Even if they lived far away from the center of the fighting, people saw their lives changed as some men went off to fight while family members back home had to keep things running in their absence. War also produced shortages of goods as the military conflict interfered with trade and pushed prices higher due to the shortages. But people also continued to engage in normal day-to-day activities such as weddings and parties in an effort to maintain some sort of normality in the midst of crisis. The American Revolution constituted a major event on a national scale, but its impact on individuals varied depending on their location and interest in the changes produced by the war. Trying to ascertain the various ways the American Revolution affected people's daily lives helps us better understand the overall impact of the war in ways that extend beyond its military and political results. For some people, it was a new beginning in life, while others sought to continue to live their lives as they had always done. But almost no one could ignore the Revolution because its impact forever changed the settlements along the eastern coast of North America, and that result impacted everyone's life to some extent.

How to Evaluate Primary Documents

Historians depend heavily on primary sources to gain insight into how people felt about events impacting them. Primary sources are letters, diaries, and other documents produced at the time an event occurred or by people who lived through the event. In evaluating such documents, it is always important to consider a number of questions in order to adequately access the validity of a document's content.

First, historians consider who wrote the document. It is useful to investigate the author in an effort to understand who the author was, where the author came from, and how that might have affected what the author wrote. It is also important to know when and where the document was written, and how that might have affected what was written. A document written in the heat of battle provides a very different account of a battle than one written years after the conflict occurred. The intended audience of a document is also important. Is the document a letter for a family member or a piece intended to be published for wider public consumption? People often appear to be more honest in personal documents, but that is not always true in wartime as people often downplay problems or conflicts in order to protect loved ones from a brutal truth. Finally, why did the author write the document? Was the author trying to report an event or preserve a memory, make some money through a publication, or change public opinion about some event or action? The purpose in writing always influences the story that is told. Collecting answers to all these questions helps the historian assess the historical context for the document and evaluate any potential bias that exists in the document being studied.

Once these questions have been answered, the historian considers the actual content of the document. It is important to understand what is being said by the author, so the reader should look for key words and passages as well as the main thesis. Also, the reader should consider what assumptions influenced the writer because of the writer's personal history and background. People are always influenced by their social and economic background as well as the culture they have grown up in, and these influences can be ascertained in people's writings. Also important is the method of dissemination of the document. In this modern age of almost instantaneous communication, it is important to remember that in the past, sharing news and information took much longer because of the slowness of travel. However, a letter or newspaper was still welcome news whenever it arrived because it was fresh for the recipient (even if weeks had passed since its production).

Ultimately, a primary source document can provide a window into the thoughts and actions of people in the past. But there are always limitations because of the reality that people's experiences influence what they think and how they react. That holds true for the author of the document as well as the reader. So, it is important for the modern reader to carefully evaluate historical documents in an effort to remove the biases of the present as well as of the past in the hopes of gaining as accurate a sense of past events as possible. The documents included in this volume are intended to provide some insight into the day-to-day experiences of people who lived in the North American colonies during the Revolution. Some documents may be difficult to read because the original spelling and punctuation have been maintained, but this adds to the sense of historical accuracy.

Front page of the *Connecticut Courant,* November 25, 1776, Hartford, CT.

Title page of *Narrative…of a Revolutionary Soldier,* by Joseph Plumb Martin.

Page one of a letter from Abigail Adams to John Adams, July 13, 1776.

CHRONOLOGY OF EVENTS FROM THE ACCESSION OF GEORGE III TO THE THRONE OF GREAT BRITAIN TO THE END OF THE AMERICAN REVOLUTION, 1760–1783

1760	October 25	George III ascends to the throne of Great Britain.
1763	February 10	The Treaty of Paris ends the Seven Years War between Great Britain, and France and Spain. A 7,000-man army remains in the colonies because no one orders them home to Britain.
	October 7	The Proclamation Line drawn along the Appalachian Mountains by British authorities forbids settlement in the West by white settlers.
1764	April 5	The Sugar Act is passed by Parliament, reducing the duty on foreign molasses. The colonial response produces cries of "no taxation without representation."
	September 1	The Currency Act prohibits issues of legal-tender currency in the colonies.
1765	March 22	The Stamp Act is passed. It requires the purchase of stamps for all printed materials produced in the colonies. Protests and riots occur throughout the colonies.
	March 24	The Quartering Act is passed, forcing colonials to pay to house and feed the army stationed in the colonies.
	October 19	The Stamp Act Congress meets in New York and adopts a non-importation agreement to protest the Stamp Act.
1766	March 18	The Stamp Act is repealed by Parliament, which then passes the Declaratory Act, asserting its authority to bind the colonies "in all cases whatsoever."
	March–September	Anti-rent riots by tenant farmers occur in New York.
1767	June 29	The Townshend Duties are passed, placing taxes on paper, paint, glass, lead, and tea.
	June 29	The American Board of Customs is established.

	November 30	The first of John Dickinson's 12 *Letters from a Farmer in Pennsylvania* protesting the Townshend Duties is published in the *Pennsylvania Chronicle*.
1768	January	The office of secretary of state for the colonies is established in Britain. It is the first executive department with exclusively colonial concerns. Lord Hillsborough, the president of the Board of Trade, is appointed to fill the post.
	February 8	Dickinson's 12th letter is published. These letters were published as a pamphlet in March 1768. A new edition of the pamphlet appeared in April 1768 with one essay added.
	February 11	The Circular Letter is adopted by the Massachusetts House of Representatives. It becomes a cause célèbre because of a British order in April for its repeal.
	April 9	John Hancock's sloop *Liberty* is seized.
	October 1	Four regiments of British troops arrive in Boston.
1770	January 28	Lord North's ministry is formed.
	March 5	The Townshend Duties are repealed, except for the duty on tea. The repeal took effect on December 1.
	March 5	The Boston Massacre occurs, leaving five dead as troops fire into the crowd.
1772	June 9	The British schooner *Gaspee* is burned in Rhode Island.
	November 2	The Boston Committee of Correspondence is formed. The idea for similar committees later spread throughout all the colonies.
1773	May 10	The Tea Act is imposed, establishing a monopoly on the colonial tea trade for the East India Company in order to save it financially.
	December 16	The Boston Tea Party occurs to protest the Tea Act.
1774	March–June	Parliament passes the Coercive Acts as punishment for the Boston Tea Party. These laws were seen as a threat by all the colonies because of their interference with local government.
		Parliament adopts the Quebec Act, organizing a government for French Canada. It was wise legislation, but it was grouped by the colonials along with the Coercive Acts as the Intolerable Acts.
	September 5	The First Continental Congress meets in Philadelphia.
	September 28	Joseph Galloway submits his Plan of Union to the Continental Congress. It was voted down on October 22, 1774.
	October 20	The Continental Congress adopts the Continental Association (a non-importation/non-exportation agreement). It took effect on December 1.

1775	April 14	Pennsylvania Quakers form the first antislavery society in the world.
	April 19	The Battles of Lexington and Concord occur.
	May 10	Fort Ticonderoga is taken by American forces.
	May 10	The Second Continental Congress meets in Philadelphia.
	June 14	The Continental Army is created by the Continental Congress.
	June 17	George Washington is appointed commander in chief of the Continental Army.
	June 17	The Battle of Bunker Hill occurs.
	July 6	Congress adopts its Declaration of the Causes and Necessity for Taking up Arms.
	August 23	King George III proclaims the colonies in open rebellion.
	December 31	American forces fail to take Quebec. Colonial general Montgomery is killed.
1776	January 10	Thomas Paine publishes *Common Sense*.
	March 17	British troops evacuate Boston.
	May 15	Congress calls on the colonies to suppress all British authority, and to establish governments under the authority of the people.
	July 2	The Second Continental Congress declares independence.
	July 3	The British take New York City.
	July 4	The Second Continental Congress adopts the Declaration of Independence to explain why they were breaking away from Great Britain.
	August 27	The Battle of Long Island, New York, occurs. The Americans are defeated by troops under General William Howe.
	December 26	The Battle of Trenton occurs.
1777	January 3	The Battle of Princeton occurs.
	September 11	The Battle of Brandywine, Pennsylvania, occurs. Washington is defeated in his effort to protect Philadelphia.
	September 26	The British occupy Philadelphia.
	October 4	The Battle of Germantown, Pennsylvania, occurs. Howe repulses Washington's attack.
	October 7	British general Burgoyne surrenders at Saratoga.
	November 15	The Articles of Confederation are adopted by the Continental Congress but not ratified by all states until 1781.
	December 19	Washington retires his troops to Valley Forge for the winter. The Continental Army remained there until June 19, 1778.

1778	February 6	The now united former colonies conclude a military alliance and commercial treaty with France. This would be the first and only military alliance by the United States until the adoption of the North Atlantic Treaty Organization in 1949.
	June 18	The British evacuate Philadelphia.
	June 28	The Battle of Monmouth, New Jersey, occurs. Although the outcome was indecisive, Washington's troops stand up to British regulars.
	December 29	The British seize Savannah, Georgia.
1779	February	General George Rogers Clark captures Vincennes and ends British control of the Northwest.
	June	Spain enters the war against Britain.
1780	May 12	The Continental Army surrenders 5,500 men and the city of Charleston, South Carolina, following a six-week siege.
	August 16	Major General Horatio Gates is defeated by British troops under Lord Cornwallis at Camden.
	October 7	The Battle of King's Mountain, South Carolina, occurs. The British and Tories are defeated.
1781	January 17	The Battle of Cowpens, South Carolina, occurs. The British under Lieutenant Colonel Banastre Tarleton are defeated by troops under Colonel Daniel Morgan.
	March 15	The Battle of Guilford Courthouse, North Carolina, occurs. The outcome is indecisive, but Cornwallis withdraws to the Atlantic coast.
	October 19	Cornwallis surrenders to Washington at Yorktown, Virginia.
1782	March 20	The fall of Lord North's ministry in Great Britain occurs.
1783	September 3	The Treaty of Peace with Great Britain is signed, recognizing American independence.

DISRUPTION
AND CONTINUATION
OF DAILY LIFE

1. REGULAR ROUTINES IN LIFE: NEWSPAPER OBITUARIES (1768–1782)

INTRODUCTION

Even in the midst of a war like the American Revolution, life continues in a routine of sorts as births, weddings, and deaths occur on a regular basis. Part of the process of saying goodbye to the dead has always revolved around remembering their lives. Printed obituaries in newspapers have played a part in that remembering process from the moment printers began publishing newspapers in the 17th century. The events of the American Revolution often interfered with the production of newspapers because printers had to flee an approaching army or had difficulty acquiring the needed materials for publication, but obituaries continued to be published throughout the war whenever newspapers appeared. What is said in an obituary not only tells the reader something about the deceased, but also tells the reader much about the society in which the deceased person lived. Generally, in the 18th century, only the leading members of the community or members of their families would have obituaries published. Obituaries during the Revolutionary era clearly indicated the gender divisions of the time because obituaries of men were almost always longer and more detailed than obituaries of women. The obituaries here first appeared in the *Connecticut Courant,* a newspaper published in Hartford, Connecticut.

KEEP IN MIND WHILE YOU READ

1. Hartford was the capital of Connecticut and thus the center of business for a good portion of the central part of the state.
2. Most of the towns where these people lived did not have a locally printed newspaper, so the *Connecticut Courant* was probably the closest publication available in which to publish an obituary.

Documents: Newspaper Obituaries from the Connecticut Courant (1768–1782)

Connecticut Courant (Hartford), June 20, 1768

Last Monday died at Middletown, in the 41st Year of her Age, Mrs. Sarah Easton, Wife of Capt. John Easton of that Place.

Connecticut Courant (Hartford), April 26, 1774

On the 4th day of instant April died at his House in Wethersfield, Col. ELIZUR GOODRICH, had just compleated his 81st year. He bore a fair and honourable character thro' life, and particularly in the various and important offices he sustained in the service of the public. He was many years a justice of the peace, and in the year 1745 served as Lieutenant-Colonel in the expedition against Louisboroug, where, by his general conduct his great humanity and benevolence, he obtained the estimation and love of the officers and soldiery. In the year 1755 he was appointed a Colonel of a regiment raised in this colony for the expedition against Canada, and during the campaign was taken sick and returned home, and continued a long time in a low state of health. He has been many times a member of our **General Assembly,** but for some time before his death declined all public business. He was long time a member of the Church of Christ in this place, a constant and devout attender on the public worship of God and so continued to the last. His fear and love of God, his universal kindness and tenderness to his neighbour, render his memory truly precious.

> **General Assembly:** legislative assembly, particularly of some states in the United States

Connecticut Courant (Hartford), October 9, 1775

Last Tuesday died at his Seat in Wethersfield, greatly lamented, Doct. EZEKIEL PORTER, AT 68. He was a celebrated Surgeon, and particularly excelled as a Setter of broken and dislocated Bones, was very extensively improved, and in difficult Cases, most remarkably successful. Favoured with an uncommonly healthy, vigorous and robust Constitution of Body, he was enabled to undergo extraordinary Fatigues and Self-Denials, to which, from a deep rooted Principle of Tenderness and Compassion, he readily submitted to the last, by Night as well as by Day, whenever he was called to administer to the Relief of the distressed.

As a Christian, he was very exemplary, punctually and devoutly attending upon the Institutions of the Gospel, as he could, without neglecting Mercy for Sacrifice; paying a conscientious Regard to ALL the Precepts of Christ, and particularly abounding in Works of Charity.

As a Member of the Common-Wealth, he was inoffensive, public-spirited, and a hearty Friend to that Liberty with which God and the Constitution have made us free. His natural Temper was very modest, even, amiable and engaging. In his House he was exceeding hospitable. As an Husband, he was faithful, kind, tender and endearing. As a Parent, wise, indulgent, generous and affectionate. As a Master, condescending, humane, and obliging. In short, he was a sincere Lover of God and Mankind, and was greatly esteemed and beloved by all who had the Happiness of being acquainted with him; and it may be truly said that it is rare to find a Man, that has done less Hurt, and more Good in the World than Doctor PORTER. After six Days confinement with a severe complicated Disorder, he rested from his Labours, and is (we trust) gone to reap the blessed Fruits of them.

Connecticut Courant (Hartford), January 29, 1776

Died, on the 23d inst. after a short conflict, with the throat distemper, at Northampton, aged 18, Miss Electa Hunt, youngest daughter of Mr. John Hunt, of that town, and sister to the late Rev. Mr. Hunt. May this repeated stroke of divine providence be sanctified to that greatly afflicted family, and to the surviving acquaintance of the deceased. A noble generosity of mind, and a charming simplicity and sweetness of manners were some of the many virtues with which the glorious original and fountain of all excellence had adorned this amiable young lady.

The following Character of the Rev. Mr. Hunt, is inserted by particular Desire.

The 20th of last month, about 9 in the morning, died of a lingering **consumption,** at his father's house in Northampton, the Rev. Mr. JOHN HUNT; whose decease is justly es-teemed a heavy loss, not only to his relatives and friends there, but the public in general, and to that society of christians in special, to whom he ministred in Boston, till by the tyranny of the times he and they were forced to leave their habitations, and scatter them-selves throughout the country; Since which the house where they usually met for the worship of God, has, with indecency, not to be parallelled by the conduct even of barbarous pagans, been turned into a *training place* for a number of light horse, sent from England to trample on the constitutional rights of the people in these lands.

> **consumption:** progressive wasting away of the body

It would be inglorious to the memory of so worthy a Gentleman as Mr. Hunt was, not to take public notice of his character, as it was eminently excellent and distinguishing.

The God of nature endowed him with intellectual powers far exceeding the common standard. Few were favored with a brighter understanding, a quicker invention, a more sprightly imagination, and a more sound and solid judgement. His acquirements in the learned sciences, considering his youthful age, reflected honour on him; and had the Lord of life been pleased to have continued him in existence, he would have made as shining a figure as perhaps any of his predecessors in the office he was placed in after them.

The moral framework of his mind was peculiarly amiable. He had nothing in his tem-per that made him morose, peevish, captious, wrathful, or unreasonably selfish; but ever ex-hibited a disposition that was meek, mild, calm, placid, and universally benevolent: And as the effect of their assemblage of good qualities, he approved himself a dutiful son, a loving brother, an agreeable companion, a kind friend, and hearty well wisher to the peace, liberty, and happiness of his country, and mankind in common.

As he sustained the office of a pastor to one of the most noble churches in Boston, it would be a faulty omission, if it was not said of him, that he was worthy of so important a trust, and that he acted in it with prudence, diligence, fidelity, and a becoming concern for the spiritual welfare of the people of his charge. His addresses to them from the pulpit were wisely calculated to enlighten their minds, affect their hearts, and engage them in the practice of pure and undefiled religion before God and the Father. Few exceeded him as a preacher. The subject of his sermons were the most momentous points of christianity, rela-tive both to faith and practice; their composition easy, natural and accurate; and the man-ner of their delivery grave, serious, solemn, and awakening. But beyond all that has been said, he really believed those christian truths he preached to others; and his faith purified his heart, governed his affections and passions, and had a constraining influence to make him a man of God happily furnished unto all good works. And as he lived by faith, so he died in the exercise of it; looking for the mercy of God, thro' our Lord Jesus Christ, to eternal life.

Connecticut Courant (Hartford), April 24, 1781

DIED, At Middletown, last Monday evening, Miss Persis Deshon, late of Boston, on a visit of friendship to that place; after being unwell for about eight weeks, but not confined to the house, was seized with a fit, and expired instantly, to the great grief of her friends and all who had the happiness of her acquaintance.—A loud call to survivors to be prepared to meet the king of terrors.

On Friday the 6th instant, departed this life SAMUEL COBB, Esq. of Tolland, in the 65th year of his age, after a very long and painful sickness, which he endured with very exemplary patience. He descended from a very respectable family in Barnstable, and was by nature, or rather the God of nature, furnished with a sprightly and penetrating genius, which was greatly improved by a collegiate education. When he had finished his academical studies and received the usual honors of college, he applied himself to the study of divinity, and commenced preacher of the gospel; in this sacred employment he was much esteemed, and especially by the best judges—But his voice being low, he found it inconvenient to continue in that business. He then determined to serve mankind as a physician, and became a practitioner in the healing art; in this he shone with distinguished lustre, and was imminently useful in his profession for many years. He was also improved as a minister of justice, and in this character was indeed a terror to evil doers, and a praise to such as did well. He was a firm friend to his country, and early took a determinate part in favor of American liberty. And what was peculiarly amiable, he well supported the character of a christian, as a preacher of the gospel, as a member of society, and as the head of a family. As Divine Providence blessed him with an affluent estate, so also with numerous and respectable family, he has left a disconsolate widow, and nine children, to bewail the loss of a tender consort, and affectionate parent. He died in full belief of the great and all supporting doctrines of the gospel; and with his last dying breath, professed a humble hope and firm reliance on the grace of God, and merits of a Saviour.

The memory of the just is blessed.

Connecticut Courant (Hartford), May 21, 1782

DIED on the 29th of April, in the 57th year of his age, the Rev. Mr. DANIEL WELCH of Mansfield—The disorder which put a period to his life was of short duration, tho' distressing. ON Sunday afternoon, while performing divine service, he was suddenly taken ill, and before sunrise the next morning a breathless corpse—He met death with composure, christian fortitude and a firm reliance on the merits of the Redeemer, whose unsearchable riches he had been displaying in the course of his ministry—He has left a numerous offspring dissolved in tears, who deeply lament the loss of a tender parent, in whose councils, guidance and guardianship they safely confided. The many gifts and endowments which Mr. Welch possessed, commanded esteem and rendered him the delight of his friends and acquaintance. His conversation easy, free, animating and instructive, liberal to the poor, given to hospitality, a lover of good men.—By his death a dark cloud is drawn over the church and society, and a great part of their strength and glory departed. He lived in great harmony and friendship with his people, and was universally esteemed by them as a valuable and useful minister—But his work is done, and we trust he is gone from a world of darkness and sorrow to the regions of unclouded day.

Connecticut Courant (Hartford), May 28, 1782

On Friday the 7th instant departed this life, in the 52d year of her age, Mrs. ELIZA-BETH LEE, the amiable and greatly beloved wife of Col. ISAAC LEE, of Farmington. Her disorder was the small pox, which put a period to her life after enduring extreme distress for about twenty days, with a christian patience and submission. She was peculiarly adorned with social and friendly virtues, and well supported the character of a christian. Her behavior as a wife, a mother-in law, a neighbour and friend, was such as gave the highest satisfaction, and commanded the esteem of all her acquaintance. Has left her consort overwhelmed in tears, and is greatly lamented by her friends and acquaintance.

Connecticut Courant (Hartford), July 2, 1782

Departed this life, on Friday the 21 of June last, the amiable Consort of WILIAM GOODRICH, Esq. of Stockbridge: She was the third daughter to the Hon. TIMOTHY WOODBRIDGE, Esq. late of that Town—She Died in the 40th Year of her Age, after a lingering Illness; in whose Death the Poor have lost a Friend, and the great Circle of her Acquaintance an agreeable Companion, as she lived beloved, she died universally lamented, has left her Husband and three Children, with her Acquaintance to lament her loss—as she lived so she died in the full belief of the great Day of Retribution, whatever degrees of Virtue she possessed, that day will fully discover.

AFTERMATH

One of the reasons that obituaries appeared in newspapers during the American Revolution (and continue to do so today) was because they provided a good method for spreading the word about someone's death. Printing obituaries, as well as birth and wedding announcements of prominent people in the community, provided a major reason for printers to struggle to keep their newspapers going during the war. They knew that people would want this sort of news, and so they would continue to buy the newspapers as long as possible. Newspapers grew in size and frequency of publication during the 19th century, and obituaries continued to be an important part of each issue.

ASK YOURSELF

1. What do you think were the reasons for the different lengths of the obituaries? Gender obviously played a role, but was that the only factor?
2. What characteristics were emphasized in the obituaries? Why do you think they were emphasized?

TOPICS AND ACTIVITIES TO CONSIDER

- Printed obituaries have been appearing for centuries. Investigate how they have changed over the years and how they have remained the same.
- Prior to the invention of the printing press, remembrances of the dead were still created. Investigate how the recently deceased were remembered prior to the appearance of the printing press and newspaper obituaries.
- These obituaries clearly indicate a difference in roles for men and women in 18th century society. Investigate the expected roles for men and women during the Revolutionary era, and see how the people discussed in the obituaries fit the models.

LOUISBURG

Louisboroug, or Louisburg, was the site of a French fortress in Canada. In 1745, during the War of the Austrian Succession, an event occurred that surprised many people in Europe and America. An army made up of men from New England attacked the fort and successfully captured it. New Englanders rejoiced at their success initially, but their elation turned to frustration and disgust in 1748. The Treaty of Aix-la-Chapelle, which ended the war, returned Louisburg to France in exchange for the British trading post at Madras in India. The men from New England who fought at Louisburg thought that British officials had betrayed them and that their sacrifices had been in vain. The Americans believed that their colonies were the most important part of the British Empire, but increasingly areas such as India were becoming more important to leaders in Great Britain. Such misunderstandings helped set the stage for the disagreements that led to the American Revolution.

Further Reading

Hume, Janice. *Obituaries in American Culture.* Jackson: University Press of Mississippi, 2000.

Kann, Mark E. *The Gendering of American Politics: Founding Mothers, Founding Fathers, and Political Patriarchs.* Westport, CT: Praeger, 1999.

Kann, Mark E. *A Republic of Men: The American Founders, Gendered Language, and Patriarchal Politics.* New York: New York University Press, 1998.

Kitch, Carolyn L., and Janice Hume. *Journalism in a Culture of Grief.* New York: Routledge, 2008.

McNulty, Bard. *Older Than the Nation: The Story of the* Hartford Courant. Stonington, CT: Pequot Press, 1964.

Schloesser, Pauline E. *The Fair Sex: White Women and Racial Patriarchy in the Early American Republic.* New York: New York University Press, 2002.

Smith, James Eugene. *One Hundred Years of Hartford's* Courant, *from Colonial Times through the Civil War.* New Haven, CT: Yale University Press, 1949.

2. A FACT OF LIFE: NEWSPAPER REPORTS OF ACCIDENTAL DEATHS (1773–1783)

INTRODUCTION

Accidents happen to people, whether in the midst of a war or during a time of peace. People take precautions against accidents, but it does not always work. Buildings collapse and hurt people, or people eat something they find in the woods and get sick. And driving down the street has always been dangerous, whether using a horse, a wagon, or an automobile. Newspapers have always reported such accidents, partially because their readers want to know what has happened, and partially to warn people so that this sort of accident will not happen again. In each of the news reports below, the writer stated or implied that he hoped that readers would take the tragedy as an example so as to avoid such problems in the future.

KEEP IN MIND WHILE YOU READ

1. Building construction was often carried out by a group of people in the community in order to speed up the process. So, the background for the first accident reported was a common occurrence.
2. Public knowledge about what plants were safe to eat was often limited, so accidental deaths like the ones in the last two reports would have been fairly common.
3. Riding a horse was a common way for an individual to get around in the 18th century, so the person in the second report was probably an experienced rider.

Documents: Newspaper Reports of Accidental Deaths (1773–1783)

Essex Gazette (Salem, Massachusetts), September 21, 1773: *Extract of a letter from New Ipswich, September 13, 1773*

Last Tuesday the most melancholy Accident, of the kind, happened at Wilton, in New-Hampshire Government, that perhaps has been known in the Country:—A large Company was collected there to raise a Meeting-House, and they got up the Body of it, the Beams and Joists, and on these had laid a large quantity of Boards for the more convenient standing; they had also raised part of the Roof, in doing which they had occasion for a number of Crow-bars and Axes, which rested on the Building while the People got together and were in the act of raising another double pair of Principals with a King-Post, when on a sudden the Beam under them broke at the Mortise in the middle, by which upwards of 50 Persons fell to the bottom of the House with the Timber, Boards, Bars, Axes, &c. and exhibited a Scene to the astonish'd Spectators around the House (for there were no Persons in the Bottom of it, all having withdrawn thro' fear of what might happen) which can't be describ'd; and could only be equalled by the Blood and Brains, Shrieks and Groans of the dead and wounded, which were immediately seen and heard.—Three were killed outright, another survived but a short time, and several others have since died of their Wounds; of fifty three that fell not one escap'd without broken Bones, terrible Bruises, or Wounds from the Axes, &c. And as they were Men pick'd from that and the neighbouring Towns, and many of them heads of Families, the News of their Catastrophe filled those Places with Weeping, Lamentation and Woe, and may fitly mind us all that "Man knoweth not his time," but "at such an hour as we think not the Son of Man cometh," and it therefore concerns us to be always ready.

Connecticut Courant (Hartford), March 29, 1774

Last Wednesday the following sorrowful accident happened at East Windsor, **viz.** As Mr. John Huntington of Tolland was attempting to pass a Cart which he met, there being just Room for a Horse to pass between the Cart and a Ditch, the Horse took Fright as he was passing the wheel, run back against the Cattle, and they taking Fright, flung him from his Horse, under the wheel which passed over his Head and Breast, which instantly put an End to his Life. He has left a sorrowful widow, and a large family of Children.

Connecticut Courant (Hartford), August 14, 1775

A few days since three children belonging to Sharon, playing in a meadow, pulled up the hemlock, or wild parsnip root, and eat of it, and in about five hours they all expired, and were buried in one grave the next day. This root is thought by some one of the greatest poisons in nature, & that an extract from it of three grains, would be sufficient to kill any person—great care ought to be taken by parents to prevent their children going among it.

Connecticut Courant (Hartford), October 21, 1783

Cholera Morbus: intestinal disturbance characterized by cramping, diarrhea, and sometimes vomiting resulting from overeating or from eating contaminated foods
viz.: namely

Died at Coventry, one Elias Kreamer, a German; the manner of his death being somewhat singular, it is thought proper the circumstances of it should be made public:—On Sunday the 4th of August last, he in company with a young man of the family in which he resided, made a collection of a quantity of *Toad-stools,* under the notion of *Mushrooms,* which having fryed they eat the evening following; but not having made proper discrimination in their collection, their supper proved a poison to them, operating much like a ***Cholera Morbus,*** of which said Kreamer expired on Wednesday morning of the 7th; the other one happily recovered though affected in the same manner except in degree.

AFTERMATH

Such accidental deaths proved very common well into the 19th century, and they spurred efforts to try to improve controls in order to prevent them. By the 20th century, restrictions had been put in place in an effort to prevent as many such accidental deaths as possible. Communities adopted building codes to try to ensure that construction sites were as safe as possible, and that the completed structures were safe as well. Efforts to identify poisonous plants were publicized so that people could be better informed about what was safe to eat. And rules about traffic in the streets (even before automobiles appeared) tried to control travel in an effort to reduce the accidents on the road. But even the best rules and guidelines cannot eliminate all accidents, so reports such as these continue to appear today.

ASK YOURSELF

1. Why do you think newspaper readers would be interested in stories such as these?
2. Why do you think the people who were killed in each accident failed to see the potential problems they were dealing with?
3. Why do you think the story from the construction accident received more coverage than the other accidents? Was it more unexpected? Or was it because it involved more people? Do you think this is still true in reports of accidents today?

TOPICS AND ACTIVITIES TO CONSIDER

- Many critics have stated that people like to read about accidents because they are bloody and stir up one's emotions. Investigate how accidents and deaths resulting from them have been covered in the media over time. What has changed? What has remained the same?
- Many people have died from eating poisonous plants, which has encouraged efforts to spread knowledge about such things in order to reduce the number of accidental deaths. Investigate the history of efforts to spread general knowledge about poisonous plants.

Further Reading

Copeland, David. *Colonial American Newspapers: Character and Content.* Newark: University of Delaware Press, 1997.

Kingsbury, John Merriam. *Poisonous Plants of the United States and Canada.* Englewood Cliffs, NJ: Prentice Hall, 1964.

Sloan, W. David, and Julie Hedgepeth Williams. *The Early American Press, 1690–1783.* Westport, CT.: Greenwood Press, 1994.

Wilbur, C. Keith. *Home Building and Woodworking in Colonial America.* Old Saybrook, CT: Globe Pequot Press, 1992.

3. Trials of Daily Life: Newspaper Advertisements about Spousal Abuse and Abandonment (1775–1776)

INTRODUCTION

Obviously, war can produce strains on families and marriages as people attempt to deal with the problems brought on by the conflict. But in many cases, turbulent events only add to strains that already existed. In the 18th century, there were not many options for couples who had major marital problems. Wives had no legal identity, and all the property they brought to the marriage became the property of their husbands, so wives generally had no independent source of income. A husband was considered the legal representative for his wife in all cases, and thus he was responsible for any debts she entered into, whether he knew about them or not. There were also few legal outlets in cases of spousal abuse because such issues were considered to be ones that should be dealt with primarily within the home. For women with abusive husbands, there were few options. As indicated by the newspaper advertisements, some women chose to leave in order to escape the abuse.

KEEP IN MIND WHILE YOU READ

1. Husbands were legally responsible for any debts their wives incurred, but taking out advertisements such as these could help if sued in court.
2. The modern concepts of spousal abuse and sexual harassment did not exist in the 18th century.

Documents: Newspaper Advertisements about Spousal Abuse and Abandonment (1775–1776)

Connecticut Courant (Hartford), August 21, 1775

WHEREAS Abigail my wife, has without any cause or provocation deserted my bed and board, and has and still doth refuse to return and live with me; I do therefore strictly forbid all and every person or persons harbouring, or in any way entertaining or detaining her, or crediting her on my account, or having any deal whatsoever with her: And I do now stand ready to receive her if she will return, and provide for her to the utmost of my abilities, and in every respect treat her as a kind and tender husband. TIMOTHY HUBBARD, jun.

Connecticut Courant (Hartford), August 28, 1775

WHEREAS my husband, Timothy Hubbard, has advertised me in the public prints, and forewarned all persons entertaining me, &c,—Altho' 'tis very disagreeable to expose to public view, the miseries and calamities of a distracted family, yet self-defence obliges me to tell the world, That about three years since, I was married to a certain Timothy Hubbard; the whole of which time since I have suffered intolerable abuse and cruelty from him, mostly in secret—have been in constant fear of losing my life; threatening to have it destroyed by violence has been common. About six months since (my patience being spent) I applied to the civil authority of this town for direction; they sent for him, when, before two Justices, he confessed all I laid to his charge, and most faithfully promised reformation—I was advised to make tryal a second time—I accordingly made a sufficient trial, and found I must either quit my life or my husband—I made my choice, which produced the foregoing advertisement, and in which he promises fair, indeed!—he always was excellent at promising, but very forgetful to perform. He invites me to return and live with him—if he has perform'd his engagement to his country, I must go to the camp before Boston to do it, but should not be surprised to find him as perfidious to his officers as to me. He has left no house or estate to return to, to which he has any title—this inconvenience I have been no stranger to since my marriage. 'Tis not possible for me to involve him in debt, where he is known. I hope he will disgorge all his thirst for blood in the cause of his country, and return home a human creature, which would greatly rejoice his much injured wife, who would then be willing to live with and maintain him, or (if he should choose) would give my consent that any person should harbour, entertain, detain or credit him, that was willing so to do. ABIGAIL HUBBARD.

Connecticut Courant (Hartford), October 21, 1776

WHEREAS Esther, my wife, hath eloped from me, these are to forbid all persons trusting her on my account, as I will pay no debt contracted by her; and all persons are forbid harbouring or entertaining said Esther. SOLOMON GOODRICH.

Connecticut Courant (Hartford), November 4, 1776

Whereas Solomon Goodrich has advertised me his wife in the Connecticut Courant, re absenting myself from him; and has forbid all persons trusting me on his account, or entertaining me on any account. I am under a necessity, in the same way, to publish to the world the reasons why I have so absented myself: for there is great blame somewhere, either he or I have acted exceeding wickedly in this affair—he, in so acting, as to make it impossible for me to dwell with him; or I, in absenting myself from him without any just cause. That the impartial world may judge, I now publish a few of the many instances of his injurious conduct toward me.

He has frequently, in instances too many to be enumerated, cruelly pulled my hair—pinch'd my flesh—kick'd me out of the bed—dragged me out by my arm and my heels—dragged me across the room and flung ashes upon me to smother me—haul'd me out of bed in the dead of the night, and flung cold water from the well upon me till I had not a dry thread about me, and was obliged to flee to any of the neighbors for help. His general conduct, and the conduct of his family, and especially his son Solomon's, for these six months back, has manifested the greatest aversion to my being in the family. He has commanded me to be gone out of his family, or he would horsewhip me like a dog, and if that would not compel me, he would kick me to hell. This is a literal, though very concise representation of the ill treatment I have had; the innumerable instances of his other injurious treatment, false representations, and abominable language, I suppress for the present. The truth of the above, I solemnly attest. ESTHER GOODRICH

Sharon, October 22, 1776. THEN Mrs. Esther Goodrich, the subscriber of the foregoing advertisement, made solemn oath to the truth of the facts charged in the same, before me, DANIEL GRISWOLD, Jus. Pac.

AFTERMATH

For the two women involved in the above advertisements, the American Revolution did not seem to help their situations at all. And that proved true for many other women whose day-to-day lives involved dealing with invading armies as well as the everyday problems of producing what was needed to live and survive. But the American Revolution did have an impact on the lives of women in the long run. Ideas about women's roles began to change as people realized that women had contributed to the war effort through their support of boycotts and their running of family businesses in the absence of their husbands. So, general ideas and attitudes about the role of women changed for the better as a result of the American Revolution. But for women who suffered spousal abuse as these two women apparently did, help was a long time in coming. Laws that dealt directly with spousal abuse did not appear on the books until the 20th century.

ASK YOURSELF

1. Why do you think the women chose to flee their homes when they did? Why did they not flee further away? Did they have any other options you can identify?
2. In both cases, each woman resorted to some sort of legal avenue once her husband had published his advertisement denying he was at fault. Doing so was somewhat unusual at the time. Why do you think these women resorted to such an approach? How have efforts to deal with spousal abuse changed since the 18th century?
3. Why do you think the husbands chose to take out the advertisements? Was it primarily to save money if their wives incurred debts, or was it more of a face-saving measure because their wives had abandoned them?

TOPICS AND ACTIVITIES TO CONSIDER

- Ideas about the roles of women have changed over time. Investigate what was considered to be appropriate behavior for women at the time of the American Revolution. How did the Revolution change these ideas?
- Ideas about marital relationships have changed over time. Research what was considered to be the ideal marriage in the 18th century. Include a consideration of how one found a spouse and how marriage changed one's life and expectations at the time.
- Research the ways in which attitudes toward spousal abuse have changed over time. Consider how these attitudes have changed and why these changes have occurred.

Further Reading

Hoffman, Ronald, and Peter J. Albert, eds. *Women in the Age of the American Revolution.* Charlottesville: University of Virginia Press, 1989.

Kerber, Linda K. *Women of the Republic: Intellect and Ideology in Revolutionary America.* Chapel Hill: Published for the Institute of Early American History and Culture by the University of North Carolina Press, 1980.

Mays, Dorothy A. *Women in Early America: Struggle, Survival, and Freedom in a New World.* Santa Barbara, CA: ABC-CLIO, 2004.

Norton, Mary Beth. *Liberty's Daughters: The Revolutionary Experience of American Women, 1750–1800.* Boston: Little, Brown and Company, 1980.

Salmon, Marylynn. *Women and the Law of Property in Early America.* Chapel Hill: University of North Carolina Press, 1986.

4. The Dangers of Daily Life: Newspaper Accounts of Fires (1771–1776)

INTRODUCTION

A major fear of people throughout the colonies in the 1700s was the potential destruction from fires. Once a fire took hold in a community, it was often very difficult to put it out because there were no city-employed fire fighters as there are today. Often, people would actively tear down surrounding buildings in an effort to keep a fire from spreading any farther. Sometimes that helped, but frequently wind would keep blowing the embers around, and the fire would continue to spread and burn until it burned itself out.

Accidental fires were generally started by misuse of candles or cooking fires or because a building was struck by lightning. During the Revolution, some would be started when one side in the conflict began shelling the other side, and people's homes would get caught in the cross-fire. Also, both sides accused each other of purposely setting fires in order to hurt the other. Destroying the buildings in which the opposing army lived would help win ultimate victory. For many people who lived in towns and cities during this period, it really did not matter how the fire started—the result was the loss of their homes and belongings.

KEEP IN MIND WHILE YOU READ

1. The first account was published in a paper in Hartford, Connecticut, but describes a fire in Wilmington, North Carolina, over 700 miles away.
2. The British had pushed George Washington and the Continental Army out of New York City in August 1776, so the fire that is described started only a few weeks after the British occupied the city.

Documents: Newspaper Accounts of Fires (1771–1776)

Connecticut Courant (Hartford), April 2, 1771—Report on a Fire in Wilmington, North Carolina

Last Tuesday morning about two o'clock, a dreadful fire broke out at Capt. Oldfield's fleet, at the south side of the dock. The same moment, that discovered the flames, shew'd the impossibility of extinguishing them. The fire raged with its utmost violence until all the houses in that square, fifteen in number, were totally consumed. Upon the first alarm by the fire bell, the engines were immediately brought to the spot and work'd, but without effect. The inhabitants of the town, and the people from the vessels that lay at the wharfs, shewed utmost alacrity in endeavouring to stop the progress of the flames, and removing what could possibly be saved, but notwithstanding every effort, a very great quantity of dry goods, rum, sugar molasses, flaxseed, and provision was consumed.

The rapidity of the flames threatening the immediate destruction of Mr. Burgwin's [illegible] house, and all the wharfs, houses and stores below the dock, a number of gentlemen exerted themselves at the utmost risque, inciting others by their example, manifested that they preferred the preservation of so great a part of the property of others, to any consideration of their own safety. By this laudable conduct a quantity of naval stores and lumber were removed amidst an almost suffocating smoak, and within the scorching heat of the fire, which was thus prevented from further devastation. Happily the wind was easterly, to this circumstance and to the opposite house being of brick, was in a great measure owing the preservation of the house and store of John Lyon, Esq; Had the fire extended itself to that part of Front-street, the whole of Dock-street, and in all probability the greatest part of the town, must have been reduced to ashes; the loss on this melancholly occasion is computed at Ten Thousand pounds **Proclamation money.** Mr. Robeson lost above 1000l [1,000 pounds]. This is the second time that he has unhappily been a considerable sufferer in this country, by fire.

> **Proclamation money:** coins that were valued according to a proclamation issued by Queen Anne on June 18, 1704. This value was in effect until 1775.

New York Mercury, September 30, 1776

On Saturday, the past Instant, we had a terrible Fire in this City, which consumed about One Thousand Houses, or nearly a fourth of the whole City. The following is the best account we can collect of this melancholy event. The Fire broke out first at the most southerly Part of the City, near White-Hall, and was discovered between 12 and 1 o'Clock in the Morning, the Wind blowing very fresh from the South, and the Weather exceeding dry. The Rebel Army having carried off all the Bells of the City, the Alarm could not be speedily communicated, and very few of the Citizens were in Town, most of them being driven out by the Calamities of War, and several, of the first Rank, sent Prisoners to New England, and other distant Parts. A few Minutes after the Fire was discovered at White Hall, it was observed to break out in five or six other Places, at a considerable Distance.

In this dreadful Situation, when the whole City was threatened with Destruction, Major-General Robertson, who had the Chief Command, sent immediately for two regiments that were encamped near the City, placed Guards in the several Streets, and took every other Precaution that was practicable to ward off the impending Ruin. Lord Howe ordered the Boats of the Fleet to be manned, and after landing a large Number of Officers and Seamen to assist us, the Boats were stationed on each Side of the City in the North and East Rivers, and the Lines near the Royal Army were extended across the Island, as it manifestly appeared the City was designedly set on Fire.

The Fire raged with inconceivable Violence, and in its destructive Progress swept away all the Buildings between Broad Street and the North River, almost as high as the City Hall; and from thence, all the Houses between Broad-Way and the North River, as far as King's College, a few only excepted. Long before the main Fire reached Trinity Church, that large, ancient, and venerable Edifice was in Flames, which baffled every Effort to suppress them. The Steeple, which was 140 Feet high, the upper Part of Wood, and placed on an elevated Situation, resembled a vast Pyramid of Fire, exhibiting a most grand and awful Spectacle. Several Women and Children perished in the fire; their Shrieks, joined to the roaring of the Flames, the Crush of falling Houses, and the widespread Ruin which everywhere appeared, formed a Scene of Horror great beyond Description, which was still heightened by the Darkness of the Night. Besides Trinity Church, the Rector's House, the Charity School, the Old Lutheran Church, and many other fine Buildings, were consumed. St. Paul's Church and King's College were directly in the Line of Fire, but saved with very great Difficulty. After raging about 10 Hours, the Fire was extinguished between 10 and 11 o'Clock, A.M.

During this complicated Scene of Devastation and Distress, at which the most savage Heart might relent, several persons were discovered with large Bundles of Matches, dipped in melted Rosin and Brimstone, attempting to set Fire to the Houses. A New England Man, who had a Captain's Commission under the **Continental Congress,** and in their Service, was seized, having these dreadful Implements of Ruin—on being searched, the Sum of 500l [500 pounds]. was found upon him. General Robertson rescued two of those **Incendiaries** from the enraged Populace, who had otherwise consigned them to the Flames, and reserved them for the Hand of deliberate justice. One Wright White, a Carpenter, was observed to cut the Leather Buckets which conveyed Water; he also wounded, with a **Cutlass,** a Woman who was very active in handing Water. This provoked the Spectators to such a Degree, that they instantly hung him up. One of those Villains set Fire to the College and was seized; many others were detected in the like Crime and secured.

The Officers of the Army and Navy, the Seamen and Soldiers, greatly exerted themselves, often with the utmost Hazard to themselves, and showed all that Alertness and Activity for which they are justly celebrated on such Occasions. To their vigorous Efforts in pulling down such Wooden Buildings as would conduct the Fire, it is owing, under Providence, that the whole City was not consumed; for the Number of Inhabitants was small, and the Pumps and Fire-Engines were very much out of Order. This last Circumstance, together with the Removal of our Bells, the Time and Place of the Fire's breaking out, when the Wind was South, the City's being set on Fire in so many different Places nearly at the same time, so many Incendiaries being caught in the very Fact of setting Fire to Houses; These, to mention no other particulars, clearly evince, beyond the Possibility of Doubt, that this diabolical Affair was the Result of a preconcerted, deliberate Scheme. Thus, the Persons who called themselves our Friends

Continental Congress: body that governed the colonies and later the states during the conflict with Great Britain. The First Continental Congress met in Philadelphia in 1774. The Second Continental Congress met from 1775 to 1781, primarily in Philadelphia.
Cutlass: short, heavy curving cutting sword formerly used by sailors on war vessels
Incendiaries: people who excite or inflame factions and promote quarrels or sedition

and Protectors, were the Perpetrators of this atrocious Deed, which in Guilt and Villany, is not inferior to the Gun-powder Plot; Whilst those who were held up as our Enemies, were the People who gallantly stept forth, at the Risque of their Lives, to snatch us from destruction! Our distresses were very great indeed before, but this Disaster has increased them tenfold. Many Hundreds of Families have lost their all, and are reduced from a State of Affluence to the lowest Ebb of Want and Wretchedness—destitute of Shelter, Food, and Cloathing.

Surely "there must be some chosen Curse—some secret Thunder in the Stores of Heaven, red with uncommon Wrath to blast" the Miscreants who thus wantonly sport with the Lives, Property, and Happiness of their Fellow Creatures, and unfeelingly doom them to inevitable ruin.

AFTERMATH

Accusations of deliberate setting of fires occurred throughout the Revolutionary War period. Fires occurred in a number of major cities during the war, and the people in the city always wondered if the enemy had set the fire in an effort to weaken their opponents. It was not possible to accurately determine the cause of a fire, so most of the time people never knew exactly why a fire started. But as is shown in the description of the New York City fire given above, people often reacted and punished people they were suspicious of even if they did not really know if these people were guilty of starting the fire in the first place. Thus, fires became a part of wartime and added to people's fears in the face of the enemy.

Communities throughout the world have tried to create organizations to help deal with fires, and the American colonies were no different in this matter. As early as 1647, towns appointed FIRE WARDENS to spread the word more quickly so that a fire could be extinguished as quickly as possible. In 1736 BENJAMIN FRANKLIN organized the first volunteer fire department in the American colonies. Called the Union Fire Company, the members personally furnished buckets and bags so they would have the necessary equipment to fight the fires when they occurred. Other towns followed this example, so communities throughout the colonies became more capable of fighting fires when they occurred. As cities grew in the 19th and 20th centuries, local governments would organize government-run fire departments that would serve the entire community. But volunteer fire departments continue to exist today in smaller communities that cannot afford an official organization.

THE GUNPOWDER PLOT

The Gunpowder Plot was a failed assassination attempt by a group of Roman Catholics against James, King of England and Scotland, in 1605. The plan had been to blow up the Houses of Parliament and thus kill the king and most of the Protestant aristocracy. Robert Catesby led the plotters while Guy Fawkes prepared the explosives. Fawkes managed to get the explosives in the room beneath the chamber of the House of Lords, but the plot was discovered before he could set them off. The discovery of the plot on November 5, 1605, led to public trials of a number of the conspirators who were found guilty and hanged. Since 1605, November 5 has been celebrated in Britain as Guy Fawkes Night, and usually involves the setting off of fireworks and the holding of public bonfires.

ASK YOURSELF

1. Was there anything else that could have been done to fight these two fires? Why do you think people stayed and fought the fire rather than getting out of harm's way? Did the losses from the fire increase because people failed to leave soon enough?
2. Why do you think people in New York City were so ready to blame spies for starting the fire? Did they really have enough evidence to support the charge, or were they just reacting to what was happening around them?

TOPICS AND ACTIVITIES TO CONSIDER

- Read additional accounts of fires during the American Revolution. People believed the enemy was setting fires, but is there credible evidence to support such a claim? Why or why not?
- Investigate the development of organized methods to fight fires, beginning with the 17th-century fire wardens and the 18th-century volunteer fire brigades. How have these methods changed over time? How and why have they improved over time?

Further Reading

Ditzel, Paul C. *Fire Engines, Fire Fighters: The Men, Equipment, and Machines, from Colonial Days to the Present.* New York: Crown, 1976.

Hoffer, Peter Charles. *Seven Fires: The Urban Infernos That Reshaped America.* New York: Public Affairs, 2006.

Smith, Dennis. *History of Firefighting in America: 300 Years of Courage.* New York: Dial Press, 1978.

5. The Difficulties of Running a Household during Wartime: Temperance Smith's Account (1775)

INTRODUCTION

Living from day to day can be tough during a war, even if a person does not live near where the battles take place. This proved true for many people during the American Revolution because supplies became difficult to acquire. Obviously, goods normally acquired from Great Britain became scarce as trade declined during the war. But even supplies produced in the colonies could be difficult to obtain as the fighting and movement of the armies interfered with the normal trade routes throughout the country. Because of such problems, many families experienced shortages and other problems during the American Revolution. In many cases, husbands and fathers were off fighting the war, and wives and mothers were forced to deal with acquiring the necessities of life for their families in ways that they had never previously experienced.

The wife of a pastor from Sharon, Connecticut, faced such problems when her husband went off to serve as chaplain for a regiment involved in the Canada campaign in 1775. Pastor COTTON MATHER SMITH strongly encouraged his congregation to help in the fight against the British after word of the Battles of Lexington and Concord arrived in Sharon. He led them in their initial training and then went with them as they marched northward to join the fight. In his absence, his wife, Temperance, had to oversee the acquisition and production of what the household needed to survive. As the wife of a pastor, her responsibilities included not only her own children, but also orphans that needed care and young men studying for the ministry, who depended on the local pastor for help to survive. At the time Pastor Smith marched off to war, 22 people (not including the servants) lived in his house. Years later, his wife described what it was like to oversee such a large household in the middle of a war.

KEEP IN MIND WHILE YOU READ

1. As the wife of a clergyman, it was almost impossible for Mrs. Smith to deny help to anyone who needed it.
2. Running such a large household was normal in many ways for a woman in Mrs. Smith's position in the 18th century, but the absence of her husband increased her responsibilities.

3. News from the battlefront would have been difficult to acquire on a regular basis because of the length of time it took for letters to be delivered in the 18th century. So, lack of knowledge of her husband's fate would have added to Mrs. Smith's worries and concerns.

Document: Temperance Smith's Account (1775)

Your dear Father was among the very first to volunteer and received the honored post of Chaplain to the Fourth Connecticut Regiment, commanded by Colonel Hinman, and ordered to march to Ticonderoga. In common with many other well qualified Pastors my Husband had been in the habit of receiving into his family from time to time such young men as might wish, after leaving college, to fit themselves for the Gospel Ministry. At this time there were five such students in our house. My Husband provided for them by engaging his beloved friend, the Rev. Dr. Bellamy, of Bethlehem, to come and reside in our house, prosecute the education of the young theological students, supply the Sharon pulpit and attend to pastoral duties; a young friend of Dr. Bellamy engaging to perform like brotherly services for him in his parish. As Dr. Bellamy had two students of his own he brought them with him, which added to those already in our house made my family to consist of twenty-two persons besides servants.

In our present state of peace and plenty [1795] this does not seem so very great a burden; but at that time when the exactions of the Mother Country had rendered it impossible for any but the wealthiest to import anything to eat or wear, and all had to be raised and manufactured at home, from bread stuffs, sugar and rum to the linen and woollen for our clothes and bedding, you may well imagine that my duties were not light, though I can say for myself that I never complained even in my inmost thoughts, for if I could even give up for the honored cause of Liberty, the Husband whom I loved so dearly that my constant fear was lest I should sin to idolatry, it would assuredly have ill become me to repine at any inconvenience to myself. And besides, to tell the truth, I had no leisure for murmuring. I rose with the sun and all through the long day I had no time for aught but my work. So much did it press upon me that I could scarcely divert my thoughts from its demands even during the family prayers, which thing both amazed and displeased me, for during that hour, at least, I should have been sending all my thoughts to Heaven for the safety of my beloved Husband and the salvation of our hapless Country; instead of which I was often wondering whether Polly had remembered to set the **sponge** for the bread, or to put water on the **leach tub**, or to turn the cloth in the dying vat, or whether wool had been carded for Betsey to start her spinning wheel in the morning, or Billy had chopped light-wood enough for the kindling, or dry hard wood enough to heat the big oven, or whether some other thing had not been forgotten of the thousand that must be done without fail or else there would be a disagreeable hitch in the house-keeping; so you may be sure that when I went to bed at night, I went to sleep and not to lie awake imagining all sorts of disasters that might happen. There was generally enough that had happened to keep my mind at work if I stayed awake, but that I very seldom did. A perfectly healthy woman has good powers of sleep....

> **leach tub:** wooden tub in which ashes or bark are washed in order to get alkali water needed to make soap
> **sponge:** bread dough after it has been raised or converted into a light, porous mass by yeast or leaven

On the third Sabbath in September Dr. Bellamy gave us a sound and clear sermon in which God's watchful Providence over his People was most beautifully depicted and drew tears from the eyes of those who were unused to weeping, and during the prayer-meeting in the evening the same thought was dwelt upon in a way showing that all who spoke and prayed felt that our God is indeed a Father to all who trust him; so that on that night I went to bed in a calmer and more contented frame of mind than usual. I had, to be sure, been much displeased to find that our supply of bread (through some wasteful misman-agement of Polly's) had grown so small that the baking would have to be done on Mon-day morning, which is not good house-keeping; for the washing should always be done on Monday and the bakings on Tuesday, Thursday and Saturday. But I had caused Polly to set a large sponge and made Billy provide plenty of firing so that by getting up betimes in the morning we could have the brick oven heated and the baking out of the way by the time Billy and Jack should have gotten the clothes pounded out ready for boiling, so that the two things should not interfere with each other. The last thought on my mind after com-mitting my dear Husband and Country into our Maker's care for the night, was to charge my mind to rise even before daylight that I might be able to execute my plans. . . .

As early as three o'clock in the morning I called Nancy and Judy, Jack and young Billy, but would not allow old Billy to be disturbed; whereat the rest marvelled, seeing that I was not used to be more tender of him than of any of the other ser-vants, but rather the less so in that he was my own slave that my Fa-ther had given to me upon my marriage. But I let them marvel, for truly it was no concern of theirs, and by five o'clock the bread was ready to be moulded, the hickory coals were lying in a great glow-ing mass on the oven bottom, casting a brilliant light over its vaulted top and sending such a heat into my face when I passed by the oven mouth that it caused me to think then, as it always does, of Nebu-chadnezzar's fiery furnace, seven times heated. Young Billy was al-ready pounding out the clothes and over the fire Jack was hanging the great brass kettles for the wash, while Nancy and Judy had made ready the smoking hot piles of **Johnny cake,** the boiler of wheat coffee (which was all we could get in those days, and a poor substitute it was for good Mocha) and the big platter of ham and eggs and plenty of good potatoes roasted in the ashes, which is the best way that potatoes can be cooked, in my opinion.

> **Johnnycake:** bread made of white or yellow cornmeal mixed with salt and water or milk; either baked thin in a pan or dropped by spoonfuls onto a hot greased griddle

Source: Smith, Helen E. *Colonial Days and Ways.* New York: The Century Company, 1900, pp. 226–229.

AFTERMATH

Such trials continued for Mrs. Smith and many others throughout the war years, but they eased up a bit in New England when the fighting moved south to New York and Pennsylva-nia in 1776 and then further south to the Carolinas in 1779. Mrs. Smith's situation probably eased a bit because her husband returned home after the Canadian campaign and remained in Sharon for the rest of the war. He still encouraged support for the cause and urged the citizens to serve when called upon to do so. The movement of the fighting away from New England reduced the need for active military duty, but Pastor Smith and the citizens of Sha-ron tried to keep up with what was going on in the war in case their services were needed.

JOSEPH BELLAMY

Joseph Bellamy, the preacher who filled in for Pastor Smith while he marched off to war, had been born and raised in Connecticut. He attended Yale University and graduated in 1735 at the age of 16. A student and supporter of Jonathan Edwards, he was licensed to preach in 1737 at the age of 18. In November 1738 he moved to Bethlehem, Connecticut, where he served as pastor until his death in 1790. A strong supporter of the GREAT AWAKENING revival of the 1740s, Bellamy wrote in support of the New Light theology that developed out of the revival. In 1750 he published *True Religion Delineated,* which became one of the best written expressions of the ideas of the Great Awakening and the focus on the need for personal salvation by all people. Bellamy opened a seminary of sorts in his home and trained many of the next generation of religious leaders in New England. He also increasingly worried about the direction of society with its increasing emphasis on making money and financial success. In an effort to deal with what he considered to be the growing sinfulness of the people, he founded one of the first regular Sunday schools in order to teach moral living to the entire community. Bellamy also grew to support the Revolution as it developed because he believed British rule encouraged immorality and injustice. Thus, he was very willing to help Pastor Smith in his efforts to support the troops from Sharon, Connecticut.

And the deprivations caused by the lack of supplies continued until after the fighting ended in 1781.

ASK YOURSELF

1. Why do you think Pastor Smith thought it necessary to serve in the army when the Revolution broke out?
2. Mrs. Smith expressed frustration with her servants at times. Do you think her frustrations were worsened by the times, or would she have been this frustrated during peacetime as well? Why or why not?
3. Were Mrs. Smith's problems worse than those that might be faced by the spouse of a soldier today? Why or why not? If so, in what ways were Mrs. Smith's problems more difficult?

TOPICS AND ACTIVITIES TO CONSIDER

- Investigate the various chores that Mrs. Smith refers to. What would be involved in carrying out these tasks on a regular basis?
- Investigate accounts of other women running households in the absence of husbands who were off fighting. Compare and contrast these others experiences to those of Mrs. Smith.
- Mrs. Smith refers to the fact that seven young men studying to be ministers lived in her house in 1775. Investigate the education of clergyman in the 18th century, focusing on when and why they would be trained in the house of an active pastor.
- Mrs. Smith refers to owning a slave. Investigate the existence of slavery in New England in the 18th century.

Further Reading

Roth, David Morris. *Connecticut: A Bicentennial History.* New York: W. W. Norton, 1979.

Roth, David Morris. *From Revolution to Constitution: Connecticut: 1763–1818.* Chester, CT: Pequot Press, 1975.

Sedgwick, Charles F. *General History of the Town of Sharon, Litchfield, County, Conn. From Its First Settlement.* Amenia, NY: Charles Walsh, Printer and Publisher, 1877.

Wrong, George M. *Canada and the American Revolution: The Disruption of the First British Empire.* New York: MacMillan Company, 1935.

6. LIVING UNDER FIRE DURING WAR: TIMOTHY NEWELL'S JOURNAL (1775)

INTRODUCTION

Whenever and wherever fighting took place during the American Revolution, people who lived near the battlefield suffered as a result of the conflict. This proved particularly difficult when one army caught the other army inside a town and laid siege to the town in order to force the opposing army to leave or surrender. Sieges, by definition, involve constant harassment and attack, along with attempts to cut off supplies to the town that is surrounded in hopes of forcing surrender. The first community to experience this sort of warfare during the American Revolution was Boston.

Following the Battles of Lexington and Concord on April 19, 1775, the British Army withdrew into the city of Boston while the colonial MILITIA surrounded the city and began to lay siege to it. The Second CONTINENTAL CONGRESS created the CONTINENTAL ARMY in June 1775 and appointed GEORGE WASHINGTON as its commander. Washington took command of the men laying siege to Boston and organized their efforts in hopes of forcing the British to surrender.

For the people living in Boston at the time, the siege was a time of great fear and suffering. The two armies regularly fired cannons at each other, and food and supplies were difficult to acquire. Timothy Newell, a member of the Boston Selectmen (18th-century equivalent of a city council), described what it was like to live in a city under siege in his personal journal.

KEEP IN MIND WHILE YOU READ

1. The colonies had not declared independence at this time, which makes it more complicated to determine who was on which side of the conflict.
2. As selectman, Newell had a responsibility to protect the city of Boston and its inhabitants.

Document: Journal of Timothy Newell reporting on living in a town occupied by the British (1775)

July 2nd. Sabbath morning. I waked up by a cannonade from the lines, which continued two hours. A house on the Neck burnt down thereby, which belonged to the town.

July 8th. Saturday morning at half past 2 waked up with roaring of cannon and small arms upon the lines which continued about two hours. Brown's house burnt.

July 9th. The **Regulars** last night made an advance battery near Browns on the Neck.

July 10th. **Provincials** last night attacked the **Centinels** at the lines, and burnt Brown's shop.

July 12th. Two men of war made a heavy fire on Long Island. The Provincials last night in 65 whale boats and 500 men went over to Long Island and took off 31 head of cattle, with a number of Sheep and quantity of hay and likewise seized on and brought off fourteen of the **Kings Mowers** with the family belonging to the Island—The next day they returned again and set fire to the Mansion house and barn &c.—this within sight of the **Man of war,** who kept up a constant fire on the them.

July 14th. Last night was awoke by the discharge of cannon on the lines—Master James Lovell, Master Leach, John Hunt, have been imprisoned some time past—all they know why it is so is they are charged with free speaking on the public measures; Dorrington his son and daughter and the nurse for blowing up fires in the evenings, they are charged with giving signals in this way to the army without.

July 20th. Mr. Carpenter was taken by the night Patrole—upon examination he had swam over to Dorchester and back again, was tried here that day and sentence of death passed on him and to be executed the next day,—his coffin brought into the **Goal-yard,** his halter bought and he dressed as criminals are before execution. Sentence was respited and a few days after was pardoned.

July 23d. **The Castle,** it is publicly talked, will be dismantled. This evening many guns fired at and from the man of war at N. Boston. Ten or twelve transports it is said sailed this day with 150 soldiers upon a secret expedition for provisions.

August 1st. This week passed tolerably quiet. Last night at half past 12 oclock was awoke with a heavy firing from a Man of War at the Provincials on Phip's farm. From the lines at Charlestown and Boston it appeared as if a general attack was made,—the firing continued till 6 oclock. The George Tavern was burnt by the Regulars and the house at the lighthouse by the Provincials (about 300) who took about 30 soldiers and a number of Carpenters. This morning half past 4 oclock awoke with cannonade and small arms from Charlestown which lasted till eleven oclock after that.

Very trying scenes.

This day was invited by two Gentlemen to dine upon rats.—The whole of this day till sunset a constant fire up Mistic River from the lines and our Centinels at Charlestown and the Provincials from Mount Prospect.

August 4th. John Gill imprisoned, charged with printing **sedition** treason and rebellion.

Castle, the: Fort William and Mary on an island in Boston harbor. Originally built in 1643, it was renamed Fort Independence in 1779.

Centinels: one that watches or guards; sentries

Goal-yard: jail yard

Kings Mowers: unit of men who cut hay and other crops for use by the British Army

Man of war: armed naval vessel

Provincials: soldiers recruited from the North American colonies prior to the American Revolution

Regulars: soldiers in a regular army

sedition: stirring up of rebellion against the government

August 6th. Skirmishing up Mistic river, several Soldiers brought over here wounded. The House at Penny ferry Malden side, burnt.

August 13th. Several **Gondaloes** sailed up Mistic river, upon which the Provincials and they had a skirmish, many shots exchanged but nothing decisive.

August 15th. Cannonade from the lines most of this afternoon on both sides. The General's fleet of Transports arrived from their cruise having taken from the Islands of Gardners &c. about two thousand sheep—one hundred and ten oxen, butter, eggs &c. &c.

August *16th*. Cannonade from both lines.

August 17th. Cannonade again.

August 19th. Ditto. A **42 pounder** split on the lines, killed a **bombardier** and wounded one or two men.

August 20th to 25th. Daily firing from the lines and from the Centinels on both sides.

August 27th. Sabbath. Cannonading from the lines at Charlestown on new **works**—a nearer approach, also much firing of small arms.

August 29th. Several bombs from Ditto on Ditto in the night.

August 30th. Ditto. In the night—ditto. Bombarding from the lines on Bunkers Hill.

September 1st. Ditto. Almost constant firing from the Centinels at each other. New works arise upon the Neck by the Provincials who approach very near.

September 11th. A sergeant and 5 men taken by the Provincials at Dorchester.

September 12th. Went in a boat to relieve a lad blown off in a Canoe....

September 14th to 19th. Began taking down houses at the South end, to build a new line of Works—A good deal of cannonading on both sides the lines for many days past. Several shots came thro' houses at the South end. Capt. Poulet lost his leg, &c. &c. &c.

September 27th. These several days past have been tolerably quiet. The works at the Southward go on. Yesterday the Cerberus Man of war arrived in 7 weeks from London—brings advices of coercive measures by Administration—5 Regiments—one thousand Marines, another Admiral with a fleet of men of war &c.—and General Gage called home.

October 3d. This morning two bomb **Ketches** and several armed vessels with some soldiers sailed on a secret expedition, it is said to demand a Ship belonging to Portsmouth, retaken by our whale boats, and carried into Cape Ann—also to demand of that town 40 seamen which they took from the man of war—if not delivered in 24 hours to bombard the town.

October 6th. The Provincials from Lams Dam discharged their cannon at the Regulars, as they relieve guard at the lines—One Corporal killed with a cannon ball.

October 10th. A negro man belonging to [illegible] wheeling a barrow load of [illegible] in the Streets, the Provost came up to him and **caned** him to a great degree. The negro conscious of his innocence asked him why he did so—he was told it was for wheeling his barrow at the side of the street and not in the middle.—General Gage sailed this day for London and left several thousand Inhabitants in town who are suffering the want of Bread and every necessary of life.

October 13th. Colonel Birch of the **Lighthorse Dragoons** went to view our Meetinghouse which was destined for a Riding School for the Dragoons. It was designed to clear the floor, to put two feet of tan covered with horse dung to make it elastic.—But when it was considered that the Pillars must be taken away, which would bring down the roof, they altered their mind,—so that the Pillars saved us.

bombardier: soldier who runs the cannons and artillery during battle

caned: beat someone with a stick

42 pounder: type of cannon

Gondaloes: heavy, flat-bottomed boats used on New England rivers as gunboats during the American Revolution

Ketches: sailing vessels with sails in the front and back

Lighthorse Dragoons: heavily armed cavalryman

works: fortified structure

batteries: basic tactical and administrative artillery units

grape shot: cluster usually consisting of nine small iron balls put together by means of cast-iron circular plates at top and bottom with two rings and a central connecting rod, and used as a charge for a cannon

Old South Meeting house: largest building in Boston at the time, the church that served as the organizing point for the Boston Tea Party on December 16, 1773

October 17th. Two floating **batteries** from the Provincials from Cambridge river fired a number of cannon into the camp at the Common, the shot went thro houses by the Lamb Tavern, &c.—A deserter who came in this morning, says one of the Cannon split, and killed and wounded several. 5 or 6 hats, a waistcoat and part of a boat came on shore at the bottom of the Common.

October 25th. Several nights past the whole army was ordered not to undress—the cannon all loaded with **grape shot** from a full apprehension the Provincials would make an attack upon the town. The streets paraded all night by the Light Horse.

October 27th. The spacious **Old South Meeting house**, taken possession of by the Light horse 17th Regiment of Dragoons commanded by Lieut Col Samuel Birch. The Pulpit, pews, and seats, all cut to pieces and carried off in the most savage manner as can be expressed and destined for a riding school. The beautiful carved pew with the silk furniture of Deacon Hubbard's was taken down and carried to [illegible]'s house by an officer and made a hog stye. The above was effected by a solicitation of General Burgoyne.

October 30th. A soldier, one of the Light-horse men, was hanged at the head of their camp for attempting to desert. Proclamation issued by General Howe for the Inhabitants to sign an Association to take arms &c.

November 4th. A Proclamation issued for people to give in their names to go out of town, but before the time limit expired a stop was put to it. This like others of the kind seems only designed to continue the vexation of the people.

November 9th. Several Companies of Regulars from Charlestown went over to Phips's farm to take a number of Cattle feeding there. The Provincials came upon them and soon drove them on board boats after an engagement—it is said several are wounded and none killed, but they supposed many of the Provincials killed.

November 16th. Many people turned out of their houses for the troops to enter. The keys of our Meeting house cellars demanded of me by Major Sheriff by order of General Howe. Houses, fences, trees, &c., pulled down and carried off for fuel. My wharf and barn pulled down by order of General Robinson. Beef, Mutton, Port at 1/6 per pound, Geese 14/Fowls 6/8. L. M.

November 19th. A large ship arrived from Plymouth in England with almost every kind of provisions dead and alive, hogs, sheep , fowls ducks, eggs, mince meat, &c. Gingerbread &c. 25 regiments of Kings troops now in this distressed town.

Source: Newell, Timothy. "A Journal Kept during the Time That Boston Was Shut up in 1775–6." *Collections of the Massachusetts Historical Society Collection.* 4th Series, Vol. 1. Boston: Published by the Society, 1852, pp. 264–266, 268–270.

AFTERMATH

The siege of Boston lasted for almost a year. The siege had started on April 19, 1775, following the Battles of Lexington and Concord. The British forces in Boston managed to withdraw on March 17, 1776. It was either withdraw or surrender because the British were unable to break the siege of the city. The British forces went to Nova Scotia to regroup.

JOHN GILL

John Gill was a printer in Boston during the Revolutionary era. On April 7, 1755, he and Benjamin Edes began to publish the *Boston Gazette and Country Journal.* As tensions increased with Great Britain, the *Boston Gazette* became one of the major print outlets for the radicals led by Samuel Adams. While the leaders of the radicals often met at the office of the *Boston Gazette,* Gill concentrated his efforts on the business. Following the Battles of Lexington and Concord, the partnership was dissolved. Edes escaped to Watertown, where he continued the *Gazette.* Gill remained in Boston and was arrested on August 4, 1775, for encouraging sedition and treason in his publications. He was released on October 2, 1775. He started the *Continental Journal and Weekly Advertiser* on May 30, 1776, but it was a much less radical production than the *Gazette* had been. Gill sold the *Journal* on April 28, 1785, as a protest against the state's stamp act. He could not believe Massachusetts would adopt a piece of legislation so similar to the one that had helped spark the Revolution when Great Britain had adopted it 20 years earlier. Gill died on August 25, 1785.

People in the city of Boston who remained loyal to Great Britain also left at this time in order to avoid punishment at the hands of the PATRIOTS. Many went to Canada or to Great Britain. Timothy Newell supported the Patriot side in the conflict, but not in the active and outgoing manner of his fellow selectman JOHN HANCOCK. Rather, Newell perceived his primary responsibility to be to look after the city of Boston and its residents. Thus, he remained in the city throughout the siege. For the city of Boston, the fighting was over. There was no more large-scale fighting in Massachusetts during the American Revolution. The center of the conflict moved south into the middle colonies of New York and Pennsylvania and then further south into the Carolinas and Virginia.

ASK YOURSELF

1. Why do you think Timothy Newell thought it was more important for him to remain in Boston during the siege than attempt to flee?
2. How do you think you would react to the reality of a siege like this one? How might one deal with all the bombings and the shortages of necessary supplies?

TOPICS AND ACTIVITIES TO CONSIDER

- Sieges of major cities have been a common way to fight wars throughout history, and people who live through them have recorded their experiences. Investigate other sieges in American history (such as of New Orleans during the War of 1812, or of Vicksburg or Atlanta during the Civil War). Compare reports of what it was like to live in these cities at the time of the sieges to the experiences reported by Newell.
- City leaders react in different ways when facing crises such as the siege of Boston. Investigate how city leaders have reacted to other crises throughout American history. Have they encouraged their citizens to fight back or tried to calm them down as Newell seemed to do? What explains the variety of reactions over time?

Further Reading

Allison, Robert J. *A Short History of Boston.* Beverly, MA: Commonwealth Editions, 2004.

Carr, Jacqueline Barbara. *After the Siege: A Social History of Boston.* Boston: Northeastern University Press, 2005.

Frothingham, Richard. *History of the Siege of Boston and the Battles of Lexington, Concord, and Bunker Hill.* New York: Da Capo Press, 1970 (1903).

Stephenson, Michael. *Patriot Battles: How the War of Independence Was Fought.* New York: Harper Collins, 2007.

Web Sites

The American Revolution: http://www.nps.gov/revwar

Boston in 1775: http://www.Boston1775.blogspot.com

Events of the American Revolution: http://www.historyplace.com/unitedstates/revolution/

7. Some Things in Life Continue, Even in War: Newspaper Accounts of Weddings (1767–1775)

INTRODUCTION

Regular rituals of life like weddings, births, and deaths continue even in times of war and conflict. This proved true during the American Revolution, but there were differences in how these events were dealt with. This was particularly true for weddings because the military conflict often interfered with the timing for such events as well as the method by which they were conducted and the response to them by the people of the community. Throughout the 18th century, weddings involving people from the middle and lower echelons of society generally were not noted in any public manner. Weddings involving the upper crust of society, however, generally were announced in the local newspaper. These weddings were often a time of celebration or public enjoyment, as indicated by several of the announcements that follow.

But as the fighting with Great Britain got underway, even these formal announcements disappeared as the pages of the local newspaper were taken up with news reports related to the war. Weddings still occurred as people tried to continue on with their lives, but the fight for independence produced strains and often interfered with traditional customs and practices. But there were those who tried to show that life continued even in the face of war, as indicated by the announcement of JOHN HANCOCK's wedding in September 1775. Hancock, a Boston merchant, represented Massachusetts in the Second CONTINENTAL CONGRESS meeting in Philadelphia in 1775. But Hancock, even in the midst of war and government service away from home, found time to get married. The newspaper writer praises him for continuing on with his life even in the midst of such turmoil.

KEEP IN MIND WHILE YOU READ

1. Because of their social status in the community, the readers of the newspapers would have known who all the people mentioned in wedding announcements were, even if they did not know them personally.
2. Even though the focus audience for any newspaper would have been the people in the local community, newspaper printers exchanged copies with each other as a source of news from other regions. These notices would have been read and maybe republished in other parts of the country.

Documents: Newspaper Accounts of Weddings (1767–1775)

Connecticut Courant (Hartford), December 28, 1767

Last Thursday Evening Mr. SAMUEL TALCOTT, jun. Merchant, was married to Miss ABIGAIL LEDYARD, Daughter of JOHN LEDYARD, Esq; of this Town; a young Lady possessed of every Accomplishment necessary to render the Marriage State most agreable and happy.

Connecticut Courant (Hartford), June 20, 1768

We hear from New-Brunswick, in New Jersey, that on the 20th of May last, the Rev. ABRAHAM BEACH, formerly of this Place, was married to the amiable and accomplished Miss NANCY VAN WINCKLE, a lady whose shining virtues and sweet disposition, must render the married state truly happy.

Essex Gazette (Salem, Massachusetts), April 13, 1773

We hear from Cambridge, that on April Fools Day, was married there by the Rev. Dr. Appleton, Mr. Thomas Reed, aged 89 Years, to the agreeable Mrs. Alice Pine, aged 87 Years, who for a long time supported the Office of College Sweeper with great Dignity and to general Approbation of the Students; he has lately resigned that Post and retired from Business with a handsome Fortune.—In the Evening, an elegant Supper was provided, at which were present some eminent Personages.—During the Ceremony, minute Guns were fired by the whole artillery of that Place; and a Bell was rung for Three Hours on the happy Occasion—The next Morning by Day break another royal Salute was given, and the Bell rung as before.—A general invitation was given the next Day to an elegant entertainment and the whole was conducted with great Decency and Decorum.—Expectations of a numerous Progeny are very great.

Happy! Happy! Happy Pair!
None but the brave,
None but the brave,
None but the brave, deserve the Fair.

New York Gazette, September 4, 1775

Fairfield, Connecticut, column dated August 29—
Last evening was married, at the Seat of Thaddeus Burr, Esq., by the Reverend Mr. Eliot, the Honourable John Hancock, Esq, President of the Continental Congress, to Miss Dorothy Quincy, daughter of Edmund Quincy, Esq., of Boston
Florus informs us, that "in the second Punic War, when Hannibal besieged Rome and was very near making himself Master of it, a Field upon which part of his Army lay, was offered for Sale, and was immediately purchased by a Roman, in a strong Assurance that the Roman Valour and Courage would soon raise the Siege." Equal to the conduct of that illustrious Citizen was the Marriage of the Hon. John Hancock, Esq.; who, with his amiable Lady, has paid as great a Compliment to *American* valour, and discovered equal Patriotism,

by marrying now while all the Colonies are as much convulsed as Rome when Hannibal was at her Gates.

AFTERMATH

Once the Revolution ended, local newspapers once again published announcements of weddings of the well-to-do people in the community. Their publication was, for many people, a sign that day-to-day life was returning to normal. Over time, as newspapers grew in size, wedding announcements also grew in size. The average Revolutionary era newspaper was only four pages, while newspapers in the 19th century included multiple sections. Over time, wedding announcements went from a few sentences to more like the several paragraphs that are common today.

John Hancock is the only person in these announcements who is well known today. He had served as president of the Massachusetts Provincial Congresses prior to the Battles of Lexington and Concord. He represented Massachusetts in the Second Continental Congress from 1775 to 1780, serving as its president in 1776 and thus being the first person to sign the Declaration of Independence. He also served as governor of Massachusetts and filled a number of other public posts prior to his death in 1793.

ASK YOURSELF

1. Do you think the third announcement about the elderly people getting married was a real announcement, or was it just an April Fool's Day joke? Why?
2. In these announcements, the men are often identified by their profession while the women are identified by character traits. Is that still common today? Why or why not?
3. Today, wedding announcements often contain fairly detailed descriptions of the wedding party. This is not true of these announcements from the 18th century. Why do you think that is so?

TOPICS AND ACTIVITIES TO CONSIDER

- Wedding practices have changed over the years. Investigate what an 18th-century wedding would have been like in detail, and compare it to modern weddings.
- The fact that the men in these announcements are identified by their profession while the women are identified more by character traits reflects ideas about the roles of men and women in the 18th century. Investigate these ideas. What other activities in society at the time reflect these ideas?

Further Reading

Bloch, Ruth H. *Gender and Morality in Anglo-American Culture, 1650–1800.* Berkeley: University of California Press, 2003.

"The Freshest Advices: The Advancement of Matrimonial Felicity." *Colonial Williamsburg Journal* 21.6 (Dec. 1999/Jan. 2000): 3–8.

Unger, Harlow G. *John Hancock: Merchant King and American Patriot.* New York: John Wiley and Sons, 2000.

8. THE TRIALS OF LIFE: NEWSPAPER ADVERTISEMENTS FOR LOST AND FOUND ANIMALS (1775–1776)

INTRODUCTION

For Americans during the Revolutionary era, owning animals was usually a necessity of daily life. Horses provided the primary form of transportation, either by being ridden or used to pull wagons. Cattle were often a mainstay of life because they provided both milk and meat for families. To lose these animals could be a devastating blow because of their essential role in the family economy. And to have to take care of stray animals could also prove problematic because of the cost and effort involved.

Animals often strayed under the best of circumstances because fences did not always hold up, and horses and cattle managed to break out. The value of such animals also encouraged thieves to steal them in the hopes of making some money. When horses and cattle disappeared, their owners tried to locate them, and people who found stray animals tried to return them to their rightful owners. Both groups hoped to carry out this process as quickly as possible, and they sought the most efficient means to communicate the information about the animals to the public at large. At the time of the Revolution, the best way to get the word out was to publish an advertisement in the local newspaper describing the lost or found animal in the hopes that it would be recognized by someone. Such advertisements ran in practically every issue of any newspaper published at the time, indicating how widespread the problem of lost and straying animals was.

KEEP IN MIND WHILE YOU READ

1. The *New England Chronicle or Essex Gazette* was published in Cambridge, Massachusetts; regiments from the CONTINENTAL ARMY were stationed there during the siege of Boston following the Battles of Lexington and Concord.
2. Photographs did not exist at this time, so detailed descriptions were needed in order to clearly identify missing animals.

———————

Documents: Newspaper Advertisements for Lost and Found Animals (1775–1776)

New England Chronicle or Essex Gazette (Cambridge, Massachusetts), September 14, 1775

STRAYED or stolen from the Subscriber, since Monday the 11th Inst. a large black HORSE, raw boned, the Top of his right Ear cut off, and the left Ear two thirds off, his Tail cut off close, and his Foretop cut short off. Whoever will take up said Horse and bring him to Capt. Wentworth Stuart, in Col. Phinney's Regiment, at Fort No. 2 shall be handsomely rewarded. WENTWORTH STUART, Captain

STRAYED or stolen from me the Subscriber, on the Night of the 2d Instant, out of Col. Royall's Pasture, a large black MARE, about 15 Hands high, 11 or 12 Years old, her Mane hangs on her right Side, paces and trots well, but chiefly inclines to pace, except when fretted: Whoever takes up said Mare and conveys her to Capt. Henry Dearborn, on Winter-Hill, in Col. John Stark's Regiment, or to me the Subscriber at Epping, in New-Hampshire, shall be handsomely rewarded for his Trouble, and all necessary Charges paid him, by me. SIMON DEARBORN.

STRAYED or stolen, a dark red MARE, about 8 Years old, middling sized, has a white Spot or two on her Shoulders, a ring Bone on each hind Foot, paces and trots.——Whoever will take up said Mare, and bring her to Lieut. Nathaniel Nichols, in Capt. Job Cushing's Company, in General Heath's Regiment, at Fort No. 2, in Cambridge, shall be handsomely rewarded, and all necessary Charges paid.

STRAYED or stolen from the Subscriber, out of Temple's Pasture at Winter-Hill, on the Night of the 25th of August, a red MARE, 4 Years old, between 14 and 15 Hands high, shod all round, a white Face and both hind Feet white, with a lightish Spot on the fore Part of the off gambrel Joint, and two black Spots on her near Buttock. Whoever will take up said Mare, and deliver her to me in Goffe's Town, New-Hampshire, or Capt. Samuel Rickard in Camp, on said Winter-Hill, shall receive a handsome Reward. ALEX. WALKER.

STRAYED or stolen from a Pasture in Dorchester, near Col. Ward's Quarters, on the 25th of August, a light bay MARE, near 15 Hands high, with a black Mane and Tail, a large white Stripe in her Face, one wall'd Eye, one white hind Foot, with some white on the other, also some white Spots on one of her Buttocks, was full of Flesh when she went away, trots and paces; also a brown HORSE, about 14 Hands high, with a Star in his Forehead, had a sore Back when he went away, low in Flesh, and is a natural Pacer. Whoever will take up said Mare and Horse, or either of them, and returns them to the Owner in Westborough, or give Intelligence to Capt. Josiah Fay, in Col. Ward's Regiment at Dorchester, where they may be found, or to the Owner in Westborough, shall be handsomely rewarded and all necessary Charges paid by me. JONATHAN FAY.

STRAYED or stolen out of the Common, near Cambridge Meeting-House, on or about the 17th Instant, a dark brown HORSE, about 12 or 13 Years old, about 14 Hands and an Half high, paces and trots, and is handy to his Hand gallop, a cut Main, something low in Flesh, the hinder Part of his Back on each Side gall-d by the Pad of the Saddle. Whoever will take up said Horse and deliver him to Lieut. John Keys, in General Putnam's Regiment, at Cambridge, shall have one Dollar Reward and all necessary Charges paid by me. EBENEZER WALES.

STRAYED or stolen from Winter-Hill, last Friday Night, a grey MARE, about 8 Years old, 14 Hands high, with a Scar across each of her Thighs, and another on her right Buttock. Whoever will take up said Mare, and bring her to Capt. Abbot, in Col. Stark's Regiment, shall be well rewarded for their Trouble.

STRAYED or stolen from the Pasture of Lemuel Child of Roxbury, Innholder, a large brown HORSE with a Star in his Forehead, and wall Eyes, and has been nick-d. Whoever will take up said Horse and bring or send him to said Child shall have three Dollars Reward, paid by me. LEMUEL CHILD.

TAKEN up in Uxbridge, a black Horse, with a Star in his Forehead, about 14 Hands high, a natural Trotter, which answers to an Advertisement in the Essex Gazette, July 6. The owner may have him again, by applying to BENJAMIN COGSWELL of Uxbridge, paying all Charges.

Connecticut Courant (Hartford), November 25, 1776

TAKEN up by Solomon Woodford of Farmington, a white and red lined steer, two years old past, marked with a hollow crop in the off ear and a hole through the same, and has a large bell on, the owner is desired to pay charges and take him away.

TAKEN up, and now in the hands of the subscriber, of Newington, a bright bay horse, about 15 hands high, about 12 years old, paces and trots, shod all round.—The owner may have him on paying charges, by applying to THO'S WHITE.

Taken up by the subscriber a black horse colt, one year old past, about midling in height for one of his age.—The owner is desired to prove property, pay charges and take him away. ISAAC WRIGHT.

Strayed from the subscriber about the last of October, from Barkhemstead, five cattle, all two years old, two stears marked with a swallow's tail in the left ear, and a slit under side the same, one side black and white, more than half white, the other all red, one stear and heifer, marked with a crop on the end of both ears, and a slit in the end of the same, the stear red with a white face, and four white feet, the heifer red, with a white belly and flank, the other mark'd with a swallow's tail in the left ear, and slit under the same, with a half-penny under the right, the stear a pale red, with bug horns. Whoever will take up the same, and given notice to the owner, shall be well rewarded, and all charged paid, by SAMUEL TREAT.

Taken up by the subscriber of North Bolton, the 2d inst. a black mare about 5 years old, natural trotter, high liv'd, near 14 hands high, branded D M on her left hoof.—The owner is desired to prove his property pay charges and take her away. ELIAKIM ROOT.

Stolen out of the inclosure of landlord Smith of Renport, the night following the 20th of October, a black roan or iron-grey mare, 12 or 13 years old, about 14 hands high, a natural trotter, but paces some, a very small white spot in her forehead, carries her head pretty high, was some gauld with a collar on her breast, something crooked hind legs, supposed to be branded with the letter B on one thigh. Whoever will take up and return said mare to the subscriber or send me word where she may be had, shall have two dollars reward and all necessary charges paid and no questions asked. NATHANIEL WHITE.

Strayed or Stolen from the pasture of David Commins, of Ashford, in the night after the 6th instant, a black horse, with a star in his forehead and white streak on his nose, his hind feet white, about 15 hands high, about 12 years old, paces and trots but mostly inclined to pace.—Whoever shall take up said horse and thief, and secure said thief so that he may be brought to justice, and return said horse to the subscriber, or inform him where he may find said horse, shall have TEN DOLLARS reward and all necessary charges, or if said horse without the thief, THREE DOLLARS reward and all necessary charges paid by GIDEON HALE.

Broke into my field the 28th of September, 1776, a two year old red and white lined bur-horn'd stear, marked with a half-penny the under side the off ear. The owner may have him, paying cost and damage, by applying to SAMUEL OWEN, at Turkey Hills in Windsor.

Strayed from the subscriber last July, two colts, one two year old past, and the other one year old past, both black, with one of their hind feet white—the two year old is branded thus 9 on the left shoulder. Whoever will take up said colts, and give notice to me that I may have them again, shall be reasonably rewarded. LABAN BEACH.

Taken up at Enfield, on the 4th inst. a horse, three years old, about 14 hands and 18 inches high, the owner is desired to pay charges and take him away. PHINEAS LOVEJOY.

AFTERMATH

Loss of animals was a common occurrence in the 18th century, but the disruptions caused by the fighting during the Revolution added to the problems. The noise of the guns often spooked animals and caused them to run away, while the presence of armies often made it difficult to search for the animals as thoroughly as possible. Besides the general use of horses and cattle, both were very important for the armies because of the need for transportation and food for the soldiers. The Continental Army constantly sought more horses because of their losses in battle as well as through theft and straying. As a result, advertisements such as these became more prolific during the Revolution because the number of strayed and missing animals increased greatly.

Although the problem of straying animals never completely disappeared, the situation did improve in the years after the American Revolution because of improvements in fencing. Wire fences appeared in the first half of the 19th century throughout the United States. These helped keep animals fenced in, but there were still problems. The introduction of barbed wire fences in the 1870s improved the situation even more and greatly reduced the number of strays. Barbed wire fences are still widely used to help keep horses and cattle fenced in.

ASK YOURSELF

1. Why do you think there was a great diversity in the amount of reward offered for the return of a strayed animal? Does it reflect the wealth of the owner or the worth of the animal, or both?
2. Why do you think people who found stray animals spent the money to take out an advertisement looking for the owner? Were they just seeking compensation for their trouble, or were they trying to be good neighbors? Or was it a little of both?

TOPICS AND ACTIVITIES TO CONSIDER

- Investigate the use of horses in the Revolutionary War by the Continental and British armies. Were there similarities and differences? Are horses still used by military forces today? In what way?
- Investigate what breeds of horses and cattle would have been in the colonies during the Revolutionary War. If possible, identify some of the breeds described in the advertisements and consider why those particular breeds were used at the time.

Further Reading

Barrow, Robert Mangum. *Newspaper Advertising in Colonial America, 1704–1775*. PhD Dissertation, University of Virginia, 1967.

Becker, R. B. *Dairy Cattle Breeds: Origins and Development*. Gainesville: University of Florida Press, 1973.

Carlson, Laurie M. *Cattle: An Informal Social History*. Chicago: Ivan R. Dee, 2001.

Hutson, James A. *Logistics of Liberty: American Services of Supply in the Revolutionary War and After*. Newark: University of Delaware Press, 1991.

Lawrence, John. *The History and Delineation of the Horse, in All His Varieties*. London: Albion Press, 1809.

Nosworthy, Brent. *The Anatomy of Victory: Battle Tactics, 1689–1763*. New York: Hippocrene Books, 1990.

Web Site

History of the Quartermaster Corps: http://www.qmfound.com/history.html

9. WARS EVENTUALLY END: ANNA RAWLE'S DIARY (1781)

INTRODUCTION

Throughout the course of the American Revolution, many people were divided in their loyalties and their hopes for the outcome of the war. In some parts of the country (particularly in the South), fighting broke out between the PATRIOTS who supported independence and the LOYALISTS who wanted to remain part of Great Britain. Even in parts of the country where such infighting did not occur, the Loyalists often suffered at the hands of the Patriots because of their failure to support the fight for independence. This happened in Philadelphia when news of the British surrender at Yorktown reached there, as Anna Rawle described in her diary.

Anna Rawle grew up in Pennsylvania in a wealthy family. Her father, FRANCIS RAWLE, had died in 1761 when Anna was a young child and her mother, Rebecca, remarried in 1767. Her new husband, SAMUEL SHOEMAKER, also came from a wealthy family and served in many offices in Philadelphia prior to the Revolution. The family supported the British government and opposed the Revolution. In 1781 Mrs. SHOEMAKER traveled to New York to see her husband, while her daughter Anna remained in Philadelphia. During their separation, Anna kept a diary in order to provide her mother information and entertainment about events in Philadelphia during her absence. Included among these records was the following description of the events following the arrival of the news of the CONTINENTAL ARMY's victory at Yorktown.

KEEP IN MIND WHILE YOU READ

1. The city of Philadelphia had been the capital of sorts for the American colonies in revolt because it was the site of the meetings of the CONTINENTAL CONGRESS. But it also had been occupied by the British from 1777 to 1778. So, the divisions between supporters of independence and supporters of Great Britain had been pretty clear for some time.
2. Anna Rawle's family had had money, power, and influence prior to the Revolution. The British defeat in the Revolution might have been a sign that those days were over.

Document: Anna Rawle's Diary (1781)

October 22, 1781.—Second day. The first thing I heard this morning was that Lord Cornwallis had surrendered to the French and Americans—intelligence as surprizing as vexatious. People who are so stupidly regardless of their own interests are undeserving of compassion, but one cannot help lamenting that the fate of so many worthy persons should be connected with the failure or success of the British army. Uncle Howell came in soon after Breakfast, and tho' he is neither Whig nor Tory, looked as if he had sat up all night; he was glad to see all here so cheerful, he said. When he was gone Ben Shoemaker arrived; he was told it as he came along, and was astonished. However, as there is no letter from Washington, we flatter ourselves that it is not true....

October 24.—Fourth day. I feel in a most unsettled humour. I can neither read, work or give my attention one moment to anything. It is too true that Cornwallis is taken. Tilghman is just arrived with dispatches from Washington which confirm it. B. S. came here and shewed us some papers; long conversations we often have together on the melancholy situation of things.

October 25.—Fifth day. I suppose, dear Mammy, thee would not have imagined this house **to be illuminated** last night, but it was. A mob surrounded it, broke the shutters and the glass of the windows, and were coming in, none but forlorn women here. We for a time listened for their attacks in fear and trembling till, finding them grow more loud and violent, not knowing what to do, we ran into the yard. Warm Whigs of one side, and Hartley's of the other (who were treated even worse than we), rendered it impossible for us to escape that way. We had not been there many minutes before we were drove back by the sight of two men climbing the fence. We thought the mob were coming in thro' there, but it proved to be Coburn and Bob. Shewell, who called to us not to be frightened, and fixed lights up at the windows, which pacified the mob, and after three huzzas they moved off. A number of men came in afterwards to see us. French and J. B. nailed boards up at the broken pannels, or it would not have been safe to have gone to bed. Coburn and Shewell were really very kind; had it not been for them I really believe the house would have been pulled down. Even the firm Uncle Fisher was obliged to submit to have his windows illuminated, for they had pick-axes and iron bars with which they had done considerable injury to his house, and would soon have demolished it had not some of the Hodges and other people got in back and acted as they pleased. All Uncle's sons were out, but Sammy, and if they had been at home it was in vain to oppose them. In short it was the most alarming scene I ever remember. For two hours we had the disagreeable noise of stones banging about, glass crashing, and the tumultuous voices of a large body of men, as they were a long time at the different houses in the neighbourhood. At last they were victorious, and it was one general illumination throughout the town. As we had not the pleasure of seeing any of the gentlemen in the house, nor the furniture cut up, and goods stolen, nor been beat, nor pistols pointed at our breasts, we may count our sufferings slight compared to many others. Mr. Gibbs was obliged to make his escape over a fence, and while his wife was endeavouring to shield him from the rage of one of the men, she received a violent bruise in the breast, and a blow in the face which made her nose bleed. Ben. Shoemaker was here this morning; tho' exceedingly threatened he says he came off with the loss of four panes of glass. Some Whig friends put candles in the windows which made his peace with the mob, and they retired. John Drinker has lost

> **to be illuminated:** to be decorated with lights

half the goods out of his shop and been beat by them; in short the sufferings of those they pleased to style Tories would fill a volume and shake the credulity of those who were not here on that memorable night, and to-day Philadelphia makes an uncommon appearance, which ought to cover the Whigs with eternal confusion. A neighbour of ours had the effrontery to tell Mrs. G. that he was sorry for her furniture, but not for her windows—a ridiculous distinction that many of them make. J. Head has nothing left whole in his parlour. Uncle Penington lost a good deal of window-glass. Aunt Burge preserved hers thro' the care of some of her neighbours. The Drinkers and Walns make heavy complaints of the Carolinians in their neighbourhood. Walns' pickles were thrown about the streets and barrells of sugar stolen. Grandmammy was the most composed of anybody here. Was I not sure, my dearest Mother, that you would have very exaggerated accounts of this affair from others, and would probably be uneasy for the fate of our friends, I would be entirely silent about it, but as you will hear it from some one or another, not mentioning it will seem as if we had suffered exceedingly, and I hope I may depend on the safety of this opportunity.

People did nothing to-day but condole and enquire into each others honourable losses. Amongst a great variety who were here was Aunt Rawle; next to her sisters this was the family, she said, whom she felt most interested for; her visit was quite unexpected. Uncle and Aunt Howell went from here to Edgely this morning. Aunt Betsy to tea. Becky Fisher and her brother in evening.

October 26.—Sixth day.—Neighbor Waln and Ben. Shoemaker were here in the afternoon. Juliet, Polly Foulke and James Fisher came to see us in the evening; the conversation as usual on the late disturbances. It seems universally agreed that Philadelphia will no longer be that happy asylum for the Quakers that it once was. Those joyful days when all was prosperity and peace are gone, never to return; and perhaps it is as necessary for our society to ask for terms as it was for Cornwallis.

Source: Rawle, Anna. "Diary, October 25, 1781." *Pennsylvania Magazine of History and Biography* 16 (Philadelphia: Historical Society of Pennsylvania, 1892): 104–107.

AFTERMATH

Anna Rawle and her family remained in Pennsylvania following the end of the Revolution. Her stepfather had been declared guilty of high treason by the Pennsylvania state legislature in 1778 and much of their property had been seized once the British abandoned Philadelphia. This included property that actually had belonged to Anna's father. Because of the laws at the time, all property that a woman brought to a marriage belonged to her husband. This was true even if the property had originally belonged to a previous spouse. Thus, Anna and her brother William and sister Margaret lost most of their inheritance from their father because of the internal conflicts of the Revolution. Anna's stepfather died in 1800, and her mother passed away in 1819. Anna married John Clifford and lived a comfortable life by the standards of the day. It seems that the family was able to put most of the troubles and sufferings of the Revolution behind them.

ASK YOURSELF

1. Why do you think that the Patriots destroyed the property of Loyalists in the midst of their celebrations following the victory at Yorktown? Is that a usual type of behavior following a military victory?

2. Why would some people become Patriots while others remained Loyalists? What sorts of reasons would influence which side a person joined in such an internal conflict like the American Revolution?

TOPICS AND ACTIVITIES TO CONSIDER

- The conflicts between the Patriots and Loyalists constituted a civil war of sorts. Investigate other similar conflicts in history. Did they all result in destruction such as Anna Rawle describes? Do all civil wars have something in common? If so, what would that be?

- Anna talks of a relative who is neutral in the Revolution. Consider why one would be neutral in any military conflict such as the Revolution. Investigate how people who tried to be neutral were treated in other wars and compare that to how they were treated during the Revolution.

Further Reading

Berkin, Carol. *Revolutionary Mothers: Women in the Struggle for America's Independence.* New York: Alfred A. Knopf, 2005.

Calhoon, Robert M. *The Loyalists in Revolutionary America, 1760–1781.* New York: Harcourt Brace Jovanovich, 1973.

Ellet, Elizabeth Fries. *Revolutionary Women in the War for American Independence: A One-Volume Revised Edition.* Westport, CT: Greenwood Publishing Group, 1998.

Evans, Elizabeth. *Weathering the Storm: Women of the American Revolution.* New York: Paragon House, 1975.

Fleming, Thomas. *The Battle of Yorktown.* New York: American Heritage Publications, 1968.

Gerb, George Winthrop. *A History of Philadelphia, 1776–1789.* Madison: University of Wisconsin Press, 1973.

Glenn, Thomas Allen. *Some Colonial Mansions and Those Who Lived in Them, Second Series.* Philadelphia: Henry T. Coates & Company, 1900, pp. 123–198.

Jackson, John W. *With the British Army in Philadelphia.* San Rafael, CA: Presidio Press, 1979.

Kerber, Linda K. *Women of the Republic: Intellect and Ideology in Revolutionary America.* Chapel Hill: Published for the Institute of Early American History and Culture by the University of North Carolina Press, 1980.

Martin, David G. *The Philadelphia Campaign, June 1777–1778.* Conshohocken, PA: Combined Books, 1993.

Nelson. William H. *The American Tory.* Oxford: Clarendon Press, 1961.

Norton, Mary Beth. *Liberty's Daughters: The Revolutionary Experience of American Women, 1750–1800.* Boston: Little, Brown and Company, 1980.

Weigley, Russell Frank. *Philadelphia: A 300-Year History.* New York: W. W. Norton, 1982.

Web Sites

American Loyalists: http://www.redcoat.me.uk

History of Philadelphia: http://www.ushistory.org/philadelphia/index.html

The On-Line Institute for Advanced Loyalist Studies: http://www.royalprovincial.com

United Empire Loyalists' Association of Canada: http://www.uelac.org

ECONOMICS AND EMPLOYMENT

10. Headaches during Wartime: Government Efforts to Deal with Economic Problems (1774–1782)

INTRODUCTION

As the arguments with Great Britain increased in the 1760s and 1770s, more people in the American colonies worried about the state of the local economy because of the potential problems resulting from the cutoff of trade with the mother country. Increasing numbers of colonial leaders called on people to break their economic ties with Great Britain in an effort to develop economic independence. And the outbreak of war only made these concerns and problems worse because the presence of the armies interfered with local trade as well as with the trans-Atlantic trade. The war also increased INFLATION, which made acquiring supplies expensive as well as difficult. Leading the way in working to develop the economy were the members of the CONTINENTAL CONGRESS. But each colony or state also tried to encourage economic development. Efforts to organize the economy ranged from plans to increase production of goods to the establishment of a national bank intended to stabilize the local currency. Overall, such efforts did not accomplish very much, but the local economy survived primarily because most people in the American colonies were self-sufficient and produced the basic necessities of life anyway.

KEEP IN MIND WHILE YOU READ

1. Most citizens of the time produced what they needed to live, so proposals such as the ones in the first document were aimed primarily at the wealthier people who could afford to import goods from Great Britain and elsewhere.
2. The call for support of local production and financial institutions would serve two purposes: it would help boost the local economy and also serve as a way to assist efforts against British tyranny.

Document 1: Manufacturing Proposals (1774)

AS THE HAPPINESS of particular families arises in a great degree from their being more or less dependent upon others; and as the less occasion they have for any article belonging to others, the more independent; and consequently the happier they are; so the happiness of every political body of men upon earth is to be estimated in a great measure upon their greater or less dependence upon any other political bodies; and from hence arises a forcible argument, why every state ought to regulate their internal policy in such a manner as to furnish themselves, within their own body, with every necessary article for subsistence and defense. Otherwise, their political existence will depend upon others who may take advantage of such weakness and reduce them to the lowest state of vassalage and slavery. For preventing so great an evil, more to be dreaded than death itself, it must be the wisdom of this colony at all times, more especially at this time, when the hand of power is lashing us with the scorpions of despotism, to encourage agriculture, manufactures, and economy, so as to render this state as independent of every other state as the nature of our country will admit. From the consideration thereof, and trusting that the virtue of the people of this colony is such that the following resolutions of this congress, which must be productive of the greatest good, will by them be effectually carried into execution. And it is therefore resolved:

1. That we do recommend to the people the improvement of their breed of sheep, and the greatest possible increase of the same; and also the preferable use of our own woolen manufactures; and to manufacturers, that the manufacturers ask only reasonable prices for their goods; and especially a very careful sorting of the wool, so that it may be manufactured to the greatest advantage, and as much as may be, into the best goods.

2. We do also recommend to the people the raising of hemp and flax; and as large quantities of flaxseed, more than may be wanted for sowing, may be produced, we would also further recommend the manufacturing the same into oil.

3. We do likewise recommend the making of nails; which we do apprehend must meet with the strongest encouragement from the public, and be of lasting benefit both to the manufacturer and the public.

4. The making of steel, and the preferable use of the same, we do also recommend to the inhabitants of this colony.

5. We do in like manner recommend the making tinplate, as an article well worth the attention of this people.

6. As firearms have been manufactured in several parts of this colony, we do recommend the use of such, in preference to any imported. And we do recommend the making gunlocks, and furniture and other locks, with other articles in the iron way.

saltpeter: potassium nitrate, which is a necessary ingredient for the manufacture of gunpowder

7. We do also earnestly recommend the making of **saltpeter,** as an article of vast importance to be encouraged, as may be directed hereafter.

8. That gunpowder is also an article of such importance that every man among us who loves his country must wish the establishment of manufactories for that purpose, and, as there are the ruins of several powder mills, and sundry persons among us who are acquainted with that business, we do heartily recommend its encouragement by repairing one or more of said mills, or erecting others, and renewing said business as soon as possible.

9. That as several paper mills are now usefully employed, we do likewise recommend a preferable use of our own manufactures in this way; and a careful saving and collecting of rags, etc., and also that the manufacturers give a generous price for such rags, etc.

10. That it will be the interest, as well as the duty of this body, or of such as may succeed us, to make such effectual provision for the further manufacturing of the several sorts of glass, as that the same may be carried on to the mutual benefit of the undertaker and the public, and firmly established in this colony.

11. Whereas buttons of excellent qualities and of various sorts are manufactured among us, we do earnestly recommend the general use of the same; so that the manufactories may be extended to the advantage of the people and the manufacturers.

12. And whereas salt is an article of vast consumption within this colony, and in its fisheries, we do heartily recommend the making the same, in the several ways wherein it is made in several parts of Europe; especially in the method used in that part of France where they make bay-salt.

13. We do likewise recommend an encouragement of **hornsmiths** in all their various branches, as what will be of public utility.

14. We do also recommend the establishment of one or more manufactories for making wool-comber's combs, as an article necessary in our woolen manufactures.

15. We do in like manner heartily recommend the preferable use of the stockings and other hosiery woven among ourselves, so as to enlarge the manufactories thereof, in such a manner as to encourage the manufacturers and serve the country.

16. As **madder** is an article of great importance in the dyer's business, and which may be easily raised and cured among ourselves, we do therefore earnestly recommend the raising and curing the same.

> **hornsmiths:** artisans who flattened animal horns into sheets to make into combs, buttons, and sheet protectors for hornbooks (thin piece of wood with a handle that usually contained the alphabet or numbers to help children learn)
> **madder:** herb that produced roots used in dye production

17. In order the more effectually to carry these resolutions into effect, we do earnestly recommend that a society or societies be established for the purposes of introducing and establishing such arts and manufactures as may be useful to this people and are not yet introduced, and the more effectually establishing such as we already have among us.

18. We do recommend to the inhabitants of this province to make use of our own manufactures, and those of our sister colonies, in preference to all other manufactures.

Source: Force, Peter, ed. *American Archives: Fourth Series Containing a Documentary History of the English Colonies in North America from the King's Message to Parliament of March 7, 1774, to the Declaration of Independence by the United States.* Vol. 1. Washington, DC: 1837–1846, pp. 1001–1002.

Document 2: Robert Morris, Incorporation of the Bank of the United States (1782)

I HAVE THE HONOR TO TRANSMIT herewith an ordinance passed by the United States in Congress assembled the 31st day of December, 1781, incorporating the subscribers of the Bank of North America, together with sundry resolutions recommending to the several states to pass such laws as they may judge necessary for giving the said ordinance its full operation. The resolutions of the 26th of May last speak so clearly to the points necessary to be established by those laws that I need not enlarge on them. Should anything more be found necessary upon experience, the president and directors will no doubt make suitable applications to Congress, or to the states respectively, as the case may require.

It affords me great satisfaction to inform you that this bank commenced its operations yesterday, and I am confident that with proper management it will answer the most sanguine expectations of those who befriend the institution. It will facilitate the management of the finances of the United States. The several states may, when their respective necessities require, and the abilities of the bank will permit, derive occasional advantages and accommodations from it. It will afford to the individuals of all the states a medium for their intercourse with each other, and for the payment of taxes more convenient than the precious metals, and equally safe. It will have a tendency to increase both the internal and external commerce of North America, and undoubtedly will be infinitely useful to all the traders of every state in the Union, provided, as I have already said, it is conducted on principles of equity, justice, prudence, and economy. The present directors bear characters which cannot fail to inspire confidence, and as the corporation is amendable to the laws, power can neither sanctify any improper conduct nor protect the guilty.

Under a full conviction of these things, I flatter myself that I shall stand excused for recommending in the strongest manner this well-meant plan, to all the encouragement and protection which your state can give, consistently with wisdom and justice.

Source: Sparks, Jared, ed. *The Diplomatic Correspondence of the American Revolution.* Vol. XII. Boston: Nathan Hale and Gray & Bowen, 1830, pp. 76–77.

AFTERMATH

Efforts to both expand and control the economy during the American Revolution produced mixed results. When the war was over, many Americans eagerly began importing goods from Great Britain once more, and inflation soared. The ARTICLES OF CONFEDERATION, adopted during the Revolution, had established a very weak central government. The result was little ability to regulate the economy at the national level. The economic problems of the 1780s helped produced calls for changes in the national government that eventually resulted in the adoption of the CONSTITUTION in 1787.

ASK YOURSELF

1. Why do you think the calls for increased manufacturing dealt with so many different types of products? Were they all necessary for a stable lifestyle, or were some luxury goods that would appeal to the more wealthy people in America?
2. What was the Congress hoping to accomplish with the establishment of a national bank when the national government did not really have any means to regulate the economy?

TOPICS AND ACTIVITIES TO CONSIDER

- ◈ Inflation has often been a problem during wartime. Investigate the impact of inflation during the American Revolution and the various ways in which people and governments attempted to deal with the problem.
- ◈ National banks have often been proposed as a means to regulate the money supply and the economy. The United States has had three national banks: the one created in 1782, a second one created while GEORGE WASHINGTON was president, and one created after the War of 1812. Investigate these three banks; compare and contrast what the proponents hoped to accomplish and how each bank operated.

Further Reading

Backman, Jules A. *Business in the American Economy, 1776–2001.* New York: New York University Press, 1976.

Nettels, Curtis Putnam. *The Emergence of a National Economy.* New York: Holt, Rinehart and Winston, 1962.

Perkins, Edwin J. *The Economy of Colonial America.* New York: Columbia University Press, 1980.

Samuels, Warren J., and Malcolm Rutherford. *The Emergence of a National Economy: The United States from Independence to the Civil War.* Brookfield, VT: Pickering & Chatto, 2004.

Williamson, Harold F. *The Growth of the American Economy.* New York: Prentice-Hall, 1944.

11. THE DAILY NECESSITIES OF LIFE GET CAUGHT UP IN THE REVOLUTION: NEWSPAPER ADVERTISEMENTS FOR CLOTH (1773–1775)

INTRODUCTION

During the American Revolution, many aspects of daily life became politicized as people sought to stand up against what they perceived to be persecution by British authorities. One such aspect was the production of cloth. Prior to the Revolution, merchants in American cities imported a variety of types of cloth for the making of clothes. For many of these merchants, cloth constituted a major part of their business because many people increasingly chose to buy cloth instead of making their own. But the growing conflict with Great Britain in the 1760s and 1770s pushed people to stop buying goods from overseas. In fact, non-importation agreements constituted a major mechanism used by colonial leaders to protest British actions. People sought to support the protests against Britain by producing more goods locally. To produce and buy goods locally became a sign of patriotism and support for the Revolution. The newspaper advertisements that follow reflected this change. The first two advertisements show the variety of goods imported by merchants for sale to the public, a practice that continued off and on right up to the outbreak of the war. The third advertisement provided a call for women to help the effort by spinning thread. Through such efforts, a normal day-to-day activity became a sign of one's patriotism.

KEEP IN MIND WHILE YOU READ

1. Being able to buy cloth and other goods like those advertised would be a sign of financial success.
2. Most women would know how to spin because it was a necessary skill, but it was an activity done at home and not in a public setting or for public reasons.

Documents: Newspaper Advertisements for Cloth (1773–1775)

Connecticut Courant (Hartford), November 23, 1773

William Beadle,
At WETHERSFIELD,
Has just received a good Assortment of
Goods, suitable for the present Season,
Amongst which are

Broad Cloths, **Duffles, Coatings, Serges,** Velvets, Serge Denims, Womens Velvet, Scarlet Broad Cloths, Flower'd Drawboys, Everlasting India **Taffaties, Ducapes, Lutestrings Smitting, Persians,** Thin Silks of all Sorts, Figur'd Stuff for Gouns, **Callimancoes, Camblets, Russels, Bombazeen, Crapes, Durants** and **Tamies** of all colours, **Irish Linnens, Sheeting, Dowlass, Baze** and Flannel, the best of TEA, Coffee, Chocolate, Spices of all Kinds, Nails of all Sizes, Large Brass Kettles, Frying Pans, Spades and Shovels, **Crowleys Steel,** Powder and Shot, Pewter of all Sorts, Wool Cards, China, Glass and Earthen Ware, Indigo, Raisins, West India Rum, Molasses, **Teneriff Wine** best quality. French Brandy, A quantity of Wild Cherry Rum very rich, Loaf and Brown Sugars, Painters Colours, Cotton Wool, Whale Bone, and a variety of other Articles, as CHEAP as Possible, But NO TRUST.

Wethersfield, Nov. 19, 1773.

Connecticut Courant (Hartford), July 10, 1775

THOMAS GREEN,
From NEWPORT,
TAKES this method to notify the public, that he has taken a shop (of Mr. *Ward's*) opposite the Town-House in *Middletown,* where he has to sell,
CHEAP FOR CASH,
A good assortment of English, India, West-India, and Home-made GOODS, whereof the following particulars are a part, viz.
CALLICOES; **CHINTZES***;* PATCHES
and printed Cottons; Stamped Linnens and Damaskus's for Waistcoats; **Wiltons;** Jeans and **Fustians;** Corduroys; Breeches Patterns; Striped Cottons and Cotton **Hollands.——**A Variety of Silks for Gowns, viz. Persians; India Taffaties of all Colours; Lutestrings, **Padusays** and figur'd Sattins; Plain Sattins; Pelongs and **Sarsanets** of all Colours. A Variety of flowered **Lawns** and Apron Patterns; Sprig'd and book Muzlins; Plain Lawns and **Cambrick;** Long Lawns; Irish Hollands; Laces and **Gimps;** A Variety of figur'd and plain Ribbons; Black and white plain Gauzes; Silk, Linen and Gauze Handkerchiefs; Broad Cloths; Plains and German Serges; Velvets & Velveretts of all Kinds; **Lastings; Shalloons; Tammies;** Durants; Camblets; Crapes; **Staffs;** Callamanco's; Silk Gloves and

---

Allum: chemical compound used to fix dyes in cloth

Baze: woolen fabric that was often used to cover tables or to line drawers

Bombazeen: silk fabric with a twill weave that was dyed black for mourning wear

Callimancoes: glossy woolen fabrics checkered or brocaded in the warp so that the pattern shows on one side only—much used in the 18th century

Camblets: European fabric of silk or wool meant to copy an Asiatic fabric made out of camel's hair or Angora wool or garments made out of silk and wool

Cambrick: fine, thin, closely woven plain white fabric made out of linen or cotton

Chintzes: glazed cotton fabric with colorful printed designs

Coatings: cloth for making coats

Coperas: green dye that was often used to dye trousers

Crapes: lightweight fabric of silk or cotton with a crinkled surface

Mitts; Necklaces; Wool and Cotton, worsted, thread and cotton Stockings. All sorts of common School Books; Watts' Psalms and Hymns; Green and scarlet Plush, and Trimmings for Saddles; Looking Glasses; Cutlary; **Haberdashary;** thick Woollens; Bazes; Hollow Iron Ware; Womens and Girls Stuff Shoes and Clogs; Felt and Castor Hats; Assortment of Nails; Pepper; Spices of all sorts; **Allum; Coperas; Redwood, Logwood;** best Indigo; Coffee, Chocolate; Loaf and Brown Sugar, Rice; Pipes, &c. &c. &c.

Pennsylvania Journal (Philadelphia), August 16, 1775

To the SPINNERS in this City, the Suburbs, and Country.

Your services are now wanted to promote the AMERICAN MANUFACTURY, at the corner of Market and Ninth-streets, where Cotton, Wool, Flax, &c. are delivered out;—strangers, who apply, are desired to bring a few lines, by way of recommendation, from some respectable person in their neighbourhood.

One distinguishing characteristic of an excellent Woman, as given by the wisest of men, is, "That she seeketh wool and flax, and worketh willingly with her hands—She layeth her hands to the spindle, and her hands holdeth the distaff."—In this time of public distress, you have now, each of you, an opportunity, not only to help to sustain your families, but likewise to cast your mite into the Treasury of the public good. The most feeble effort to help to save the state from ruin, when it is all you can do, is as the widow's mite, entitled to the same reward as they who, of their abundant abilities, have cast in much.

AFTERMATH

As the war progressed, many goods became hard to acquire because colonists could not produce everything needed, and imports from Great Britain had been cut off. Women were increasingly urged to spin thread and weave cloth to help the war effort, and wearing clothes made out of homespun (as homemade cloth was called at that time) became a badge of honor for people supporting the revolt against Great Britain. Once the war ended, merchants resumed importing goods from Great Britain. But in the postwar era, people also continued to produce goods at home. By the 19th century, machines such as the SPINNING JENNY and the WATER FRAME became more common and factories developed to centralize production of cloth in a more efficient manner.

ASK YOURSELF

1. The advertisements list a variety of different types of cloth for sale. Why do you think so many different types of cloth would have been popular during the 1700s? Is that still true today?

Crowleys Steel: type of steel made in England by a company founded by Ambrose Crowley in the early 18th century

Dowlass: coarse linen cloth originally made in Brittany

Ducapes: heavy corded silk dress fabric that was very popular in the 18th century

Duffles: coarse, heavy woolen material with a heavy nap that is often used for blankets or overcoats

Durants: strong felted cloth intended to be an imitation of buff leather

Fustians: strong cotton linen fabric used for clothing

Gimps: braid used to trim clothes and upholstery

Haberdashary: goods sold by a dealer in small wares or notions such as needles, thread, and buttons

Hollands: plain cloth used for window shades and clothing

Irish Linnens: fine, lightweight linen fabric made in Ireland and used especially for clothing

Lastings: special sturdy cloth used in the shoe and luggage trades

Lawns: sheer plain woven linen or cotton fabric used for clothing

Logwood: dye made out of brown and red heartwood from trees that grew in Central America and the West Indies

Lutestrings Smitting: fancy silk used to make ribbons

Padusays: rich, heavy silk fabric with a corded effect

Persians: thin, soft plain or printed silk used especially for linings

Redwood: wood that yielded a red dye

Russels: strong twilled woolen cloth for clothing and shoes

Sarsanets: soft, thin silk of oriental origin that was used for dresses, veils, and trimmings

Serges: durable twill fabric of various weights that could be made from wool, cotton, silk, or rayon. It was used for suits, coats, and dresses.

Shalloons: lightweight fabric used to make linings of coats and uniforms

Sheeting: sturdy cloth of cotton or linen often used for bedsheets

Staffs: strong, rigid bards and rods used in corsets

Taffaties: crisp plain woven fabric made of silk, rayon, or linen. It was used especially for women's clothing.

Tammies or Tamies: cloth used to make curtains and linings

Teneriff Wine: wine made in the Canary Islands

Wiltons: heavy carpet woven with loops

2. The first advertisement stated that there will be "no trust," which means no selling on credit. Most of this merchant's customers would have been neighbors, so why do you think he would not sell on credit?

3. The last advertisement quotes Proverbs 31:13, 19. Why do you think the author of this advertisement decided to quote from the Bible? What did he hope to accomplish?

TOPICS AND ACTIVITIES TO CONSIDER

- Spinning has traditionally been a woman's occupation. Investigate how spinning developed and how a woman's role in the process changed over time.

- The advertisements listing goods for sale enumerate long lists of different types of cloth. Investigate what different types of cloth have been produced since the American Revolution and what they have been used for.

- Throughout the Revolution, PATRIOT leaders urged Americans to do various things to support the war effort. Investigate what Americans were urged to do and what they were urged not to do as signs of support for the Revolution.

Further Information

Barnes, Patricia. *Spinning Wheels and Spinning: The Definitive Book on Spinning Wheels, Spinners, and Spinning.* New York: Scribners, 1978.

Carter, Phyllis Ann, and Kathleen Voute. *Spin, Weave, and Wear: The Story of Cloth.* New York: McBride, 1944.

Hoffman, Ronald. *Women in the Age of the American Revolution.* Charlottesville: Published for the U.S. Capitol Historical Society by the University of Virginia Press, 1989.

Kann, Mark E. *The Gendering of American Politics: Founding Mothers, Founding Fathers, and Political Patriarchs.* Westport, CT: Praeger, 1999.

Meyer, Carolyn. *People Who Make Things: How American Craftsmen Live and Work.* New York: Atheneum, 1975.

Perica, Esther. *The American Woman: Her Role during the American Revolution.* Monroe, NY: Library Research Associates, 1981.

Film and Television

Early American Textiles. Washington, DC: The Lab, 1975. Filmstrip.

Web Sites

Clothing: http://www.history.org/history/clothing/intro/clothing.cfm

Parker, Keith W. The Involvement of "The Ladies": Economic Support of Women During the American Revolution: http://www.earlyamerica.com/review/2006_summer_fall/women-revolution.html

Trades of Milliners and Weavers: http://www.history.org/Almanack/life/trades/tradehdr.cfm

12. GETTING NEEDED INFORMATION: NEWSPAPER ADVERTISEMENTS FOR ALMANACS (1775)

INTRODUCTION

During the 18th century, the predominant segment of the colonial American economy involved agriculture and farming. In order to be as successful as possible at farming, information about weather, sunrise and sunset, and other astronomical events proved useful, so farmers often sought out such information. One source that had become popular in Europe and continued to be popular in America was the annual almanac. By the 17th century, almanacs in Great Britain were bestsellers, second only to the Bible. The first almanac published in America appeared in 1639 in Cambridge, Massachusetts. From that point on, more and more different editions appeared throughout the colonies. Probably the most famous almanac published in the colonies was *Poor Richard's Almanac,* printed in Philadelphia by BENJAMIN FRANKLIN from 1733 to 1758.

Franklin, like most printers in the colonies, realized that a successful almanac could provide a great boost to the annual income of any print shop. Thus, every printer desired to print an almanac every year in order to have a dependable source of income. Besides the usual astronomical information, printers would include other items that they thought would be of interest to readers and thus boost sales of the almanac. A good example of this can be seen in the advertisement for almanacs published in October 1775 by JAMES ADAMS, a printer in Wilmington, Delaware. He advertised his almanacs in Philadelphia newspapers because they would circulate throughout Delaware as well as Pennsylvania, and by doing so, he hoped to increase the sales of both editions.

If the printer also published a newspaper, he would advertise his new almanac in ways designed to grab the attention of his readers and hopefully increase sales of the almanac. In November 1775, EBENEZER WATSON, printer of the *Connecticut Courant* in Hartford, advertised his new almanac, which he hoped to publish shortly. Although the Revolution had begun only a few months earlier, and independence had not yet been declared, the war was already having an impact because the advertisement indicated that publication of the almanac would take place only if paper could be acquired. Such shortages would continue to be a problem for some printers throughout the course of the war, particularly for those who were close to the fighting. At the time Watson ran his advertisement, the fighting was centered around Boston, Massachusetts, only 100 miles from Hartford.

KEEP IN MIND WHILE YOU READ

1. A successful almanac could mean a financially good year, so Adams and Watson wanted to make their almanacs sound as appealing as possible in their advertisements.
2. For many people in colonial America, the annual almanac would be one of the few things (if not the only thing) that they would read besides the Bible.

Documents: Newspaper Advertisements for Almanacs (1775)

Pennsylvania Journal (Philadelphia), October 18, 1775

JUST PUBLISHED,
and to be sold by JAMES ADAMS, at his Printing-Office,
IN WILMINGTON,
The *WILMINGTON AND PENNSYLVANIA*
ALMANACKS,
For the year of our LORD, 1778.

Among the contents of the Wilmington Almanack (besides the usual astronomical calculations) are; DIRECTIONS, shewing people what is their own power both with respect to the prevention and cure of diseases. An Elegy to the memory of the American Volunteers, who fell in the engagement between the Massachusetts-Bay Militia and the British Troops, April 19, 1775. Observations on Faces. The **Irishman's Epistle** to the Officers and troops at Boston. **Liberty-Tree**. A droll Dialogue between a fisherman of Poole, in England, and a countryman, relative to the trade of America, and proposed victory over the Americans, &c. A remarkable instance of American increase. Remedies for inward diseases in cattle:—Together with significant sayings, interspersed among the columns of aspects, tables of interest, &c. &c. Contents of the Pennsylvania Almanack, (besides the usual calculations) viz. Continuation of William Penn's Advice to his Children. Conclusion of Wisdom's Call to the young of both sexes. Substitutes for Tea. The Character of a true Friend. Remedy for lameness, produced by a fixed contraction of the parts effected:—This medicine has been the means of curing a gentleman of New-York, aged 63 years, whose arm, from the shoulder to his fingers ends was so withered and wasted, that no blood could come therefrom, and was one fourth in size less than the other, and is now in its full state;—as well as others in that government. The Image's Speech to the superstitious Pilgrim. Receipts in Farriery. Pithy Sayings; Tables of Interest at six and seven per cent, &c. &c.

> **Irishman's Epistle:** poem addressed to the British military in Boston
> **Liberty-Tree:** original tree that stood near the Boston Common. It served as a rallying point for growing resistance to British rule. Most towns later had their own Liberty Trees that served as symbols of popular support for liberty and resistance to tyranny.

Connecticut Courant (Hartford), November 27, 1775

In the Press, and will be published as soon as PAPER can possibly be procured. WATSON's REGISTER, and CONNECTICUT ALMANACK for 1776;

This Almanack contains, besides what is usual in Almanacks,

    I. Directions for setting and regulating Clocks and Watches, and how to know when they go true; founded on astronomical principles.

    II. An Account of the Number of Inhabitants, Males and Females in the several Counties of the Colony of *Connecticut*.

    III. Rules containing probably Conjectures concerning the Term of person's Lives.

    IV. Curious Questions for the Sons of Art to amuse themselves with in long Winter Evenings.

    V. A Table showing the Beginning of Twilight, or Break of Day throughout the Year nicely computed.

    VI. A Table of the Weight and Value of Gold and Silver.

    VII. A Table of Interest at 6 per Cent.

    VIII. An Account of the Royal Navy of Great Britain.

    IX. A complete List of Officers of the several Regiments raised by the Colony of *Connecticut* for the Defence of America, now in the Continental Army.

AFTERMATH

Ebenezer Watson was able to acquire the paper he needed, and he printed his almanac for 1776. He ran his print shop in Hartford from 1771 until his death in September 1777. Throughout this period, an annual almanac was always an important part of his business plan. Almanacs continued to be popular publications throughout the 19th century in the United States. Their popularity faded only when other sources of weather information became available in the early 20th century, primarily through the rise and development of broadcasting. But almanacs continue to be published, with *The Farmer's Almanac* and *The Old Farmer's Almanac* being very popular among people who enjoy reading them. Besides the traditional astronomical information, modern almanacs also include historical information and discussions of current issues.

ASK YOURSELF

1. What topics that Adams and Watson included in their almanacs do you think

WILLIAM PENN'S "ADVICE TO HIS CHILDREN"

William Penn founded the colony of Pennsylvania and also played an important role in the settlement of New Jersey and Delaware. Penn joined the Society of Friends (the QUAKERS) in 1666 and spent much of his adult life defending religious toleration. Born in 1644, Penn was the son of Admiral William Penn, who helped bring Charles II back to the throne in 1660. The family remained in royal favor, which was part of the reason that son William received what later became Pennsylvania as a proprietary colony. Penn established the colony as a haven for those who shared his Quaker faith as well as other groups who sought safety from religious persecution. Penn wrote his "Advice to His Children" as he prepared to depart on his first trip to America to see the land he had recently been granted. He feared that he might not return, so he used the written word to give them advice for the future. Penn did return, and moved back and forth between England and Pennsylvania over the next several decades. He died in England in 1718.

would have been included no matter when they were published? What topics do you think were included because of the conflict with Great Britain? Why do you think these additional topics were included?

2. Why do you think almanacs became such popular publications? What is it about their contents that is so attractive?

TOPICS AND ACTIVITIES TO CONSIDER

- Although almanacs are no longer as popular as they once were, people still seek out this sort of information. Consider how newspapers, news magazines, and the Internet have come to serve some of the same information functions as almanacs did in the past.

- Almanacs were often an essential part of a print shop's production in the 18th century. Investigate the printing industry as it has developed over the years in order to ascertain how it has changed over time. What types of publications became essential in the 19th and 20th centuries?

Further Reading

Drake Milton. *Almanacs of the United States.* 2 vols. New York: Scarecrow Press, 1962.

Hawkins, Dorothy Lawson. "James Adams: The First Printer of Delaware." *Papers of the Bibliographical Society of America.* Vol. 28.1. Chicago: 1934, pp. 28–63.

McNulty, Bard. *Older Than the Nation: The Story of the* Hartford Courant. Stonington, CT: Pequot Press, 1964.

Smith, James Eugene. *One Hundred Years of Hartford's* Courant *from Colonial Times through the Civil War.* New Haven, CT: Yale University Press, 1949.

Thomas, Isaiah. *The History of Printing in America.* Worcester, MA: Isaiah Thomas, Jr., 1810; reprint ed. Ed. Marcus A. McCorison. Barre, MA: Imprint Society, 1970.

Web Site

Printing Trade: http://www.history.org/Almanack/life/trades/tradehdr.cfm

13. WAR PRODUCES PROPERTY DESTRUCTION: ROBERT MORTON'S DIARY (1777)

INTRODUCTION

The armies that were engaged in the American Revolution traveled all over the colonies during the years of fighting. Making sure that they had enough supplies to feed the men and their animals was not always easy. This was particularly true for the forces fighting for Great Britain because home was three thousand miles away across the Atlantic Ocean. So, as armies had done long before the American Revolution, these troops had to "live off the land" and take what they needed from the areas in which they were camped. British officials tried to make sure that those who provided needed supplies were given receipts promising payment when the war ended, but that was not always possible. As described by Robert Morton in his diary from 1777, troops often just took what they needed in order to survive. At the time of the events he recorded in his diary, Robert Morton was 16 years old. His stepfather, JAMES PEMBERTON, was a leading QUAKER in Philadelphia, who had been exiled to Winchester, Virginia, because of his apparent opposition to the war. As a result, Robert Morton had to take care of the family plantation by himself.

KEEP IN MIND WHILE YOU READ

1. The Hessians were troops from Germany that had been hired to supplement the British army. They often did not speak English, so it was difficult for American colonists to communicate with them.
2. Robert Morton lived in Philadelphia, but his plantation was outside the city. So, traveling to it to do needed work would take some time.
3. The British were occupying Philadelphia at the time Morton recorded these events.

Document: Excerpt from Robert Morton's Diary (1777)

Oct. 19th.—A firing this morning at the fort. Went this afternoon to the Plantation. When I had got as far as I. Pemberton's Place, I see about 100 Hessians com'g down the road on a foraging, or rather plundering, party. As soon as they came to the corner of the road, their com. gave them permission to take all the cabbage and Potatoes they could find. Being afraid y't they would take our cabbage, I applied for a guard to the House and Garden, which was immediately granted, and by that means prevented our cabbage from being plundered. After they had taken all Jno. King's Cabbage and Potatoes they marched off. Bro't our cabbage home. It was surprising to see with what rapidity they run to, and with voraciousness they seized upon Jno. King's Cabbage and Potatoes, who remained a silent spectator to their infamous depredations.

Oct. 20th.—Went to the plantation to see about the potatoes, &c., and when I got to the corner of ye road I see another party of Hessians com'g down with Horses, Carts, bags, &c., to carry off Hay, potatoes, &c. The com'r rode up to Jno. King's House, and I followed him. He said he was come by orders of the General to take the Hay and Potatoes. I told him who it belonged to, but to no purpose. By this time a guard which Col. Harcourt had sent came up and declared they should not take it. From thence they went to J. Bringhurst's Place where they took all the Hay and most of ye Potatoes which belonged to the Tenant, to the great distress of the family. I went a little further and see a number of Hessians crossing over the bridge of boats lately made for that purpose, with Bennett of W——n, a prisoner. 14 of the Eng. flat bottomed boats came by the **Che-de-Frise** this morning, which occasioned some firing. I went this afternoon to see the British encampment, which extends in nearly a line from Delaware to Schuylkill. The reason of their leaving Germantown was because their lines were too extensive for the number of ye men. The troops appeared in good spirits, good health and heartily desirous for the fleets getting up that they might pursue General Washington. The most heavy firing at the fort y't we have had yet: On 1st day, the 19th, Gen'l Howe came to his quarters at Jno. Cadwalader's house in consequence of the Army contracting their lines. The B. Camp is below Kensington. We see a number of the Con. troops about 1/2 mile from the British Piquet, having exchanged several shots.

Oct. 21st.—This morning about 2500 Hessians, under the Command of Count Donop, crossed the River in order to attack Red Bank, and marched from Cooper's Ferry tow'ds Haddonfield. No firing this day at the fort.

Oct. 22nd.—Went to the Plantation this morning and found that the British had taken 1 load of hay without paying or giving a Rec't. A number of the British have crossed the lower ferry in expectation of an attack with the Continental Troops, and keeping a communication open with Chester. The British have taken 2 more loads of hay upon the same conditions as the first. Last 7th day I rec'd a Rec't for the load of hay taken for the Light Horse, which I omitted mentioning at that time. The Hessians having taken all the Stores belonging to the A. Army at Haddonfield, proceeded on tow'ds Red Bank.

Che-de-Frise: obstacle composed of barbed wire or spikes attached to a wooden frame that is used to block enemy advancement

Facine Battery: group of large guns linked together so that they can fire together

Oct. 23rd.—5th day of the week.... The Hessians this morning broke open the Plantation house, but did no considerable damages. The British that crossed Schuylkill yesterday, have returned and broke up the bridge at Gray's ferry, where they are erect'g a **Facine Battery** to defend the pass instead of carry'g it to the upper ferry, where its proximity to ye camp would render it more conveniently protected and where, from the situation of the ground, it would be impossible to demolish it from the opposite side.

Oct. 24th.—No firing this morning. The Hessians and British Soldiers have taken above 50 Bus. of our Potatoes, notwithstanding the gracious proclamation of his Excell'y to protect the peaceable inhabitants in a quiet possession of their property. The ravages and wanton destruction of the soldiery will, I think, soon become irksome to the inhabitants, as

HESSIANS

The Hessians were auxiliary troops hired by the British to fight during the American Revolution. Over 30,000 men from various states in Germany served in this way. They constituted approximately one-fourth of the British forces that served in the Revolution. They were called Hessians because the majority of them came from Hesse-Kassel and were hired out by Landgrave Frederick II, the ruler of that state. Although these men are often referred to as mercenaries, that term really does not apply to them because it implies that they voluntarily hired out their services for money. Most of the Hessians were debtors or petty criminals who served in order to excuse their debts or instead of prison terms. The money paid for their services went to the ruler of the state they lived in, so the men themselves did not receive any of it. The use of foreign troops by the British was seen by many Americans as an insult and may have pushed people who originally thought of remaining neutral in the war to join the Patriot cause and support the Revolution. When the war ended, just over 17,000 Hessians returned to their homeland. Of the remaining 12,500, over 6,000 had died from illness or accidents, while 5,000 remained in America.

many who depended upon their vegetables, &c., for the maintenance of their families, are now entirely and effectually ruined by the soldiers being permitted, under the command of their officers, to ravage and destroy their property. I presume the fatal effects of such conduct will shortly be very apparent by the discontent of the inhabitants, who are now almost satiated with British clemency, and numbers of whom, I believe, will shortly put themselves out of the British protection; I mean not to dictate to men of whose superior abilities I have a just appreciation, but had the necessities of the army justified the measures, and they had paid a sufficient price for what they had taken, then they would have the good wishes of the people, and perhaps all the assistance they could afford; but contrary conduct has produced contrary effects, and if they pursue their present system, their success will be precarious and uncertain. It is reported that Count Donop, after he had taken a view of the American Fort, found it impossible to take it without great loss; but as his orders were peremptory, he must take it or nobly fall in the attack. He del'd his watch and purse to Lord Bute's natural son, and then bro. on the attack; being soon after wounded, he fainted and he died.

Oct. 25th—Great part of this day employed at Plantation taking down the fences to prevent the soldiery taking them. A report is this day prevalent, that Gen'l Burgoyne with 4000 men, surrendered prisoners of War on the 15th inst.

Source: Morton, Robert. "Diary, September 16–December 14, 1777." *Pennsylvania Magazine of History and Biography* 1(Philadelphia: Historical Society of Pennsylvania, 1877): 19–24.

AFTERMATH

Such foraging occurred throughout the course of the Revolution as the British and their Hessian allies tried to defeat the CONTINENTAL ARMY. As feared by Robert Morton in his diary, seizures of food and supplies by the British forces angered many people who had previously supported the British cause or had at least been neutral in the conflict between Great Britain and her colonies. There is no way to measure how many of these people got angry enough to support the Patriot cause, but it is clear that it did happen in some cases. Whether this ultimately changed the course of the war is impossible to determine, but it cannot have helped. Farmers who depended on their crops to feed their own families would not have been happy when the invading armies seized their crops and supplies. Loss of the supplies made the day-to-day lives of those affected more difficult and thus added to the anger directed toward Great Britain.

ASK YOURSELF

1. Why do you think Robert Morton went into such detail about the agricultural losses brought about by the foraging efforts of the Hessians? Are such losses a normal part of war?
2. Would it have made any difference in the losses if Morton had spent more time at the plantation?
3. Why do you think the military forces just took what they needed? Why did they not offer to pay more often?

TOPICS AND ACTIVITIES TO CONSIDER

- ❧ This report is about British and Hessian seizures of crops. Investigate how much of this occurred as well as whether the PATRIOT forces seized food and supplies also. Compare and contrast the extent to which the two sides engaged in such activities. How did they justify it?
- ❧ Robert Morton and his family did not live on his plantation all the time. Investigate how farms were organized in the 18th century, and when and why people would choose not to live on the farm all the time.

Further Reading

Atwood, Rodney. *The Hessians: Mercenaries from Hesse-Kassel in the American Revolution.* New York: Cambridge University Press, 1980.

Bushman, Richard R. *Opening the Countryside: The First American Agricultural Revolution, 1750–1850.* Lecture Tape, Cornell University.

Gerb, George Winthrop. *A History of Philadelphia, 1776–1789.* Madison: University of Wisconsin Press, 1973.

Hurt, R. Douglas. *American Agriculture: A Brief History.* Ames: Iowa State University, 2002.

Jackson, John W. *With the British Army in Philadelphia.* San Rafael, CA: Presidio Press, 1979.

Kulikoff, Allan. *From British Peasants to Colonial American Farmers.* Chapel Hill: University of North Carolina Press, 2000.

Lowell, Edward J. *The Hessians and the Other German Auxiliaries of Great Britain in the Revolutionary War.* Williamstown, MA: Corner House, 1970 (reprint 1884 ed.).

Martin, David G. *The Philadelphia Campaign, June 1777–1778.* Conshohocken, PA: Combined Books, 1993.

Schlebecker, John T. *Whereby We Thrive: A History of American Farming, 1607–1972.* Ames: Iowa State University Press, 1975.

Weigley, Russell Frank. *Philadelphia: A 300-Year History.* New York: W. W. Norton, 1982.

Web Sites

Growing a Nation: The Story of American Agriculture: http://www.agclassroom.org/gan/index.htm

The Hessians: http://www.americanrevolution.org/hessians/hessindex.html

History of Philadelphia: http://www.ushistory.org/philadelphia/index.html

Myth and Reality in 18th-Century Agriculture or What 18th-Century Farming is Not!: http://www.history.org/history/teaching/enewsletter/volume2/april04/mythandreality.cfm

Patterson, Richard. What Was a Hessian? http://www.ushistory.org/WASHINGTON CROSSING/history/hessian.htm

Rural Trades: http://www.history.org/Almanack/life/trades/tradehdr.cfm

14. Trials of Wartime: Advertisements in the *Connecticut Courant* Reflect the Scarcity of Supplies (1776–1777)

INTRODUCTION

Producing or acquiring the necessities of life can be difficult during wartime. This proved true during the American Revolution for the many who struggled to feed their families in the face of shortages and destruction produced by the war. But producing desired items that were not considered essential could be even more difficult. Newspapers and other printed products often fell into this category. For most people in the 18th century, newspapers often provided the primary means of gaining knowledge about other parts of the country. Often, men would gather in the local tavern and listen while someone read the latest issue of a newspaper. It might be the paper published in their town, or it might be one from another city that had arrived in the mail (a process that could take weeks). Many historians credit the newspapers with helping the PATRIOTS win the Revolution because newspapers kept people interested and engaged in the war even when the fighting was hundreds of miles away. But producing a newspaper during wartime was not easy. EBENEZER WATSON, printer of the *Connecticut Courant,* struggled with acquiring the supplies he needed to produce his newspaper and with making enough money so that the publication could continue.

KEEP IN MIND WHILE YOU READ

1. The *Connecticut Courant* was published in Hartford, the capital of Connecticut, a place where newspapers would be eagerly sought by many people seeking information.
2. The fighting in the Revolution had shifted from Boston to New York by the time these advertisements appeared. The close proximity of both of these cities to Hartford probably meant that the citizens of Hartford were very interested in news of the fighting.

Documents: Advertisements in the Connecticut Courant *Reflecting the Scarcity of Supplies (1776–1777)*

Connecticut Courant (Hartford), October 14, 1776

RAGS.

THREE COPPERS per pound given for all kinds of Cotton and Linen Rags.

The subscriber being concern'd in a Paper Mill in this place, desires all who wish well to their country, to consider the importance of saving their Rags. The erecting paper works will turn to little account, if the materials of which paper consists, are wasted and thrown away. Double the quantity usually collected in the course of a year, might doubtless be saved in that term of time, if frugality and economy in this respect were properly and universally practised. But, tho' paper is essential to the well-being of a State, and without which the art of writing and printing would be rendered useless, yet how difficult is it to persuade many to encourage it by saving their rags! I am told that some towns in the State of Massachusetts Bay, have taken up this matter and made effectual provision for collecting them, and it is greatly to be wished that other towns would follow such laudable examples. Indeed, it is an object, by many, thought worthy the attention of the legislature of every free State on the continent. Rags, though sometimes a symptom of poverty and distress, make a beautiful figure in a paper mill, especially in large quantities; they enable the workmen to go forward with vigor in their business, that 'tis the design of this to awaken the attention of people, and if possible, persuade them to feel the *necessity* and *importance* of saving every rag in their power. EBEN. WATSON.

Ready Money (3 coppers per lb.) given for clean cotton and linen rags of any kind, coarse or fine, at the printing-office and paper mill in Hartford, and by Mr. Ambrose Nicholson, Glastonbury; Mrs. Elizabeth Hopkins, Wethersfield; Mr. Joseph King, Middletown; Mr. Jesse Austin, Durham; Mr. Samuel Smith, Farmington; Mr. Daniel Allen, Southington; Mr. William Stanton, Litchfield; Mr. Nathaniel Stanley, Canaan; Mr. Titus Watson, Norfolk; Mr. Ephraim Starr, Goshen; Mr. Daniel Hudson, Torringford; Mr. Jonathan Humphrey, Simsbury; Mr. John Sill, Windsor; Mr. Seth Austin, Suffield; Mr. Joseph Knight, Enfield; and by a number of other Gentlemen in the neighbouring towns. Any persons in the country, who are willing so far to promote the manufacture of paper, as to take in rags, shall be paid the above price of three coppers per lb. for whatever quantity they may procure, either in cash, or a beautiful writing paper, together with 20 per cent commissions, and all the expences of transportation, to the printing office or paper mill in Hartford. A little bag or basket, hung up in some convenient place, will receive the rags with the same motion that will be necessary to sweep them into the fire.

N. B. No writing paper will be sold for the use of any town that is not careful to save its rags, by E. WATSON.

Connecticut Courant (Hartford), May 5, 1777

THE unreasonable price of the necessaries of life has thrown the Printer into an unhappy dilemma. He must either fling up his business and starve his family, or increase the wages of his workmen, and the price of his News-Paper, and other work. He has hitherto sacredly adhered to his former price, by which means he has greatly suffered in his interest, especially for eight months past, whilst with indignation and surprize he has beheld the power of avarice, and the infatuation of the times. But what can be done? He has struggled against the torrent of oppression till his strength is exhausted, and must either rise in his demands, or be reduced to beggary. And is it right to neglect the means of safety, and work as it were for nothing, when every necessary of life is purchased at the most enormous price? No; the horrors of poverty, which rush on him like an armed force forbid it; the daily returning wants of his family, the irresistable calls of nature and the great law of self preservation, forbid it. As the people will not break the fatal inchantment, by reducing the price of things, he is compelled to raise the price of this work. *Twelve Shillings* a year, therefore, for the News paper, and other work in proportion, is as low as he can possibly afford it, as the times are at present, (after which the paper will be cheaper than any one of it's size on the continent.) As this price is consistent with the regulating act, to which, as he always has, so he means still to adhear, till repealed, or more universally violated, he thinks himself excusable in the step he has taken, and that no person will have just cause of complaint. Those gentlemen who are unwilling to comply with the above terms, are desired to send their names to the Printer within three weeks from this date, (at which time the proposed alteration will take place) that their papers may be stopt, otherwise they will be continued to them by their humble servant, E. WATSON.

Those persons who send their names to the Printer, desiring their papers may be discontinued in consequence of the above advertisement, are requested likewise to send the money for those they have already had.

Connecticut Courant (Hartford), September 22, 1777

To the LADIES.

THE owners of the PAPER MILL in Hartford, earnestly intreat the Ladies to consider their distress on account of the scarcity of RAGS. The business of Paper-Making and Printing is at an end if Rags are not to be had. On a former advertisement the works were plentifully supplied with this article, and the people were spirited to save every Rag in their power.—Their spirit of late has greatly declined, and the effects of it will be soon and severely felt. The News Paper must inevitably stop, or be reduced to a half sheet—The Schools will be essentially affected, and all writing business cease, unless the Ladies will exert themselves and shew their patriotism on this occasion. Money is so sunk in its credit, and the price of Rags so small, that the encouragement in this respect is trifling; but benefit accruing to the public, and the essential service hereby done to the country, it is hoped will be prevailing arguments to arouse their attention, and engage their friendship in a matter of such necessity, and so interesting to the people. It is a thousand pities to reduce the size of this paper at this critical moment, when the grandest events are turning up, and in a day of such anxious expectation, and when it often requires more than a whole sheet to convey intelligence.

AFTERMATH

Pleas such as these published by Ebenezer Watson appeared throughout the colonies and later the states during the Revolutionary period as printers struggled to keep their presses running in order to keep publishing their newspapers. Watson died of smallpox soon after the last ad appeared in the *Courant,* but the paper did not cease to exist. His widow,

PAPERMAKING

Paper has been made by human beings for many centuries, but it has become a relatively speedy process only in the last two hundred years. Prior to the 19th century, paper had to be made by hand. The basic material used to make paper in the 18th century was fiber from cotton or linen rags. The rags would be thoroughly cleaned and then reduced to a pulp in a vat. A wire mold would then be dipped into the stock vat to form the sheet of paper. Once formed, the sheet would be placed on felt or woolen cloth for pressing. Stacks of paper sheets would be pressed and reduced from two feet to six or eight inches. The paper sheets would then be hung up to dry. Once dry, the paper would be smoothed either with a glossy stone by hand or by running it through a water-powered hammer. Once this was done, the paper was ready to be used for writing or printing. Obviously, this process was slow and required a good deal of time to get a large supply of paper ready for use. The complications in producing the necessary amount of paper needed to publish a newspaper help explain why most early publications generally appeared only once a week. When daily newspapers first appeared in the 1780s, printers could do the job only through having massive stocks of paper on hand and often more than one printing press so that the speed of production could be increased.

HANNAH BUNCE WATSON, continued to publish it. In 1779 she married her neighbor, BARZILLAI HUDSON, a mason by training. He partnered with GEORGE GOODWIN in publishing the *Courant* until Hudson's death in 1823. Today, the *Hartford Courant* is the oldest continually published newspaper in the United States, having appeared regularly since its founding in 1764.

ASK YOURSELF

1. In the first advertisement, Watson tried to urge people to save rags because it was the right thing to do for the country. How do you think his readers would have reacted to such appeals to patriotism? Do such appeals still appear today?
2. In the second advertisement, Watson tried to justify the price increase for the newspaper by stating that it was necessary in order for his family to survive. Do you think that such an appeal would have worked with his subscribers? Why or why not?
3. In the third advertisement, Watson appealed to women to save rags so that the paper mill could continue to run. In what unique ways did he appeal to women? Why do you think he chose to issue this appeal? Do you think it would it have been effective? Why or why not?

TOPICS AND ACTIVITIES TO CONSIDER

- ❧ Over the years, paper has been made out of a variety of materials. Investigate the different ways paper has been made over time, being sure to compare and contrast the types of materials used and the types of paper produced.
- ❧ Newspapers performed an important role during the American Revolution because they provided a source of information about the war for people who were not close to the fighting. Investigate the types of information presented by the newspapers at the time and consider what type of impact that would have had on people's attitudes toward the Revolution.

Further Reading

Bailyn, Bernard, and John B. Hench, eds. *The Press and the American Revolution.* Worcester, MA: Northeastern University Press, 1980.

Bridenbaugh, Carl. *The Colonial Craftsman.* Chicago: University of Chicago Press, 1950.

Hunter, Dard. *Papermaking: The History and Technique of an Ancient Craft.* New York: A. A. Knopf, 1943.

Kobre, Sidney. *Development of American Journalism.* Dubuque, IA: William C. Brown Publishing Company, 1923.

McNulty, Bard. *Older Than the Nation: The Story of the* Hartford Courant. Stonington, CT: Pequot Press, 1964.

Oswald, John Clyde. *Printing in the Americas.* New York: The Gregg Publishing Company, 1937.

Silver, Rollo G. "Aprons Instead of Uniforms: The Practice of Printing, 1776–1787." *Proceedings of the American Antiquarian Society* 87 (1977):111–194.

Smith, James Eugene. *One Hundred Years of Hartford's* Courant, *from Colonial Times through the Civil War.* New Haven, CT: Yale University Press, 1949.

Tunis, Edwin. *Colonial Craftsmen and the Beginnings of American Industry.* Cleveland, OH: World Publishing Company, 1965.

Weeks, Lyman Horace. *A History of Paper-Manufacturing in the United States, 1690–1916.* New York: The Lockwood Trade Journal Company, 1916.

Wroth, Lawrence C. *The Colonial Printer.* Portland, ME: The Southworth-Anthoensen Press, 1938.

Web Sites

Brieg, James. "Early American Newspapering." *Colonial Williamsburg Journal:* http://www.history.org/foundation/journal/Spring03/journalism.cfm

Printing Trade: http://www.history.org/Almanack/life/trades/tradehdr.cfm

15. Daily Trials: Newspaper Reports of the Impact of Weather on Daily Life (1771–1780)

INTRODUCTION

Rainstorms have always been difficult to deal with because rain can produce floods, and lightning can start fires. In the midst of fighting the American Revolution, people still had to deal with the impact of storms. Meteorology, the science of weather forecasting, already existed, but it was difficult to predict anything with any accuracy. Thunderstorms and hurricanes caused many problems for people during the time of the Revolution, particularly along the Atlantic coast. People lost belongings and houses or even their lives as they fought to deal with the storms. Such losses could make people's sufferings worse because they added to the scarcity of supplies produced by the military conflict; however, storm losses also often made the war seem farther away because the war's impact did not always produce the same immediate effect as stormy weather. But storms could also slow down the movements of the armies, which was good for the people who were threatened with attack. Newspapers published during the Revolution regularly reported on storms and their impact.

KEEP IN MIND WHILE YOU READ

1. The primary type of weather forecasting that existed at the time was reading the almanac or asking longtime residents for their ideas about the current weather and what might be coming.
2. There was no easy way to communicate the coming of storms from one community to another, so people often had little or no warning of an approaching storm.

Documents: Newspaper Reports on the Impact of Weather (1771–1780)

Connecticut Courant (Hartford), August 6, 1771

Last Friday the people here were spectators of a very melancholly scene—In the afternoon, after a very sultry day, a thunder storm seemed to be gathering, whereupon the wind, before steady and strong at 8. in the space of about half an hour veer'd round to every point of the compass, whereby a most formidable collection of clouds, plentifully charged with electrical fire, was made over our heads, the effects of which were soon visible. A large tree at Mr. Amos Hinsdale's door was struck with the lightning, but little shatter'd; also the house of Mr. Elijah Clap, with no other damage than beating off part of the top of the chimney. But the greatest fury of the lightning fell on the south meeting house, the steeple of which it struck, and its principal effects were, that after being conducted by the spindle thro' a large ball, and about two feet in length of the mast, it there broke it off and shiver'd it several feet downwards; it then seems to have forsook the mast and shivered to pieces three of the rafters of the spire, from which, on the south and east sides especially, it tore off great part of the boards, and shingles; it then split three posts of the balcony; one small part of it then took a pole, that supported a winding stair-case within the steeple, and shattered it for about 20 or 30 feet, when its force seems to have been spent. A larger part of it took a main post of the steeple and house, split it from top to bottom, ripped off the casing, &c. but the largest part seems (by the effect) to have taken a studd, on the opposite side to the post, and was conducted from studd to studd to the ground, shivering them all the way in a most surprizing manner, ripping off many of the clapboards bursting out a window, and rending off one half a door casing. Happy was it for the people here, that the explosion did not happen on the sabbath, in time of public worship, as probably many lives must have been lost. May we be taught to sing rightly of mercy as well as judgment.

This sorrowful providence affords another convincing proof of the benefit of iron rods, as conductors of the lightning, against which there has been so much; I will not say reasoning, but railing; for, tho' the spindle went thro' a large wooden ball, and about two feet farther into the mast, yet both were perfectly unhurt, till we come to the end of the spindle, where the mast is snapt off, and the fatal effects begin.

Same day the steeple of the Rev'd Dr. Dana's meeting-house in Wallingford was struck by lightning, and very much shatter'd.

Connecticut Courant (Hartford), August 3, 1773

Last Sunday a large Barn belonging to the Hon. William Pitkin, of East Hartford, was set on Fire by a Flash of Lightning. It contained upwards of 20 Loads of Hay and Flax, which, with the Barn, was entirely consumed.

Essex Gazette (Salem, Massachusetts), August 17, 1773

A Correspondent at Newbury-Port has favoured us with the following Account.

Saturday, August 14, between 7 and 8 o'Clock in the Morning, a violent Tornado or Hurricane arose, took its Course from the East, first struck Salisbury Point, and following the Course of Merrimack River, spread Devastation before it, for about the Space of a Mile in Width, by levelling with the Ground several well-built Houses, almost new, unroofing others, tearing down Shops, and shattering, more or less, almost every House and Building from Salisbury Point to about a quarter of a Mile above Almsbury Ferry.—Capt. Smith, of Beverly, was setting in a Sailmaker's Loft at Almsbury, when the Hurricane came, and in a Moment he and the whole Building were carried away together, the Edifice rent to Pieces and dispersed, and the unhappy Man found lying senseless by the Side of a Piece of Timber, at the Edge of Pawaw River, ninety-four Feet distant from the Sill of the Loft he was carried from; and a large white-oak Post, fourteen Feet in Length, and 12 by 10 Inches, was transported 138 Feet. Two new Vessels, of 90 Tons Burthen, were carried sideways near

20 Feet from the Stocks, through the Air; and a very large Bundle of Shingles taken from the Ground and thrown near 330 Feet in an opposite Direction to that of the Post above-mentioned, and at right Angles to the Course the Vessels were carried. Large Trees were torn up by the Roots and cast into Pawaw River: Very large oak Planks hurled with almost the Velocity of Cannon Balls through the Roofs of Houses: Fences split into very small Pieces, and dispersed over the Ground: The Trees of whole Orchards eradicated: Many Persons buried in their Cellars, but were dug out without receiving any Hurt (except what was very slight).—— All this terrific Scene was produced in the short Space of about 5 Minutes. But notwithstanding Chimneys falling, Houses racked to Pieces, large oak Planks from the Stages of Vessels, and many more Instruments of Death, whirling with the most surprizing Rapidity through the Air, and surrounding the affrighted Inhabitants, no Lives were lost, or any Bone fractured, except Capt. Smith's, whose Leg was broke, and his Head and other Parts terribly **contused**; and an aged Woman, who, as she escaped from the Ruins of her own House, had both her Legs broken by a large oak Plank from one of the Vessels.—In fine, the Havock that amazing Element has made at Salisbury Point and Almsbury is almost past Conception or Description.

> **contused:** bruised

P. S. Since writing the above, it is credibly reported that the Number of Buildings damaged exceeds Fifty.

Pennsylvania Journal (Philadelphia), August 28, 1776

Letter Extract from New York:

AUGUST 22.—This night we have reason to expect the grand attack from our barbarian enemies; the reasons why, follow. The night before last, a lad went over to Staten-Island, supped there with a friend, and got safe back again undiscovered, soon after he went to General Washington, and upon good authority reported—That the English army, amounting to 15 or 20,000, had embarked, and were in readiness for an engagement—that seven ships of the line, and a number of other vessels of war were to surround this city and cover their landing—That the Hessians, being 15,000, were to remain on the island and attack Perth Amboy, Elizabethtown point, and Bergen, while the main body were doing their best here ; that the Highlanders expected America was already conquered, and that they were only to come over and settle on our lands, for which reason they had brought their churns, ploughs, &c. being deceived, they had refused fighting, upon which account General Howe had shot one, hung five or six, and flogged many.

Last evening, in a violent thunder storm, Mr.—— (a very intelligent person) ventured over, he brings much the same account as the above lad, with this addition:—That all the horses on the island were by Howe's orders killed, barrelled up and put on board: the wretches thinking they could get no landing here, and of consequence be soon out of provision. That the Tories were used cruelly, and with the Highlanders were compelled to go on board the ships to fight in the character of common soldiers against us. The British army are prodigiously incensed against the tories, and curse them as the instruments of the war now raging. Mr.—— further informs, that last night the fleet were to come up, but the thunder storm prevented. The truth of this appears, from the circumstance of about three thousand red coats landing at ten o'clock this morning on Long Island, where by this time it is supposed our people are hard at it. There is an abundance of smoke to-day on Long Island, our folks having set fire to stacks of hay, &c. to prevent the enemy's being benefited in case they get any advantage against us. All the troops in the city are in high spirits, and have been under arms most of the day, as the fleet have been in motion, and are now, as is generally thought, only waiting for a change of tide—Forty-eight hours or less, I believe, will determine it as to New-York, one way or the other.

The thunder-storm of last evening was one of the most dreadful I ever heard, it lasted from seven to ten o'clock. Several claps struck in and about the city—many houses damaged—several lives lost—three officers, a Captain and two Lieutenants, belonging to Col. M'Dougal's regiment encamped opposite us, were struck instantly dead—the points of their swords for several inches melted, with a few silver dollars they had in their pockets, they (the persons) were seemingly roasted, a dog in the same tent was also killed, a soldier near it struck blind, deaf, and dumb. One in the Main-street was killed, as likewise 10 on Long Island, two or three were much burnt, and greatly hurt. When God speaks, who can but fear?

Connecticut Courant (Hartford), January 18, 1780

Account from New London:

Last Sabbath night we had an exceeding hard gale of wind, attended with snow. During the space of about four hours, the wind went almost round the compass, and threw the highest tide into the harbour, by two or three feet, that ever before was known by the oldest person among us, and has done very considerable damage to the wharves, stores, and shipping. A large quantity of sugars and other goods are lost. Many vessels and boats were drove from their moorings; and one warehouse with a quantity of sugars in it, was floted away and beat in pieces. The tide came into several houses situated on the beach, and obliged the terrified people in them to move into their chambers.

AFTERMATH

Storms continue to be something that people struggle to deal with because of all the damage they can do. Over time, efforts were undertaken to try to reduce the damage, such as BENJAMIN FRANKLIN's invention of the lightning rod, which directed the force of lightning into the ground. Use of lightning rods on the tops of buildings greatly reduced the number of fires that broke out during thunderstorms. It finally became possible to spread the word about approaching bad weather with the invention of the telegraph about 1840. Since that time, technological advances have made it possible for meteorologists to become ever more accurate in predicting bad weather. But more accurate predictions do not necessarily remove the costs and losses produced by storms. People today often suffer the same sorts of losses as those described in these Revolutionary era newspaper reports.

ASK YOURSELF

1. Why do you think people wanted all the details about the impact of storms? Why are people so fascinated with the aftermath of bad weather?
2. What do you think were the worst impacts of the storms described in these newspaper accounts? Do they seem worse than the impact of similar storms today? Why or why not?

TOPICS AND ACTIVITIES TO CONSIDER

- ❧ Storms have had significant impacts throughout history. Investigate how the weather affected the fighting during the American Revolution.

☞ People have always tried to predict the weather. Investigate how that has changed over the years.

Further Reading

Cox, John D. *Storm Watchers: The Turbulent History of Weather Prediction from Franklin's Kite to El Nino*. Hoboken, NJ: John Wiley and Sons, 2002.

Eisenstadt, Peter. *Weather and Weather Forecasting in Colonial America*. PhD dissertation, New York University, 1990.

Halford, Pauline. *Storm Warning: The Origins of the Weather Forecast*. Stroud, UK: Sutton Publishers, 2004.

Laskin, David. *Braving the Elements: The Stormy History of American Weather*. New York: Doubleday, 1996.

FUN AND GAMES

16. Continuing to Learn How to Have Fun: Philip Fithian's Diary (1773)

INTRODUCTION

In the 18th century, it was important for people from the upper echelons of society to know how to behave in public society in order to show their proper breeding. Part of that knowledge consisted of being able to dance, both traditional styles and the latest, most popular versions. Parents who could afford to do so hired dance instructors so their children could be properly trained in what they would need to be able to do in the future at public functions. In order to advance in society or find the right husband or wife, people saw being able to dance appropriately as being just as important (and maybe more important to some) as being educated in subjects such as history and literature. Such ideas did not disappear even in the midst of growing conflicts with Great Britain.

Those most able to provide such instruction for their children generally lived close to cities and towns with more ties to the larger world of British society. A good example of this can be found in the family of Robert Carter III of Virginia. Carter had enough income to be able to hire a variety of instructors for his children. His children's tutor in 1773–1774 was Philip Vickers Fithian from New Jersey. In his diary, Fithian describes how his students took off a day from his instruction in order to receive their regular dance instruction, a reflection of the relative importance of more academic subjects and dance instruction.

KEEP IN MIND WHILE YOU READ

1. At the time, Fithian was 26 years old and had recently graduated from college. His family were farmers and not very wealthy.
2. The Carters lived at Nomini Hall, a plantation in northeastern Virginia. The closest city of any size would have been Williamsburg, but it was 82 miles away (a trip of several days by carriage or horse). So teachers and instructors had to come to their students at home.

Document: Excerpts from Philip Fithian's Diary (1773)

Fryday 17.

I dismissed the children this morning til monday on account of Mr Christian's Dance, which, as it goes through his Scholars in Rotation happens to be here to Day—I myself also am unwell, so as not to go out;—Mrs Carter sent me over Coffee for Breakfast; & soon after some **Spirits of Hartshorn** for my head—At twelve she sent the waiting Man to know if I was better, & what I would choose for Dinner. I thank'd her, & desired that she would give herself no trouble; She was careful, however, for her undistinguished kindness, to send me before Dinner some hot **Barley Broth.** Ben Carter before Noon introduced into my Room, Mr Billy Booth, a young Gentleman of Fortune, who is one of Mr Christians pupils -The two Master Fantleroys came in also to see me. There came to the dance three Chariots, two **Chairs,** & a number of Horses. Towards Evening I grew Better, & walked down, with a number of young Fellows to the River; after our return I was strongly solicited by the young Gentlemen to go in and dance. I declined it, however, and went to my Room not without Wishes that it had been a part of my Education to learn what I think is an innocent and an ornamental, and most certainly, in this province is a necessary qualification for a person to appear even decent in Company!—

Mrs Carter in the Evening, sent me for Supper, a Bowl of hot Green Tea, & several **Tarts**. I expected that they would have danced til late in the Night, but intirely contrary to my Expectation, the Company were separated to their respective apartments before half after nine o-Clock.

Saturday 18.

Rose by Seven, Sent for Mr Carters Barber and was drest for Breakfast. We went in to Breakfast at ten;—I confess I have been seldom more dash'd than when I entered the dining-Room, for I must of necessity be interrogated by Mr Carter before them all, about my indisposition, and if I was better; I went through the several Ceremonies with as much resolution, and speed as possible, and soon mixed with the Company in promiscuous conversation. There were present of Grown persons Mr & Mrs Carter, Mrs Lee, & Miss Jenny Corbin; young Misses about Eleven; & Seven young Fellows, including myself;—After Breakfast, we all retired into the Dancing-Room, & after the Scholars had their Lesson singly round Mr Christian, very politely, requested me to step a Minuet: I excused myself, however, but signified my peculiar pleasure in the accuracy of their performance—There were several Minuets danced with great ease and propriety; after which the whole company joined in **country-dances,** and it was indeed beautiful to admiration, to see such a number of young persons, set off by dress to the best advantage, moving easily, to the sound of well performed Music, and with perfect regularity, tho' apparently in the utmost disorder—The Dance continued til two, we dined at half after three—soon after Dinner we repaired to the Dancing-Room again; I observe in the course of the lessons, that Mr Christian is punctual, and rigid in his discipline, so strict indeed that he struck two of the young Misses for a fault in

Barley broth: whiskey or beer/ale

Chair: light, one-horse carriage

country-dances: general term referring to less formal dances such as polkas and square dances

Spirits of Hartshorn: smelling salts made from ammonia water used to treat a cold

Tarts: small pastry shells filled with jam, fruit, and so forth

the course of their performance, even in the presence of the Mother of one of them! And he rebuked one of the young Fellows so highly as to tell him he must alter his manner, which he had observed through the Course of the Dance, to be insolent, and wanton, or absent himself from the School—I thought this a sharp reproof to a young Gentleman of seventeen, before a large number of Ladies!—When it grew too dark to dance, the young Gentlemen walked over to my Room, we conversed til half after six; Nothing is now to be heard of in conversation, but the Balls, the Fox-hunts, and fine entertainments, and the good fellowship, which are to be exhibited at the approaching CHRISTMAS. . . .

When the candles were lighted, we all repaired, for the last time, into the dancing-Room; first each couple danced a Minuet; then all joined as before in the country Dances, these continued till half after Seven when Mr Christian retired; and at the proposal of several, (with Mr Carters approbation) we played Button, to get Pauns for Redemption; here I could join with them, and indeed it was carried on with sprightliness, and Decency; in the course of redeeming my Pauns I had several kisses of the Ladies! Early in the Evening came colonel Philip Lee, in a travelling Chariot from Williamsburg—Half after eight we were rung in to Supper; The room looked luminous and splendid; four very large candles burning on the table where we supp'd ; three others in different parts of the Room; a gay, sociable Assembly, & four well instructed waiters! So soon as we rose from supper, the Company formed into a semicircle round the fire, & Mr. Lee, by the voice of the Company was chosen Pope, and Mr Carter, Mr Christian, Mrs Carter, Mrs Lee, and the rest of the company were appointed Friars, in the Play call'd "break the Pope's neck"—Here we had great Diversion in the respective Judgments upon offenders, but we were all dismissed by ten, and retired to our several Rooms.

Source: Fithian, Philip Vickers. *Journal and Letters, 1767–1774.* Ed. John Rogers Williams. Princeton, NJ: Princeton University Library, 1900, pp. 62–65.

AFTERMATH

Learning how to dance appropriately would have helped Robert Carter's children advance in life by enabling them to interact in a social setting with the wealthiest and most influential people in Virginia at that time. It hopefully would help them find a good match for a husband or wife, a match that would help them advance socially. Learning how to dance appropriately could also help Philip Fithian advance himself, but probably not as far as Carter's children because Fithian was not from a wealthy and influential family. A good education, both in academic subjects and in social skills, could help one advance some in Revolutionary era society, but one's family background continued to have a major influence on one's future into the 19th century.

Philip Vickers Fithian had attended and graduated from the College of New Jersey in Princeton prior to becoming the tutor for the Carter children. Following his year as a tutor, he continued with his plans to enter the Presbyterian clergy, serving as a missionary to the Scots-Irish settlements in western Virginia in 1775 and 1776. He married ELIZABETH BEATTY in October 1775. He became the chaplain for a New Jersey state militia regiment and witnessed the fighting around New York City in 1776. He died from exposure while stationed near Fort Washington on northern Manhattan Island on October 8, 1776.

MINUET

A variety of dances existed in the 18th century, ranging from very formal types such as the minuet to more relaxed versions such as country dances. The minuet was a more formal type of dance that was very stylized in its performance. It originally developed in France. It is generally done in a ballroom and is almost always done in 3/4 time. It became very popular in the 17th century as it spread beyond France to other countries in Europe. Country dances generally included things like polkas, circle dances, square dances, and line dances, and were not always limited to ballrooms. They were much more relaxed in their performance, which made them much more suitable for outdoors or barns. In Europe, dance training among the nobility would have focused on formal dances such as the minuet, while country dances were seen as what the general population was likely to perform. Fithian mentioned both of these types of dances, which indicates that knowledge of both would be considered necessary for a well-educated person in Virginia.

ASK YOURSELF

1. Why would a young man from New Jersey decide to take a job as a tutor in Virginia? What do you think Fithian hoped to gain from the experience?
2. Clearly, learning to dance was important. How would being able to dance appropriately show good manners? What today constitutes signs of good manners and good upbringing?
3. Dancing has been seen by people as a fun activity for a long time, even though the types of dances have changed. Why do you think people think dancing is a fun activity?

TOPICS AND ACTIVITIES TO CONSIDER

- The types of dances that have been popular have changed over the years. Investigate how dances have changed and consider why that has happened. What changes or developments in society have encouraged the development of new types of dances over the years?
- Hiring tutors and special instructors for a variety of subjects was a common practice among the well-to-do in early American colonial and post-colonial times. Investigate why this was true at the time. When and how did this practice change?
- Consider what subjects would have been most commonly taught to children in the 18th century and compare that to the predominant subjects that are taught to children today. Have the important subjects changed over time? Why or why not?

Further Reading

Benson, Norman Arthur. *The Itinerant Dancing and Music Masters of 18th-Century America*. PhD dissertation, University of Minnesota, 1963.

Fea, John. *The Way of Improvement Leads Home: Philip Vickers Fithian and the Rural Enlightenment in Early America*. Philadelphia: University of Pennsylvania Press, 2008.

Glenn, Thomas Allen. *Some Colonial Mansions and Those Who Lived in Them*. Philadelphia: Henry T. Coates & Company, 1899, pp. 217–296.

Keller, Kate Van Winkle. *"If the Company Can Do It!": Technique in 18th-Century American Social Dance*. Sandy Hook, CT: Hendrickson Group, 1991.

Morton, Louis. *Robert Carter of Nomini Hall, a Virginia Planter of the 18th Century*. Williamsburg, VA: Colonial Williamsburg, 1941.

Web Site

A History of Social Dance in America: http://www.americanantiquarian.org/Exhibitions/Dance/

17. HAVING FUN EVEN DURING WARTIME: SARAH WISTER'S JOURNAL (1777)

INTRODUCTION

War can be a devastating experience because of the death and destruction involved in fighting, but people generally always try to find ways to divert their attention from the costs involved. This proved true during the American Revolution as people continued to try to have fun and laugh as much as possible. Such an effort is described in the following document, the journal of Sarah Wister.

Sarah Wister's family had wealth and influence in her hometown of Philadelphia. As a result, she attended school and had friends among the leading families of the city. When the British threatened the city in 1777, her family moved to a farm outside the city for protection. While there, Sarah began to keep a journal of her experiences. Her journal records events from September 25, 1777, to June 20, 1778. At the time, Sarah Wister was 16, and her journal reflects the outlook and sense of humor of a teenager in the midst of a war. The practical joke described in the following selection provided some relief for all involved in the midst of a war that had no clear end in sight. Even the target of the joke relaxed and laughed at himself when it was all over.

KEEP IN MIND WHILE YOU READ

1. Many of the officers described in the selection would have been young men in their twenties and thirties, while Sarah Wister was a teenager.
2. Sarah Wister's family had wealth and position and would assume that her future husband would come from a similar background. But having the rank of an officer in the CONTINENTAL ARMY would give a man a certain level of prestige that could make him a possible husband as well.
3. The farm to which Sarah Wister's family fled when the British occupied Philadelphia was only 15 miles away from the city, so the possibility of British troops showing up was very real.

Document: Excerpts from Sarah Wister's Journal (1777)

Fifth Day December 11th.

Our Army mov'd as we thought to go into **winter quarters,** but we hear there is a party of the enemy gone over Schuyllkill; so our Army went to look at them.

I observ'd to Stodard, "So you are going to leave us to the English."

"Yes, ha! ha! ha! leave you for the English." He has a certain in-difference about him sometimes that to strangers is not very pleas-ing. He somtimes is silent for minutes. One of these silent fits was interrupted the other day by his clasping his hands and exclaiming aloud, "Oh, My God, I wish this war was at an end."

winter quarters: winter residence or station for military units

Noon. The Major gone to Camp. I don't think we shall see him again.

Well, strange creature that I am; here have I been going on without giving thee an account of two officers,—one who will be a principal character; their names are Capt. Lips-comb and a Mr. Tilly; the former a tall, genteel man, very delicate from an indisposition, and has a softness in his countenance that is very pleasing, and has the finest head of hair that I ever saw; 'tis a light, shining auburn. The fashion of his hair was this—negligently ty'd, and waving down his back. Well may it be said,—

"Loose flow'd the soft redundance of his hair."

He has not hitherto shewn himself a lady's man, tho' he is perfectly polite.

Now let me attempt to characterize Tilly. He seems a wild, noisy mortal, tho' I am not much acquainted with him. He appears bashful when with girls. We dissipated the Major's bashful-ness; but I doubt we have not so good a subject now. He is above the common size, rather gen-teel, an extreme pretty, ruddy face, hair brown, and a sufficiency of it, a very great laughter, and talks so excessively fast that he often begins sentences without finishing the last, which confuses him very much, and then he blushes and laughs; and in short, he keeps me in perpetual good humour; but the creature has not address'd one civil thing to me since he came.

But I have not done with his accomplishments yet, for he is a musician,—that is he plays on the German flute and has it here.

Fifth Day Night.

The family retir'd; take the adventures of the afternoon as they occurr'd.

Seaton and Capt. Lipscomb drank tea with us. While we sat at tea, the parlour door was open'd; in came Tilly; his appearance was elegant; he had been riding; the wind had given the most beautiful glow to his cheeks, and blow'd his hair carelessly round his face.

Oh, my heart, thought I, be secure!

The caution was needless, I found it without a wish to stray.

When the tea equipage was remov'd, the conversation turned on politicks, a subject I avoid. I gave Betsy a hint. I rose, she followed; and we went to seek Liddy.

We chatted a few moments at the door. The moon shone with uncommon splendour. Our spirits were high. I propos'd a walk; the girls agreed. When we reach'd the poplar tree, we stopp'd. Our ears were assail'd by a number of voices.

"A party of light horse," said one.

"The English, perhaps; let's run home."

"No, no," said I, "be heroines."

At last two or three men on horseback came in sight. We walked on. The well-known voice of the Major saluted our hearing with, "How do you do, ladies?"

We turn'd ourselves about with one accord. He, not relishing the idea of sleeping on the banks of the Schuylkill, had return'd to the Mill.

We chatted along the road till we reach'd our hospitable mansion. Stodard dismounted, and went into Jesse's parlour. I sat there a half hour. He is very amiable.

Seaton, Lipscomb, Tilly, and my father, hearing of his return, and impatient for the news, came in at one door, while I made my exit at the other.

I am vex'd at Tilly, who has his flute and does nothing but play the fool.

He begins a tune, plays a note or so, then stops. Well, after a while, he begins again; stops again. "Will that do Seaton? Hah! hah! hah!"

He has given us but two regular tunes since he arriv'd. I am passionately fond of music. How boyish he behaves.

Sixth day, December 12th, 1777.

I ran into aunt's this morn to chat with the girls. Major Stodard join'd us in a few minutes.

I verily believe the man is fond of the ladies, and, what to me is astonishing, he has not discovered the smallest degree of pride. Whether he is artful enough to conceal it under the veil of humility, or whether he has none is a question; but I am inclined to think it the latter.

I really am of opinion that there are few of the young fellows of the modern age exempt from vanity, more especially those who are bless'd with exterior graces. If they have a fine pair of eyes they are ever rolling them about; a fine set of teeth, mind, they are great laughers; a genteel person, forever changing their attitudes to show them to advantage. Oh, vanity, vanity; how boundless is thy sway!

But to resume this interview with Major Stodard. We were very witty and sprightly. I was darning an apron, upon which he was pleas'd to compliment me.

"Well, Miss Sally, what would you do if the British were to come here?"

"Do," exclaimed I; "be frightened just to death."

He laugh'd, and said he would escape their rage by getting behind the representation of a British **grenadier** which you have upstairs. "Of all things, I should like to frighten Tilly with it. Pray, ladies, let's fix it in his chamber to-night."

> **grenadier:** member of a special regiment in the British army

"If thee will take all the blame, we will assist thee."

"That I will," he replied, and this was the plan.

We had brought some weeks ago a British grenadier from Uncle Miles's on purpose to divert us. It is remarkably well executed, six foot high, and makes a martial appearance. This we agreed to stand at the door that opens into the road (the house has four rooms on a floor, with a wide entry running through), with another figure that would add to the deceit. One of our servants was to stand behind them, others were to serve as occasion offer'd.

After half an hour's converse, in which we rais'd our expectations to the highest pitch, we parted. If our scheme answers, I shall communicate in the eve. Till then, adieu. 'Tis dining hour.

Sixth Day Night.

Never did I more sincerely wish to possess a descriptive genius than I do now. All that I can write will fall infinitely short of the truly diverting scene that I have been witness to to-night. But, as I mean to attempt an account, I had as well shorten the preface, and begin the story.

In the beginning of the evening I went to Liddy and beg'd her to secure the swords and pistols which were in their parlour. The Marylander, hearing our voices, joined us. I told him of my proposal. Whether he thought it a good one or not I can't say, but he approv'd of it, and Liddy went in and brought her apron full of swords & pistols.

When this was done, Stodard join'd the officers. We girls went and stood at the first landing of the stairs. The Gentlemen were very merry and chatting on public affairs, when Seaton's Negro (observe that Seaton, being indisposed, was appriz'd of the scheme) open'd the door, candle in his hand, and said, "There's somebody at the door that wishes to see you."

"Who? All of us?" said Tilly.

"Yes, sir," answer'd the boy.

They all rose (the Major, as he afterwards said, almost dying with laughing), and walk'd in to the entry, Tilly first, in full expectation of news.

The first object that struck his view was a British soldier. In a moment his ears were saluted with "Is there any rebel officers here?" in a thundering voice,

Not waiting for a second word, he darted like lightning out at the front door, through the yard, bolted o'er the fence. Swamps, fences, thorn-hedges, and plough'd fields no way impeded his retreat. He was soon out of hearing.

The woods echoed with, "Which way did he go? Stop him! Surround the house!" The amiable Lipscomb had his hand on the latch of the door, intending to attempt his escape; Stodard, considering his indisposition, acquainted him with the deceit.

We females ran down stairs to join the general laugh. I walk'd into Jesse's parlour. There sat poor Stodard (whose sore lips must have received no advantage from this), almost convuls'd with laughing and rolling in an arm-chair. He said nothing. I believe he cou'd not have spoke.

"Major Stodard," said I, "Go, call Tilly back. He will lose himself, indeed he will;" every word interrupt with a "Ha! ha!"

At last he rose and went to the door, and what a loud voice could avail in bringing him back, he tried.

Figure to thyself this Tilly, of a snowy even: no hat, shoes down at heel, hair unty'd, flying across meadows, creeks and mudholes. Flying from what?—why, a bit of painted wood. But he was ignorant of what it was. The idea of being made a prisoner wholly engross'd his mind, and his last resource was to run.

After a while, we being in rather more composure, and our bursts of laughter less frequent, yet by no means subsided, in full assembly of girls and officers,—Tilly enter'd.

The greatest part of my risibility turn'd into pity. Inexpressible confusion had taken entire possession of his countenace, his fine hair hanging dishevell'd down his shoulders, all splash'd with mud yet his fright, confusion and race had not divested him of his beauty.

He smil'd as he trip'd up the steps; but 'twas vexation plac'd it on his features. Joy at that moment was vanish'd from his heart. He briskly walked five or six steps, then stopt, and took a general survey of us all.

"Where have you been, Mr Tilly?" Ask'd one officer (We girls were silent.) "I really imagin'd," said Stodard, "that you were gone for your pistols. I follow'd you to prevent danger,"—an excessive laugh at each question, which it was impossible to restrain.

"Pray, where were your pistols, Tilly?" He broke his silence by the following expression: "You may all go to the D——l." I never heard him utter an indecent expression before.

At last his good nature gain'd a compleat ascendance over his anger, and he join'd heartily in the laugh. I will do him the justice to say that he bore it charmingly. No cowardly threats, no vengeance denounced.

Stodard caught hold of his coat. "Come, look at what you ran from," and drag'd him to the door.

He gave it a look, said it was very natural, and, by the singularity of his expressions, gave fresh cause for diversion. We all retir'd to our different parlours, for to rest our faces, if I may say so.

Well, certainly, these military folks will laugh all night. Such screaming I never did hear. Adieu to-night.

Source: Meyers, Albert Cook , ed. *Sally Wister's Journal: A True Narrative Being a Quaker Maiden's Account of Her Experiences with Officers of the Continental Army, 1777–1778*. Philadelphia: Ferris & Leach, 1902, pp. 119–132.

AFTERMATH

The fear that Sarah Wister and her friends expressed regarding the British army had already proved to be very real. Following the Battle of Brandywine in early September 1777, British forces under the command of General Sɪʀ Wɪʟʟɪᴀᴍ Howe occupied the city of Philadelphia on September 26. The British remained in Philadelphia until June 1778 when the new commander, Sɪʀ Hᴇɴʀʏ Cʟɪɴᴛᴏɴ, decided to abandon the city in order to concentrate his forces in the city of New York.

Sarah Wister's family returned to Philadelphia after the evacuation, and this event marked the end of her journal. The family later moved to the family estate in Germantown, Pennsylvania. Here, Sarah spent the rest of her life, occasionally writing some poetry that was published. She never married and died in July 1804 at the age of 43.

ASK YOURSELF

1. How did Sarah react to the various Continental Army officers she met? Do her reactions seem normal and appropriate for the time? Would they be normal and appropriate now?
2. Why do you think they chose to play the joke on Tilly? Do you think the joke was funny? Why or why not?
3. What items in Sarah's descriptions indicate what social class she came from?

TOPICS AND ACTIVITIES TO CONSIDER

- ↝ Veterans have always talked about how military service brings people closer together, and the interactions between the officers that Sarah describes seem to show that to be true here. Investigate descriptions of such interactions in other military conflicts and compare them to Wister's journal. Does the common experience of military experience outweigh differences in time from war to war? Why or why not?

- ↝ Women's role during wartime has often been described as one of support and encouragement. How does Sarah's description reflect that idea during the Revolution? Investigate the role of women during other wars in American history. Compare and contrast these discussions with Sarah's reflection of the role of women in wartime. How are they similar? How are they different?

Further Reading

Berkin, Carol. *Revolutionary Mothers: Women in the Struggle for America's Independence.* New York: Alfred A. Knopf, 2005.

Ellet, Elizabeth Fries. *Revolutionary Women in the War for American Independence: A One-Volume Revised Edition.* Westport, CT: Greenwood Publishing Group, 1998.

Evans, Elizabeth. *Weathering the Storm: Women of the American Revolution.* New York Paragon House, 1975.

Gerb, George Winthrop. *A History of Philadelphia, 1776–1789.* Madison: University of Wisconsin Press, 1973.

Jackson, John W. *With the British Army in Philadelphia.* San Rafael, CA: Presidio Press, 1979.

Kerber, Linda K. *Women of the Republic: Intellect and Ideology in Revolutionary America.* Chapel Hill: Published for the Institute of Early American History and Culture by the University of North Carolina Press, 1980.

Martin, David G. *The Philadelphia Campaign, June 1777–1778.* Conshohocken, PA: Combined Books, 1993.

Norton, Mary Beth. *Liberty's Daughters: The Revolutionary Experience of American Women, 1750–1800.* Boston: Little, Brown and Company, 1980.

Weigley, Russell Frank. *Philadelphia: A 300-Year History.* New York: W. W. Norton, 1982.

Web Site

History of Philadelphia: http://www.ushistory.org/philadelphia/index.html

18. SEEKING RELIEF AND RELAXATION: REPORTS OF THEATER PRODUCTIONS DURING THE WAR (1776–1778)

INTRODUCTION

Throughout the course of the Revolution, people searched for ways to relieve the stresses of living in a world at war. One method that proved popular for some was the production of plays in order to provide an evening's entertainment for all who could attend. The cities where the British army was stationed particularly experienced this because groups of soldiers produced plays in their spare time. While the British occupied Boston, Philadelphia, and New York, regular theatrical productions took place. But the British were not the only ones who engaged in such activity. The American troops also produced and attended plays on occasion, primarily as an effort to lift their spirits during the war. GEORGE WASHINGTON approved the opening of a theater at Valley Forge in the spring of 1778 in order to provide his troops with some form of relaxation after the hard winter they had just survived. The documents below describe three theatrical productions and clearly indicate that the primary reason for each event lay in its ability to cheer people up by allowing them to have a fun and relaxing evening in the middle of the war.

KEEP IN MIND WHILE YOU READ

1. Boston had originally been settled by the Puritans back in the 1630s. Historically, the Puritans had been critical of plays and tried to suppress the theater in New England.
2. Many of the officers in both armies came from families of wealth, which meant that they may have had access to a good classical education. Included in that sort of education would have been an introduction to theater and the great plays of the past (such as those of Shakespeare).
3. The first two documents describe productions in Boston and New York during the British occupation, while the third document describes a play performed at Valley Forge following the severe winter of 1777–1778.

Document 1: Letter from Lord Thomas Stanley (1776)

We acted the tragedy of 'Zara' two nights before I left Boston, for the benefit of the widows and children. The Prologue was spoken by Lord Rawdon, a very fine fellow and good soldier. I wish you knew him. We took above L100 at the door. I hear a great many people blame us for acting, and think we might have found something better to do, but General Howe follows the example of the King of Prussia, who, when Prince Ferdinand wrote him a long letter mentioning all the difficulties and distresses of the army, sent back the following concise answer: De la gaîté, encore de la gaîté, et toujours de la gaîté. [Gaiety, more gaiety, gaiety forever!] The female parts were filled by young ladies, though some of the Boston ladies were so prudish as to say this was improper.

Source: Letter from Lord Thomas Stanley to Hugh Elliot, qtd. in George O. Seilhamer, *History of the American Treatre: During the Revolution and After.* Vol. 2. Philadelphia: Globe Printing House, 1889, p. 19.

Document 2: New York Gazette *(January 27, 1777)*

On Saturday evening last, the little theatre in John-street in this City, was opened, with the celebrated Burlesque Entertainment of TOM THUMB, written by the late Mr. Fielding, to ridicule the Bathos of several dramatic Pieces that at his Time to the disgrace of the British Stage, had engrossed both the London Theatres. The Characters were performed by Gentlemen of the Navy and Army; the Spirit with which this favourite Piece was supported by the Performers, prove their Taste and strong Conception of the Humour. Saturday's Performance convince us that a good Education and Knowledge of polite Life, are essentially necessary to form a good Actor. The Play was introduced by a Prologue written and spoken by Captain Stanly; we have great Pleasure in applauding this first Effort of his infant Muse, as replete with true poetic Genius. The Scenes painted by Captain De Lancey has great Merit, and would not disgrace a Theatre, tho' under the management of a Garrick. The House was crowded with Company, and the Ladies made a brilliant Appearance.

Document 3: Letter from William Bradford Jr. (May 14, 1778)

My dear Rachel

I find by a Letter from my father that you are on a visit at Trenton. I should be happy could you extend your Jaunt as far as full view—the Camp could now afford you some entertainment. The manoeuvering of the Army is in itself a sight that would Charm you.— Besides these, the Theatre is opened—Last Monday Cato was performed before a very numerous & splendid audience. His Excellency & Lady, Lord Stirling, the Countess & Lady Kitty, & Mr Green were part of the Assembly. The scenery was in Taste—& the performance admirable.—Col. George did his part to admiration—he made an excellent die (as they say)—Pray heaven, he don't die in earnest—for yesterday he was seized with the pleurisy & lies extremely ill—If the Enemy does not retire from Philad[elphi]a soon, our Theatrical amusements will continue—The fair Penitent with the Padlock will soon be acted. The "recruiting officer" is also on foot.

I hope however we shall be disappointed in all these by the more agreeable Entertainment of taking possession of Philad[elphi]a....

Source: Letter from William Bradford, Jr., to his sister Rachel, May 14, 1778. "Selections from the Wallace Papers." *Pennsylvania Magazine of History and Biography* 40.1 (1916): 342–343.

AFTERMATH

The British troops continued to produce plays throughout the Revolution, but the American forces ceased productions because of the opposition of the CONTINENTAL CONGRESS. The Congress had first adopted a resolution opposing the theater in 1774, and members reinforced that statement with a second one in 1778 that threatened dismissal from office to any government official who supported or attended plays. These resolutions reflected an ongoing debate about whether attending a play could be good for a person, or whether it was a waste of time that bordered on immorality. Such feelings remained strong in the New England states, but the southern states protested such restrictions and continued to have local theater productions throughout the war whenever possible.

ASK YOURSELF

1. Many of the parts in these plays were played by army officers. Why do you think they would want to take the time to learn the part and participate in the production?
2. Why would some people object to the time and effort spent on producing a play while others would think it was a good idea? Does this attitude still exist today?

TOPICS AND ACTIVITIES TO CONSIDER

- ⮞ Plays have been produced in the United States since the early 18th century. Investigate the history of the theater in the United States.
- ⮞ Plays can sometimes be written or produced to try to influence people's beliefs and actions about a political concern. Investigate the writing and production of plays during the American Revolution to see if organizers tried to use the theater to influence people's political beliefs and actions.
- ⮞ The Puritans were not the only religious group to oppose the theater. Investigate what religious groups have opposed the theater and why.

Further Reading

Brown, Jared. *The Theatre in America during the Revolution*. New York: Cambridge University Press, 1995.

Dunlap, William. *History of the American Theatre*. New York: Burt Franklin, 1963.

Henderson, Mary C. *The City and the Theatre: The History of New York Playhouses*. New York: Back Stage Books, 2004.

Londré, Felicia Hardison, and Daniel J. Watermeier. *The History of North American Theater*. New York: Continuum, 1998.

Rankin, Hugh F. *The Theater in Colonial America*. Chapel Hill: University of North Carolina Press, 1960.

Web Site

American Theatre History: http://www.theatrehistory.com/american

HEALTH AND MEDICINE

19. Dealing with Illnesses: Nicholas Cresswell's Diary (1774)

INTRODUCTION

Dealing with illnesses in the 18th century could be difficult because of the limited information available. Even trained physicians could do more harm than good because of the incompleteness of medical knowledge at the time. Most people believed that the primary explanation for illness was an internal imbalance in the body. Bloodletting was a common procedure in order to restore the body's internal balance. Various drugs, from arsenic to herbal potions, were prescribed in an effort to calm the competing forces within the body. All of these efforts often made the patient's situation worse instead of better.

In June 1774, Nicholas Cresswell became ill and needed to see a doctor. A 24-year-old Englishman, Cresswell had arrived in the American colonies a month earlier seeking adventure. He recorded his experience with the doctor he went to see in his diary. The experience was not pleasant and provides a good idea of the state of medical knowledge and practice in the 18th century.

KEEP IN MIND WHILE YOU READ

1. There were no laws or regulations related to medicine or drugs in the 18th century.
2. Cresswell was a long way from home, so he could not turn to family for help or advice.

Document: Excerpts from Nicholas Cresswell's Diary (1774)

Piscataway, Maryland—Tuesday, June 7th, 1774. This morning Capn. Knox and I left Annapolis. Dined at Marlbro, Lodged at Piscataway. A most violent pain in my Head attended with a high Fever, obliged to stop and rest myself at several houses on the road. Captn. Knox behaves exceedingly kind to me.

Wednesday, June 8th, 1774. Got to Port Tobacco with great difficulty. Captn. Knox insists on me applying to Doctor Brown. I have taken his advice and he told me it is a Fever with some cussed physical name. He has given me some slops and I am now going to bed very ill.

Nanjemoy, Maryland—Thursday, June 9th, 1774. Find myself no better, However, the Doctor has given me more physic. Got to Nanjemoy. Almost dead with pain and fatigue, added to the excessive heat, which caused me to faint twice.

Wednesday, June 15th, 1774. Very ill, confined to my room. This is the first day I have been able to stir out of it. I am much reduced and very weak, but my spirits are good and I hope in God I shall get better. Captn. Knox, Mr. Bayley, and the whole neighbourhood behaves with the greatest kindness to me, some of them has attended me constantly all the time.

Friday, June 17th, 1774. Much better. The Doctor tells me I am out of all danger, but advises me to take some physic to clear my body and to drink a little more Rum than I did before I was sick. In short, I believe it was being too abstemious that brought this sickness upon me at first, by drinking water.

Saturday, June 18th, 1774. Able to walk about the house. It is such excessive hot weather or I should mend faster.

Sunday, June 19th, 1774. Dined at a certain Mr. Hambleton's. Supped and spent the evening at Mrs. Leftwiches with some young ladies from Virginia. After supper the company amused themselves with several diverting plays. This seems very strange to me, but I believe it is common in this Country. Find myself much better today. Hope I shall be able to go to Alexandria next week.

Monday, June 20th, 1774. Gathering strength very fast, the Doctor sent me a Box of Pills with directions to take two at night and two in the Morning. These are the last I intend to take. Dined at Mrs. Leftwiches. After went over to Virginia with some young ladies, but returned in the evening.

Wednesday, June 22nd, 1774. Taking the Pills the Doctor gave me, but these don't seem to work, only cause a bad taste in my mouth. Will take three this evening.

Thursday, June 23rd, 1774. This morning took 4 Pills which has caused a violent pain in my bowels all day, attended with a constant thirst and a very bad taste in my mouth. But affects me no other way. . . .

Friday, June 24th, 1774. Much worse, my throat and tongue much swollen. Have sent for the Doctor. Confined to my bed. Am afraid that I am poisoned with his confounded Pills. A continual thirst, but these people will not let me drink.

Saturday, June 25th, 1774. Captn. Knox sent an express for the Doctor, who came about eight this morning. After he had examined the Pills, he came with a truly physical face to the bedside and felt my pulse. Began to beg pardon for the mistake he said his Prentice had inadvertently committed by sending me strong Mercurial Pills, in the room of cooling ones. I immediately gave him as hard a blow as I could with my fist over the face, and would have given him a good trimming had I been able. This discomposed his physical muscles a good deal, and made him contract them into a most formidable frown. He did not attempt to resent it. Begged I would moderate my passion, follow his directions, and in a short time I should be well again. I believed myself poisoned and grew desperate, abused him most unmercifully. However, he left me some Brimstone and Salts which I took immediately after he was gone, which worked very well and has given me a great deal of ease. Tho' I am still full of pain and much swelled, spitting and slavering like a mad dog, my teeth loose and mouth very sore. I believe I have little to trust to but the strength of my constitution for my life. Much difficulty to write, but if I happen to die I hope this will appear against the rascal.

Sunday, June 26th, 1774. This morning took a dose of Brimstone, laid in bed all day and sweat abundantly. This has made me very weak and faint. Doctor came to enquire after me, but did not come into the room. Much easier.

Monday, June 27th, 1774. A great deal better but much relaxed and very weak, able to sit up most part of the day.

Wednesday, June 29th, 1774. Mending very fast, able to walk about the room. The swelling gone away, my throat got well, but my mouth is very sore, which I wash every two hours with Vinegar. I understand the Doctor sends every day to enquire how I do. Had it not been for the extraordinary care of Captn. Knox, I must certainly have died.

Thursday, June 30th, 1774. Took a dose of Salts, able to walk into the Yard.

Saturday, July 2nd, 1774. Continue mending, but very slowly.

Sunday, July 3rd, 1774. Rode out with Mr. Wallace to Colonel Taylor's Plantation. It is only two miles, but I find it has fatigued me too much....

Tuesday, July 5th, 1774. Took another dose of Salts, which I hope will be the last I shall have occasion to take at this time. Find myself pretty well. Free from pain, but very weak and much reduced. My clothes hang about me like a skeleton. The Doctor has never come in my sight since I struck him. Intend to go and pay the rascal to-morrow.

Wednesday, July 6th, 1774. Went to see the Doctor, who (contrary to my expectation) treated me with the greatest kindness and acknowledged that he had given me just cause of complaint, though inadvertantly, and absolutely refused being paid till I am quite recovered. I understand their Doctors' Bills in this country are very extravagant. Returned to Nanjemoy much fatigued.

Source: Cresswell, Nicholas. *The Journal of Nicholas Cresswell, 1774–1777* (New York: The Dial Press, 1924), pp. 22–25.

AFTERMATH

Cresswell recovered from his illness, but he never really found out what was wrong. He continued on his travels around the colonies for several years, but returned home to England in 1777 after he decided that he could not continue to live in the former colonies because of the Revolution. A loyal citizen of England, Cresswell believed that the American Revolution was a mistake that would destroy all the good that existed in the colonies. After he returned to England, he once more worked on his father's farm in Derbyshire. He married in 1781 and settled down to raise his own family.

Medical practice continued to be problematic because of the lack of knowledge about the causes of illness and disease. The connection between germs and disease would be discovered in the 1800s, and physicians would slowly gain more information about how the human body worked. Medical training also improved in the 1800s, setting the stage for the more successful medical practices of the 20th century. But, although care for the sick has improved greatly since the 1700s, there are still gaps in knowledge and information that continue to produce problems for medical practitioners and their patients.

ASK YOURSELF

1. It appears that Cresswell hesitated at first to contact the doctor. Why do you think that he would do that? Was it because he felt the doctor could not help him, or was it because he did not want to stop his travels?

2. Why do you think Cresswell reacted so violently when the doctor admitted Cresswell had been given the wrong drugs? What else could Cresswell have done?

TOPICS AND ACTIVITIES TO CONSIDER

- ∾ Cresswell mentions taking a variety of different drugs for his illness. Investigate what these drugs were and what they were prescribed for. Compare them to what would be prescribed for the same ailments today.
- ∾ Medical training has changed over the years. Investigate how doctors were trained in the 1700s and compare that to how the training has changed since that time.

Further Reading

Murphy, Lamar Riley. *Enter the Physician: The Transformation of Domestic Medicine, 1760–1860.* Tuscaloosa: University of Alabama Press, 1991.

Reiss, Oscar. *Medicine and the American Revolution: How Diseases and Their Treatments Affected the Colonial Army.* Jefferson, NC: McFarland and Company, 1998.

Toledo-Pereyra, Luis H. *A History of American Medicine from the Colonial Period to the Early 20th Century.* Lewiston, NY: Edwin Mellen Press, 2006.

Wilbur, C. Keith. *Revolutionary Medicine, 1700–1800.* Chester, CT: Globe Pequot Press, 1980.

Web Site

Medicine in the Americas, 1610–1914: A Digital Library: http://www.nlm.nih.gov/hmd/americas/americashome.html

20. Preventive Medicine: Accounts of Smallpox Inoculations in the Army (1776–1777)

INTRODUCTION

Issues of health and disease are something people have to deal with at all times, whether they are at peace or in the middle of a war. But wars can complicate health issues because the movement of armies can encourage the spread of diseases. During the 18th century, infectious diseases proved to be major killers among armies and the civilians around them. Of particular concern at times was SMALLPOX because it could spread very quickly. Because of such worries, American military leaders pushed for their troops to be inoculated against the smallpox. By the end of 1777, all of the regulars in the CONTINENTAL ARMY had received the smallpox INOCULATION.

Smallpox inoculation in the 18th century was very different from the modern vaccination. Anyone who had previously been exposed to the disease was considered to have gained immunity and did not have to receive the inoculation. Those who were inoculated were given a mild case of the disease by having the scabs of someone infected with COWPOX rubbed into scratches made on the skin of the person receiving the inoculation. Then the person would be isolated until the mild case of the disease had run its course. Soldiers generally did not like the process because it did result in fever and temporary disability. However, the procedure seldom proved fatal for people in good health. Those who received the inoculation often commented later on how the procedure had affected them. As is shown by the statements from Josiah Sabin, Samuel Larrabee, and Joseph Plumb Martin, the process of gaining immunity to smallpox was a memorable experience.

KEEP IN MIND WHILE YOU READ

1. Inoculations were relatively new in the 18th century. Most people did not really understand how to prevent disease, so the idea of purposely infecting someone with the disease could be frightening.
2. It was assumed that enlisted men would automatically follow the orders of their superior officers because that was seen as the only way that an army could work.

Document 1: Statement from Josiah Sabin (1776)

That he enlisted on or about the first day of November in the year 1775, at New Providence, in the state of Massachusetts, where he then resided, under Capt. Reuben Hinman, Lieutenants Low and Blakesly (Christian names not recollected), regiment commanded by Col. Seth Warner and Maj. Jeremiah Cady; remained at Providence until the first of January, 1776. Commenced our march on that day to Lake Champlain, at Crown Point; thence to St. Johns, down the lake, on the ice; thence to Montreal, where we remained about two weeks on account of the badness of the weather; thence to Three Rivers; thence to Quebec, where we remained until about the eighth of May, 1776.

While at Quebec, this declarant had the smallpox. He inoculated himself; got the infection from the hospital. He also inoculated many of the soldiers, but as this was against orders, they were sent into his room blindfolded, were inoculated, and sent out in the same condition. Many lives were saved by this measure, as none thus inoculated died, while three out of four who took it the natural way died. He was reprieved by General Arnold, as he was suspected of inoculating, but his conduct was approved by his colonel (Warner), and when he was taken before General Arnold, Colonel Warner went with him, and, after a considerable controversy and many sharp words between Colonel Warner and General Arnold, he was set at liberty without punishment.

Source: Revolutionary War Pension Applications, W19003, National Archives.

Document 2: Statement from Samuel Larrabee (1776)

In August the smallpox prevailed, and the three regiments were inoculated, which took in every instance in our regiment except on myself. When the regiment had recovered, we were ordered to Ticonderoga and, before marching, were drawn up on the common to hear a sermon and prayers. This day I had the symptoms of smallpox, and the day the regiment marched I was broke out with it. Not having anyone to take care of me, there being no hospitals, I was ordered back to Widow Dimond's, with whom I was quartered when inoculated, who nursed me and got me well of the smallpox though I was long after very feeble and afflicted with boils. After recovering from smallpox, I sold my watch to pay the widow and returned my gun and equipments to the gunhouse where I drew them, not being fit for military duty, and returned to Falmouth (now Portland) by water, not being able to walk that distance.

Source: Revolutionary War Pension Applications, W18076, National Archives.

Document 3: Statement from Joseph Plumb Martin (1777)

I was soon after this transaction, ordered off, in company with about four hundred others of the Connecticut forces, to a set of old barracks, a mile or two distant in the Highlands, to be inoculated with the small pox. We arrived at and cleaned out the barracks, and after two or three days received the infection, which was on the last day of May. We had a guard of Massachusetts troops to attend us. Our hospital stores were deposited in a farmer's barn in the vicinity of our quarters. One day, about noon, the farmer's house took fire and was totally consumed, with every article of household stuff it contained, although there were five hundred men within fifty rods of it, and many of them within five, when the fire was discovered, which was not till the roof had fallen in. Our officers would not let any of the inoculated men go near the fire, and the guard had enough to do to save the barn, the fire frequently catching in the yard and on the roof, which was covered with thatch or straw. I was so near to the house, however, that I saw a cat come out from the cellar window after the house had apparently fallen into the cellar; she was all in flames when she emerged from her premises and directed her course for the barn, but her nimble gait had so fanned her carcass before she reached the place of her destination that she caused no damage at all.

I had the small pox favorably as did the rest, generally; we lost none; but it was more by good luck, or rather a kind Providence interfering, than by my good conduct that I escaped with life. There was a considerable large rivulet which ran directly in front of the barracks; in this rivulet were many deep places and plenty of a species of fish called suckers. One of my roommates, with myself, went off one day, the very day on which the pock began to turn upon me, we went up the brook until we were out of sight of the people at the barracks, when we undressed ourselves and went into the water, where it was often to our shoulders, to catch suckers by means of a fish-hook fastened to the end of a rod;—we continued at this business three or four hours, and when we came out of the water the pustules of the small pox were well cleansed. We then returned to the barracks, and I, feeling a pretty sharp appetite after my expedition, went to the side of the brook where the nurses had been cooking and eating their dinners; I found a kettle standing there half full of stewed peas, and, if I remember rightly, a small piece of pork with them. I knew the kettle belonged to the nurses in our room, and therefore conceived myself the better entitled to its contents; accordingly I fell to and helped myself. I believe I should have killed myself in good earnest, had not the owners come and caught me at it, and broke up my feast. It had like to have done the job for me as it was; I had a sorry night of it, and had I not got rid of my freight, I know not what would have been the final consequences of my indiscretion.

I left the hospital on the sixteenth day after I was inoculated, and soon after joined the regiment, when I was attacked with a severe turn of the dysentery, and immediately after recovering from that, I broke out all over with boils; good old Job could scarcely have been worse handled by them than I was;—I had eleven at one time upon my arm, each as big as half a hen's egg, and the rest of my carcass was much in the same condition. I attributed it to my not having been properly physicked after the small pox; in consequence of our hospital stores being in about the same state as the commissary's.

Source: Martin, Joseph Plumb. *Memoir of a Revolutionary Soldier.* Mineola, NY: Dover Publications, 2006, pp. 37–38.

AFTERMATH

The inoculation efforts on the part of the Continental Army soldiers paid off because most of the men who received the inoculations did not die and were only out of action for a short period of time. Initially, some leaders were critical of the inoculation efforts because they thought them dangerous. In hindsight, everyone realized how beneficial it had been for the army. Sabin, Larrabee, and Martin clearly believed that receiving the inoculation

BENEDICT ARNOLD

General BENEDICT ARNOLD was Josiah Sabin's commanding officer when Sabin gave smallpox inoculations to his fellow soldiers. For Americans, the name Benedict Arnold is synonymous with treason because of his attempt to turn the fort at West Point, New York, over to the British in 1780. But before that happened, Arnold was a PATRIOT hero. Born in Connecticut, he served in a Connecticut MILITIA company during the siege of Boston in 1775. He participated in the failed attack on Canada in 1775–1776 and was wounded during the Battle of Quebec. He then put together a flotilla of ships on Lake Champlain that slowed down the British advance until winter came even though all his ships were destroyed. In the fall of 1777, troops under his command successfully stopped the British attack at the Battle of Freeman's Farm on September 19 and broke the British attack at Saratoga on October 7. The American victory at Saratoga would lead to the alliance with France, an agreement that would play a major role in the overall Patriot victory in the war. And Arnold's leadership at Saratoga helped ensure a Patriot victory in that battle. During the Battle of Saratoga, Arnold was once more wounded. Once he recovered, he was given command of Philadelphia. He was accused of corruption and demanded a court-martial. The verdict was not guilty on most charges, but GENERAL WASHINGTON was ordered to reprimand him. This event only confirmed Arnold in his efforts to change sides in the war, a process that had begun in the middle of 1779 and ended when he defected on September 25, 1780.

had been a good idea. These efforts to prevent the spread of disease on the part of the Continental Army constituted one of the first times that a military command had consciously tried to carry out such a plan of prevention. It demonstrated the potential for such efforts and produced improvements in health care for military personnel in the future. Smallpox inoculations, originally seen as crazy and dangerous, slowly became accepted practice for soldiers and civilians alike.

ASK YOURSELF

1. Josiah Sabin's efforts to inoculate his fellow soldiers produced great disagreements among the officers. Why was there such a disagreement, and why do you think those supporting inoculations won out?
2. All three of these men's experiences with inoculation were relatively mild. How might their reaction have been different had they gotten sicker?
3. All three men made a point of relating their experiences with smallpox inoculation in their reports of their military service. Why do you think they thought it was important to do this? All these reports were written years after the Revolutionary War ended. Why do you think this experience stands out so much in their memories of their wartime service?

TOPICS AND ACTIVITIES TO CONSIDER

☙ Keeping an army healthy would make it better able to fight in battle. Consider efforts by the armies involved in the American Revolution to maintain the health of the soldiers. What were some of the problems they faced in this effort? Was one army more successful than the other? Why or why not?

☙ Medical practice has changed dramatically over the years. Investigate what was common practice in the 18th century, both in terms of infectious diseases and general health care.

Further Reading

Fenn, Elizabeth A. *Pox Americana: The Great Smallpox Epidemic of 1775–1782.* New York: Hill and Wang, 2001.

Murphy, Lamar Riley. *Enter the Physician: The Transformation of Domestic Medicine, 1760–1860.* Tuscaloosa: University of Alabama Press, 1991.

Reiss, Oscar. *Medicine and the American Revolution: How Diseases and Their Treatments Affected the Colonial Army.* Jefferson, NC: McFarland and Company, 1998.

Toledo-Pereyra, Luis H. *A History of American Medicine from the Colonial Period to the Early 20th Century.* Lewiston, NY: Edwin Mellen Press, 2006.

Wilbur, C. Keith. *Revolutionary Medicine, 1700–1800.* Chester, CT: Globe Pequot Press, 1980.

Web Sites

Medicine in the Americas, 1610–1914: A Digital Library: http://www.nlm.nih.gov/hmd/americas/americashome.html

Rieldel, Stefan. Edward Jenner and the History of Smallpox and Vaccination: http://www.ncbi.nlm.nih.gov/ppmc/articles/PMC1200696

21. Impact of Smallpox Inoculations on a Family: Letter from Abigail Adams to John Adams (July 13, 1776)

INTRODUCTION

Although there was some evidence that SMALLPOX inoculations helped prevent the disease, many people still debated whether it was a good idea to undergo the procedure. Military leaders ordered the soldiers in the CONTINENTAL ARMY to receive INOCULATIONS, but they could not force private citizens to undergo the procedure. Part of the concern was the fact that it meant totally disrupting one's life for several weeks because the inoculation resulted in a mild case of the disease from which one had to recover before returning to a normal life. The general practice was to isolate those who received the inoculation so they would not spread the disease to other people.

In the summer of 1776, ABIGAIL ADAMS determined that she and her children should undergo the procedure in order to protect themselves against the disease that was popping up around New England. In a letter to her husband JOHN ADAMS, she told him about the procedure and where they were staying until they recovered.

KEEP IN MIND WHILE YOU READ

1. Legally, the children belonged to John Adams, so Abigail probably should have asked his permission before getting them inoculated for smallpox.
2. Anyone who received a smallpox inoculation would have to be isolated from those who had not received it. But they could be housed with others who had received inoculations, which was what happened to Abigail and her children.

Document: Letter from Abigail Adams to John Adams (July 13, 1776)

Boston July 13, 1776

I must begin with apoligising to you for not writing since the 17 of June. I have really had so many cares upon my Hands and Mind, with a bad inflamation in my Eyes that I have not been able to write. I now date from Boston where I yesterday arrived and was with all 4 of our Little ones innoculated for the small pox. My unkle and Aunt were so kind as to send me an invitation with my family. Mr. Cranch and wife and family, My Sister Betsy and her Little Neice, Cotton Tufts and Mr. Thaxter, a maid who has had the Distemper and my old Nurse compose our family. A Boy too I should have added. 17 in all. My unkles maid with his Little daughter and a Negro Man are here. We had our Bedding &c. to bring. A Cow we have driven down from [Braintree] and some Hay I have had put into the Stable, wood &c. and we have really commenced housekeepers here. The House was furnished with almost every article (except Beds) which we have free use of, and think ourselves much obliged by the fine accommodations and kind offer of our Friends. All our necessary Stores we purchase jointly. Our Little ones stood the opperation Manfully. Dr. Bulfinch is our Physician. Such a Spirit of innoculation never before took place; the Town and every House in it, are as full as they can hold. I believe there are not less than 30 persons from Braintree. Mrs. Quincy, Mrs. Lincoln, Miss Betsy and Nancy are our near Neighbours. God Grant that we may all go comfortably thro the Distemper, the phisick part is bad enough I know. I knew your mind so perfectly upon the subject that I thought nothing, but our recovery would give you eaquel pleasure, and as to safety there was none. The Soldiers innoculated privately, so did many of the inhabitants and the paper curency spread it everywhere. I immediately determined to set myself about it, and get ready with my children. I wish it was so you could have been with us, but I submit.

I received some Letters from you last Saturday Night 26 of June. You mention a Letter of the 16 which I have never received, and I suppose must relate something to private affairs which I wrote about in May and sent by Harry.

As to News we have taken several fine prizes since I wrote you as you will see by the news papers. The present Report is of Lord Hows comeing with unlimited powers. However suppose it is so, I believe he little thinks of treating with us as independant States. How can any person yet dreem of a settlement, accommodations &c. They have neither the spirit nor feeling of Men, yet I see some who never were call'd Tories, gratified with the Idea of Lord Hows being upon his passage with such powers.

Source: Letter from Abigail to John Adams, 13–14 July, 1776 [electronic edition]. *Adams Family Papers: An Electronic Archive.* Massachusetts Historical Society: http://www.masshist.org/digitaladams

AFTERMATH

Abigail and the children weathered the smallpox inoculation process very well and did not experience too many problems as they recovered. This proved true for many people who underwent the procedure in the 18th century and helped reduce the spread of the disease somewhat. However, it would be late in the 19th century before large reductions in the spread of the disease occurred. This would be due to the introduction of vaccinations that successfully prevented smallpox and thus helped reduce the number of cases that occurred.

ASK YOURSELF

1. Why do you think Abigail was so determined to get inoculated for smallpox?
2. What do you think would have been John's reaction to the news that his wife and children had been inoculated against smallpox?

TOPICS AND ACTIVITIES TO CONSIDER

- ❧ People have debated for years about how to prevent disease, particularly in children. Investigate the history of vaccinations for children, and discuss how the process and ideas about when and how to do them have changed over time.

- ❧ Investigate the process of smallpox inoculation as it occurred in the 18th century and smallpox vaccination as it developed in the late 19th century. How are they similar, and how are they different?

Further Reading

Akers, Charles W. *Abigail Adams: An American Woman*. Boston: Little, Brown, 1980.

Fenn, Elizabeth A. *Pox Americana: The Great Smallpox Epidemic of 1775–1782*. New York: Hill and Wang, 2001.

Gelles, Edith B. *Portia: The World of Abigail Adams*. Bloomington: Indiana University Press, 1992.

Levin, Phyllis Lee. *Abigail Adams: A Biography*. New York: St. Martin's Press, 1987.

Melchert, Dennis Don. *Experimenting on the Neighbors: Inoculation of Smallpox in Boston in the Context of 18th-Century Medicine*. PhD dissertation, University of Iowa, 1974.

Withey, Lynne. *Dearest Friend: A Life of Abigail Adams*. New York: Free Press, 1981.

Film and Television

The Adams Chronicles, television mini-series, 1976.

American Experience: John and Abigail Adams, PBS, 2005.

Biography: John and Abigail Adams, PBS, 2005.

John Adams, television mini-series, 2008.

Web Sites

Abigail Adams Biography: http://www.firstladies.org/biographies/firstladies.aspx?biography=2

Adams Resources at the Massachusetts Historical Society: http:/www.masshist.org/adams/

John Adams: http://www.hbo.com/john-adams

Medicine in the Americas, 1610–1914: A Digital Library: http://www.nlm.nih.gov/hmd/americas/americashome.html

Riedel, Stefan. Edward Jenner and the History of Smallpox and Vaccination: http://www.ncbi.nlm.nih.gov/ppmc/articles/PMC1200696

22. Death Omnipresent: Dr. Lewis Beebe's Diary (1776)

INTRODUCTION

In discussing wartime, the focus is often either on the battlefield or the home front. The daily life of the soldiers fighting in the battles is sometimes overlooked. For soldiers in the armies fighting in the American Revolution, daily life could be tough. The CONTINENTAL ARMY often faced issues of too few supplies and bad weather, but illness probably constituted the biggest problem. There were few formal medical facilities anywhere in the North American colonies in the 1770s, but what existed for the army was even more ad-hoc and thrown together. This only added to the problems faced by doctors in caring for those in the military. Dr. Lewis Beebe, a physician from Connecticut, described the problems of caring for the sick in the army. A graduate of Yale College, Beebe had studied medicine following graduation and had opened his first practice in Sheffield, Massachusetts. He joined a regiment from Connecticut that reinforced the troops that had invaded Canada in 1775. In the diary he kept during his military service, Beebe described death as a daily companion because so many men were ill, and there was very little that he was able to do to relieve their suffering.

KEEP IN MIND WHILE YOU READ

1. During this period, medical training occurred primarily through working on the job with a physician, so Beebe's knowledge of illness would have come primarily through his personal experiences in learning medicine.
2. BENEDICT ARNOLD was from Connecticut and was generally very popular with his men at the time Beebe was keeping his diary.
3. Smallpox was a greatly feared disease at this time because it was difficult to prevent it from spreading once it broke out.

Document: Excerpts from Lewis Beebe's Diary (1776)

Tuesday, June 4th: one of our Regt. died this morning very suddenly, and was intered in the afternoon, without so much as a Coffin, and with little or no ceremony. among hundreds of men it was difficult to procure 8 or 10 to bear the corps about 15 rods. Death is a Subject not to be attended to by Soldiers; Hell & Damnation is in allmost every ones mouth from the time they awake till they fall asleep again, the Stupidity of mankind in this situation is beyond all Description. This day Majr. Brewer, Majr. Thomas, & Majr. Sedgwick left this place for New England....

Friday, 7. Last evening one died of the small pox, and early this morning one of the Colic, at 10 A.M. one of the Nervous fever, here in the hospital, is to be seen at the same time some dead, some Dying, others at the point of death, some Whistleing, some singing & many Cursing and swearing, this is a strange Composition and its chief intention has not as yet been discovered; however it appears very plain that it is wonderfully calculated for a Campaign, and if applied properly and in time, is very efficatious to prevent anything that is Serious or concerning futurity. Visited many of the sick in the hospital—was moved with a Compassionate feeling for poor Distressed Soldiers, when they are taken sick, are thrown into this dirty, stinking place, and left to take care of themselves. No attendance no provision made, but what must be Loathed & abhorred by all both well & sick....

Saturday, I mean Sunday 9th: June Two of the artillery died this day of the small pox.

Monday 10th: June.... this day died two in Colo. Pattersons Regt with the small pox; No intelligence of importance comes to hand this day; except orders, from the great Mr. Brigadier Genl. Arnold, for Colo. Poor with his Regt. to proceed to Sorrell immediately: Is not this a politick plan, especially since there is not Ten men in the Regt. but what has either now got the small pox; or taken the infection. Some men love to command, however ridiculous their orders may appear. But I am apt to think, we shall remain in this Garrison for the present. It is enough to confuse & distract a rational man to be Surgn to a Regt. nothing to be heard from morning to night, but Doctr. Doctr. Doctr. from every side 'till one is deaf, dumb, & blind, and almost dead; add to all this, we have nothing to eat; thus poor Soldiers live sometimes better, but never worse....

Wednesday 12th:.... Visited many of the sick, innoculated a number, extracted 2 teeth, was much fatigued at evening. Retired to rest a little before dark....

Thursday 13th:.... the great Genl. Arnold arrived here yesterday and began to give his inconsistent orders today & for his great pity and Concern for the sick; in the first place gave particular orders that every Sick man, together with everyone returned not fit for duty should draw but half allowance. In this order is discovered that Superior Wisdom, which is necessary for a man in his exalted Station of life to be possessed of....

Fryday 14..... One of our men died early this morning with the small pox, one about 12 with the Consumption, belonging to Colo. Bond.

Saturday 15. this morning a Schooner and 13 Batteaus arrived here with provision. Lost one man with the small pox....

Monday 17. This morning had Colo. Poors orders to repair to Isle aux naux to take care of the sick there; accordingly sailed in a batteau, and arrived there about 3 P.M. was struck with amazement upon my arrival, to see the vast crowds of poor distressed Creatures. Language cannot describe nor imagination paint, the scenes of misery and distress the Soldiery endure. Scarcely a tent upon this Isle but what contains one or more in distress and continually groaning, & calling for relief, but in vain! Requests of this Nature are as little regarded, as the singing of Crickets in a Summers evening. The most shocking of all Spectacles was to see a large barn Crowded full of men with this disorder, many of which could not See, Speak or walk—one nay two had large maggots, an inch long, Crawl out of their ears, were on almost every part of the body. No mortal will ever believe what these suffered unless they were eye witnesses. Fuller appeard to be near his end....

Thursday 20. The Genl. gave orders for all the sick to be removed to Crown point. I set out with the same, about 10 A.M. arrived at Isle emot where we encamped....

Monday 24th;... Lost one man this day with the small pox. several died on the way from Isle aux naux, to this place. The batteaus Loaded with sick continually arrived....

Tuesday 25. Extracted 7 teeth, visited many with the small pox;....

Wednesday 26. The Regt is in a most deplorable Situation, between 4 & 500 now in the height of the small pox. Death is now become a daily visitant in the Camps. But as Little regarded as the singing of birds. It appears and really is so that one great lesson to be learnt from Death, is wholly forgot; (viz) that therein we discover our own picture; we have here pointed out our own mortality, in the most lively colours. Strange that the frequent instances, of so Solemn a Scene as this, should have such an effect, that it should harden, and render us Stupid, and make us wholly insensible of the great importance of so serious a matter, but herein is discovered the amazing blindness, and Stupidity which naturally possesses our minds.... Visited many of the sick, see many curious cases, find in General that I can effect greater cures by words than by medicine.

Thursday 27. Buried two of our Regt. this day. The hot weather, proves very unfriendly to those who have the small pox....

Fryday 28th. Nine were buried this day on the point, sundry on chimney point....

Saturday 29th. Buried 4 this day, 3 belonging to our Regt. on the other side, they generally, Lose more than double to what we do here. Alas! what will become of our distressed army, Death reigns triumphant—God seems to be greatly angry with us, he appears to be incensed against us, for our abominable wickedness—and in all probability will sweep away great part of our army to Destruction.

'Tis enough to make humane nature shudder only to hear the army in General Blaspheme the Holy name of God. this sin alone is sufficient to draw down the vengeance of an angry God upon a guilty and wicked army. But what is still melancholy, and to be greatly lamented is, amidst all the tokens of Gods holy displeasure, we remain insensible of our danger, and grow harder & harder in wickedness, and are ripening fast for utter destruction.

Sunday 30. I hardly know what to say, I have visited many of the sick. We have a great variety of sore arms & abscesses forming in all parts of the body, proceeding from the small pox, occasioned by the want of physic to cleanse the patients from the disorder. however we had none so bad yet, but what we have been able to cure, except the disorder otherwise was too obstinate. Buried two today. No preaching or praying as usual. The small pox rather abates in the Regt. A number are employed the other side, almost the whole of the day to dig graves & bury the dead....

Wednesday July 3d. Had prayer last evening and this morning; hope the Regt. will take a new turn of mind, and for the future give steady attendance. Buried 3 this day. How strange it is that we have death sent into our Camp so repeatedly, every day? And we take so little notice of it? Nay it will not prevent Cursing and Swearing in the same tent with the Corps.... Since I have been writing, one more of our men has made his exit. Death visits us almost every hour.

Source: Kirkland, Frederic R., ed. "Journal of a Physician on the Expedition against Canada, 1776." *Pennsylvania Magazine of History and Biography* 59 (1935): 332–339; entire article appears on pages 321–361.

AFTERMATH

Beebe felt great frustration throughout his military service because he believed that the commanders did not do enough for the men who were ill in their units. His criticisms reflected the difficulties of medical care for the troops during the Revolution. Lack of supplies and facilities made it very difficult and many men died as a result. Beebe was also one of the first people to question the motives of Benedict Arnold, several years before Arnold's attempt to sell West Point to the British. Beebe served until the end of 1776 and then returned home. He moved to Vermont where he once more opened a medical practice. In 1786 he became the pastor of the CONGREGATIONAL CHURCH in Pawlet, Vermont, where he was ordained on June 14, 1787. Following some stormy arguments with some members of the congregation, Beebe was dismissed in 1791. He then moved to Lansingburgh, New York, and opened a liquor store. He died in New York in 1816.

ASK YOURSELF

1. Why was Beebe so critical of Benedict Arnold? Was there something else that Beebe could have done to change the situation?
2. Do you think the medical situation was worse for Beebe in the army than it would have been back home in his regular medical practice? In other words, does the military situation make the medical situation worse or not?
3. Why do you think Beebe continued to list the number who died in his diary? Was this for his own recollection, or do you think he thought others would read his diary in the future and he wanted to make sure they understood how high the death rate was at the time?

TOPICS AND ACTIVITIES TO CONSIDER

- ☙ During the American Revolution, Benedict Arnold was originally considered a hero, but later he betrayed the United States. Investigate his career during the American Revolution. Pay particular attention to people like Beebe who early on questioned Arnold's dedication to the fight for independence.
- ☙ Training for doctors in the United States has changed over the years. Investigate how doctors have been trained over the years, focusing on what changes have occurred and why they have occurred.

Further Reading

Fenn, Elizabeth A. *Pox Americana: The Great Smallpox Epidemic of 1775–1782*. New York: Hill and Wang, 2001.

Murphy, Lamar Riley. *Enter the Physician: The Transformation of Domestic Medicine, 1760–1860*. Tuscaloosa: University of Alabama Press, 1991.

Reiss, Oscar. *Medicine and the American Revolution: How Diseases and Their Treatments Affected the Colonial Army*. Jefferson, NC: McFarland and Company, 1998.

Toledo-Pereyra, Luis H. *A History of American Medicine from the Colonial Period to the Early 20th Century*. Lewiston, NY: Edwin Mellen Press, 2006.

Wilbur, C. Keith. *Revolutionary Medicine, 1700–1800*. Chester, CT: Globe Pequot Press, 1980.

Web Site

Medicine in the Americas, 1610–1914: A Digital Library: http://www.nlm.nih.gov/hmd/americas/americashome.html

23. Epidemics an Ongoing Problem: Joseph Plumb Martin Describes a Yellow Fever Epidemic in the Continental Army (1782)

INTRODUCTION

Although SMALLPOX was probably the most feared disease in the 18th century, it probably was not the most dangerous. More difficult to deal with were various infectious diseases that were passed through the food and water supply or by the bites of animals or insects such as mosquitoes. What made these diseases more dangerous was the lack of complete understanding about how they were spread and the lack of any sort of INOCULATION against them. TYPHOID FEVER, YELLOW FEVER, and other diseases spread like wildfire among the general population and the soldiers in the army whenever they appeared. Such epidemics proved difficult to deal with because the diseases were easily spread and because the facilities to care for the sick were not very good.

In 1782 Joseph Plumb Martin experienced such an epidemic when he came down with yellow fever. At the time the Revolution began, Martin lived in Milford, Connecticut. He had originally joined the state MILITIA in 1775, but he joined the CONTINENTAL ARMY in June 1776. He served with the 8th Connecticut Regiment from 1776 to 1780, participating in the Battles of White Plains and Monmouth, as well as spending the winter of 1777–1778 at Valley Forge. In 1780 he joined the corps of SAPPERS AND MINERS and served in this unit until the end of the war. Following the Battle of Yorktown, Martin's unit was sent to winter quarters in Burlington, New Jersey. It was while stationed there that he became ill with yellow fever, an experience that he described in great detail in his memoirs.

KEEP IN MIND WHILE YOU READ

1. Understanding of the causes of diseases and how to care for the ill was primitive in the 18th century, at least by modern standards.
2. Martin had been in the Continental Army since 1776 and had experienced all sorts of difficult experiences and deprivations, but he described this experience as some of the worst suffering he experienced during the war.

Document: Excerpts from Joseph Plumb Martin's Memoir of a Revolutionary Soldier *(1782)*

Soon after this came on my trouble, and that of several others of the men belonging to our corps; some time in the month of January, two of our men were taken down with a species of yellow fever; one recovered and the other died. Directly after, one belonging to our room was seized with it and removed to the hospital, where he recovered; next I was attacked with it, this was in February, it took hold of me in good earnest. I bled violently at the nose, and was so reduced in flesh and strength in a few days, that I was as helpless as an infant;—O! how much I suffered, although I had as good attendance as circumstances would admit. The disorder continued to take hold of our people till there were more than twenty sick with it. Our officers made a hospital in an upper room in one of the wings of the house, and as soon as the men fell sick they were lodged there. About the first of March I began to mend, and recovered what little reason I ever possessed, of which I had been entirely deprived from nearly the first attack of the fever. As soon as I could bear it, I was removed from my room to the hospital among those that were recently taken; for what reason I was put with the sick and dying, I did not know, nor did I ask; I did not care much what they did with me, but nothing ill resulted from it that I know of. The doctor belonging to the Artillery regiment (who attended upon us, we having no doctor in our corps) went home on furlough, and it was a happy circumstance for us, for he was not the best of physicians; besides, he was badly provided to do with; the apothecary's stores in the Revo-

> **posset:** hot drink consisting essentially of sweetened and spiced milk curdled with ale or wine, and sometimes thickened with bread

lutionary army were as ill furnished as any others; the doctor, however, left us under the care of a physician belonging to the city, who was a fine man, and to his efforts, under Providence, I verily believe I owed my life; he was a skilful, tender-hearted and diligent man. There was likewise, in the city, a widow woman that rendered us the most essential service during our sickness. As we are unable to eat any thing, and had only our rations of beef and bread to subsist upon, this widow, this pitying angel, used almost every evening to send us a little brass kettle, containing about a pail full of **posset,** consisting of wine, water, sugar and crackers. O, it was delicious, even to our sick palates. I never knew who our kind benefactress was; all I ever knew concerning her was, that she was a widow. The neighbours would not tell us who she was nor where she lived; all that I, or any others who had been sick, could learn from them was, that she was a very fine, pious soul; yes, she *will* be rewarded, where it will be said to her, "I was hungry and you gave me meat; I was sick and you visited me," although she did not visit us personally, she ministered more to our comfort than thousands of idle visits, which are oftener of more detriment to sick people than they are benefit.

Four men died in the room into which I was removed, after I was carried there. One occurrence (though nothing strange in such circumstances as I was then in) I took notice of, although I could take notice of little else. We lay on sacks filled with straw, and our beds mostly upon the floor, in a rank on each side of the room, with an alley between. The first man that died, after my being conveyed there, was the first in order from the entering door of the room, on the side I lay; next, the fourth man from him died, there was then four men between this last that died and me. In my weakness I felt prepossessed with a notion, that every fourth man would die, and that, consequently, I should escape, as I was the fifth from the one that died last; and just so it happened, the man next me on the side of those that had died, died next. I believe this circumstance contributed a great deal in retarding my recovery, until the death of this last man, and that after his death, when I thought myself exempted, it helped as much toward my recovery.—Such strange whims will often work great effects both in hindering and forwarding in such cases. When the body is feeble and the head weak, small causes often have great effect upon the sick; I know it by too frequent experience.

Eight men died at this time, the rest recovered, though the most of them very slowly; some were as crazy as coots for weeks after they had gained strength to walk about. My hair came off my head, and I was as bald as an eagle; but after I *began* to gain strength I soon got about. But it was a grievous sickness to me, the sorest I had ever undergone. Although death is much nearer to *me* now than it was then, yet I never had thought myself so near *death* as I did then.

Source: Martin, Joseph Plumb. *Memoir of a Revolutionary Soldier.* Mineola, NY: Dover Publications, 2006, pp. 144–146.

AFTERMATH

Martin's experience of yellow fever was not unusual for someone in the 18th century. As indicated by his description, some people survived and some people did not when such epidemics occurred, and it was generally not easy to determine why some lived and why others died. Martin clearly believed that he was lucky (hence his reference to being in the correct bed to survive).

Joseph Plumb Martin was discharged from military duty when the Continental Army disbanded in October 1783. He originally taught school in the state of New York, but eventually moved to the frontier of Maine, where he spent the rest of his life. He helped found the town of Prospect and served in a variety of positions in the town government (including 25 years as town clerk). He married Lucy Clewley in 1794, and they had five children. Martin died on May 2, 1850, at the age of 89.

ASK YOURSELF

1. Martin described a variety of people involved in efforts to care for the sick. He believed that some of these people did a good job while others did not. Why was this so? Was it a matter of more or less medical knowledge? Or did Martin respond primarily to people's personalities and their reactions to him as a sick man?
2. Martin believed that he survived because he happened to be in the right bed (not being the fourth man in any direction). How important was this attitude to his survival? Do doctors today believe that one's attitude plays a role in recovering from illness?

TOPICS AND ACTIVITIES TO CONSIDER

- Martin described the hospital that was set up to care for the ill in his unit. Field hospitals are often set up quickly and thus do not have everything one would hope to have in a hospital. Investigate the field hospitals of the American Revolution and the Civil War, and compare how they were similar and how they were different.

> Martin was particularly grateful to the widow who helped take care of the sick. In the 18th and 19th centuries, women were generally considered to be more caring and thus would be better nurses. Investigate the ideas about women's nature that provided support for this outlook and how those ideas developed over time.

Further Reading

Black, John Bullard. *Yellow Fever in 18th-Century America.* New York: New York Academy of Medicine, 1968.

Buel, Richard. *Dear Liberty: Connecticut's Mobilization for the Revolutionary War.* Middletown, CT: Wesleyan University Press, 1980.

Cal, Paul L. *Connecticut Soldiers in the American Revolution: A Society's Approach to War.* Thesis, United States Military Academy, 1994.

Martin, Joseph Plumb. *Memoir of a Revolutionary Soldier.* Mineola, NY: Dover Publications, 2006.

Raphael, Ray. *Founders: The People Who Brought You a Nation.* New York: The New Press, 2009.

Reiss, Oscar. *Medicine and the American Revolution: How Diseases and Their Treatments Affected the Colonial Army.* Jefferson, NC: McFarland and Company, 1998.

Film and Television Portrayals of Martin

Aaron Carter in *Liberty's Kids,* television series, 2002–2003.

Philip Seymour Hoffman in PBS series *Liberty! The American Revolution*, television mini-series, 1997.

Rick Schroder in *The American Revolution,* television mini-series, 1994.

Web Sites

Liberty! The American Revolution: http://www.pbs.org/ktca/liberty

Medicine in the Americas, 1610–1914: A Digital Library: http://www.nlm.nih.gov/hmd/americas/americashome.html

LOVE, MARRIAGE, AND FAMILY

24. RAISING CHILDREN: ELEAZAR MOODY'S *THE SCHOOL OF GOOD MANNERS* (1772)

INTRODUCTION

Even in times of conflict, parents want to raise their children in such a way that they will be able to succeed as much as possible throughout the course of their lives. Parents often seek a variety of aids to help in this process. Particularly popular in the 18th century were published books that provided guidelines on how to behave properly in public. One publication that proved particularly successful was *The School of Good Manners* by ELEAZAR MOODY, a Boston schoolmaster. Moody's book was a compilation of guidelines based primarily on an English book of the same title by JOHN GARRETSON, but Moody also included materials from a number of older French and English books on civility and proper behavior. Moody's book proved so successful that it was reprinted a number of times, including in 1772 when the Fleet brothers of Massachusetts published it. The FLEET brothers, THOMAS AND JOHN, were successful printers who published a variety of types of publications in the years prior to the American Revolution.

KEEP IN MIND WHILE YOU READ

1. Although these sorts of guidelines were aimed primarily at the more well-to-do people in American colonial society, the rules were considered good ones for everyone to follow if they wanted to be successful.
2. Even though it was expected that boys and girls would grow up to live very different lives, the same general behavior rules applied to both groups.

Document: Moody's List of Good Manners for Children (1772)

When at Home

1. Make a bow always when you come home, and be immediately uncovered.
2. Be never covered at home, especially before thy parents or strangers.

3. Never sit in the presence of thy parents without bidding, tho' no stranger be present.
4. If thou passest by thy parents, and any place where thou seest them, when either by themselves or with company, bow towards them.
5. If thou art going to speak to thy parents, and see them engaged in discourse with company, draw back and leave thy business until afterwards; but if thou must speak, be sure to whisper.
6. Never speak to thy parents without some title of respect, viz., Sir, Madam, &c.
7. Approach near thy parents at no time without a bow.
8. Dispute not, nor delay to obey thy parents commands.
9. Go not out of doors without thy parents leave, and return within the time by them limited.
10. Come not into the room where thy parents are with strangers, unless thou art called, and then decently; and at bidding go out; or if strangers come in while thou art with them, it is manners, with a bow to withdraw.

> **carriage:** manner of carrying oneself; bearing

11. Use respectful and courteous but not insulting or domineering **carriage** or language toward the servants.
12. Quarrel not nor contend with thy brethren or sisters, but live in love, peace, and unity.
13. Grumble not nor be discontented at anything thy parents appoint, speak, or do.
14. Bear with meakness and patience, and without murmuring or sullenness, thy parents reproofs or corrections: Nay, tho' it should so happen that they be causeless or undeserved.

In Their Discourse

1. Among superiors speak not till thou art spoken to, and bid to speak.
2. Hold not thine hand, nor any thing else, before thy mouth when thou speakest.
3. Come not over-near to the person thou speakest to.
4. If thy superior speak to thee while thou sittest, stand up before thou givest any answer.
5. Sit not down till thy superior bid thee.
6. Speak neither very loud, nor too low.
7. Speak clear, not stammering, stumbling nor drawling.
8. Answer not one that is speaking to thee until he hath done.
9. Loll not when thou art speaking to a superior or spoken to by him.
10. Speak not without, Sir, or some other title of respect.
11. Strive not with superiors in argument or discourse; but easily submit thine opinion to their assertions.
12. If thy superior speak any thing wherein thou knowest he is mistaken, correct not or contradict him, nor grin at the hearing of it; but pass over the error without notice or interruption.
13. Mention not frivolous or little things among grave persons or superiors.
14. If thy superior drawl or hesitate in his words, pretend not to help him out, or to prompt him.
15. Come not too near two that are whispering or speaking in secret, much less may'st thou ask about what they confer.
16. When thy parent or master speak to any person, speak not thou, nor hearken to them.

17. If thy superior be relating a story, say not, "I have heard it before," but attend to it as though it were altogether new. Seem not to question the truth of it. If he tell it not right, **snigger** not, nor endeavor to help him out, or add to his relation.
18. If any immodest or obscene thing be spoken in thy hearing, smile not, but settle thy countenance as though thou did'st not hear it.
19. Boast not in discourse of thine own wit or doings.
20. Beware thou utter not any thing hard to be believed.
21. Interrupt not any one that speaks, though thou be his familiar.
22. Coming into company, whilst any topic is discoursed on, ask not what was the preceding talk but hearken to the remainder.
23. Speaking of any distant person, it is rude and unmannerly to point at him.
24. Laugh not in, or at thy own story, wit or jest.
25. Use not any contemptuous or reproachful language to any person, though very mean or inferior.
26. Be not over earnest in talking to justify and **avouch** thy own sayings.
27. Let thy words be modest about those things which only concern thee.
28. Repeat not over again the words of a superior that asketh thee a question or talketh to thee.

> **avouch:** to affirm, to vouch for
> **snigger:** to snicker—to laugh or utter with a sly partly stifled manner

Source: Moody, Eleazar. *The School of Good Manners, Composed for the Help of Parents in Teaching Their Children How to Carry It in Their Places during Their Minority.* Boston, MA: T. and J. Fleet, 1772, pp. 17–19.

AFTERMATH

These guidelines, if obeyed, would enable the person following them to be successful in future endeavors. For years, many in the American colonies had believed that the British looked down on them because they lived in the colonies and thus did not have access to all the benefits of civilized society. These feelings of inferiority and competition had only added to conflicts that led to the outbreak of the Revolution. Many Americans had long sought to convince people from Great Britain that they were civilized and guidebooks such as Moody's publication were intended to help with that process. Some people even developed their own list of guidelines for civil behavior. While still a young man, GEORGE WASHINGTON had developed his personal list of rules for proper behavior based primarily on an English guidebook that he had read.

ASK YOURSELF

1. The guidelines are divided into rules for home and rules for public discourse. The implication is that there are different rules for home and public. Why do you think that might be true?
2. Many of the guidelines about public discourse actually encourage the individual not to speak very much at all. Why do you think that is the focus of the guidelines?

TOPICS AND ACTIVITIES TO CONSIDER

     ∾ Parents have always tried to teach their children how to behave properly so they can succeed in life. Investigate guidelines from other time periods and compare them to Moody's. How are they different, and how are they similar? Why do you think this is so?

     ∾ Printers also often included similar guidelines in the annual almanacs, publications that would be purchased by everyone who could afford to because of all the information they provided. Probably the most famous of these types of publications from the 18th century was BENJAMIN FRANKLIN's *Poor Richard's Almanac.* Investigate the types of advice for good behavior presented in almanacs and compare them to Moody's list. How are they different, and how are they similar? Why do you think this is so? Are the differences because the publications are aimed at different audiences? Or are there other reasons for the differences?

Further Reading

Cremin, Lawrence. *American Education: The Colonial Experience, 1607–1783.* New York: Harper & Row, 1970.

Monaghan, E. Jennifer. *Learning to Read and Write in Colonial America.* Amherst: University of Massachusetts Press, 2007.

Pangle, Lorraine Smith. *The Learning of Liberty: The Educational Ideas of the American Founders.* Lawrence: University Press of Kansas, 1993.

Washington, George. *Rules of Civility.* Ed. Richard Brookhiser. Charlottesville: University of Virginia Press, 2003.

Web Site

George Washington's *Rules of Civility:* http://www.history.org/Almanack/life/manners/rules2.cfm

25. War Drives Families Apart: Letter from Benjamin Franklin to William Franklin (October 6, 1773)

INTRODUCTION

The American Revolution impacted people's families in a variety of ways. One obvious impact, particularly for people in positions of power and influence, was family division when family members ended up on different sides of the conflict with Great Britain. These sorts of divisions appeared even before the fighting actually began in 1775. A good example of this type of split can be seen in the relationship between Benjamin Franklin and his son William.

BENJAMIN FRANKLIN may have been the most famous colonial leader in Europe in the years leading up to the Revolution. He made his living as a printer, but was so successful that he was able to lease his printing business to his foreman, DAVID HALL, in 1748. From that point on, Franklin devoted his time to intellectual and political pursuits. His experiments with lightning and electricity in the 1740s had been reported and replicated in Europe in the 1750s, and had established his reputation as a scientist. He represented his home colony of Pennsylvania as colonial agent in Great Britain from 1757 until the outbreak of the Revolution. He also came to represent the colonies of Georgia, New Jersey, and Massachusetts, resulting in his being seen by many in Great Britain as a sort of ambassador from the colonies to Great Britain. As the conflict with the colonies over taxes and rights grew in the 1760s and 1770s, Franklin increasingly came to believe that Great Britain's actions infringed on colonial rights and he, like so many others in the colonies, slowly moved toward support for independence.

Franklin's son William had accompanied him to Great Britain in 1757 and there received a legal education at the MIDDLE TEMPLE. William was appointed the royal governor of New Jersey in 1763, apparently in an effort to tie the famous and influential Benjamin Franklin closer to British interests. At first, WILLIAM FRANKLIN proved a successful royal governor, but his reputation declined in the face of the growing controversy between the colonies and the mother country. He supported the British government completely. This resulted in a growing disagreement with his father, as indicated in the following letter from Benjamin Franklin to his son written in 1773.

KEEP IN MIND WHILE YOU READ

1. Benjamin Franklin's job while in London was to represent the interests of several colonies to the British authorities, while William Franklin's job as royal governor of New Jersey was to represent British authority to the citizens of that colony.

2. As a former printer, Benjamin Franklin had begun his life as an artisan. His position as the colonial agent for Pennsylvania put him in contact with the aristocracy of Great Britain in a way that would normally not have been possible for a man from his working-class background. William Franklin's legal education enabled him to move upward in society farther than would normally have been expected given his family background.

Document: Benjamin Franklin's Letter to His Son William (October 6, 1773)

TO WILLIAM FRANKLIN
London, October 6, 1773.
Dear Son,

I wrote to you the 1st of last month, since which I have received yours of July 29, from New York. I know not what letters of mine Governor H[utchinson] could mean, as advising the people to insist on their independency. But whatever they were, I suppose he has sent copies of them hither, having heard some whisperings about them. I shall however, be able at any time to justify every thing I have written; the purport being uniformly this, that they should carefully avoid all tumults and every violent measure, and content themselves with verbally keeping up their claims, and holding forth their rights whenever occasion requires; secure, that, from the growing importance of America, those claims will ere long be attended to and acknowledged.

From a long and thorough consideration of the subject, I am indeed of opinion, that the parliament has no right to make any law whatever, binding on the colonies; that the king, and not the king, lords, and commons collectively, is their sovereign; and that the king, with their respective parliaments, is their only legislator. I know your sentiments differ from mine on these subjects. You are a thorough government man, which I do not wonder at, nor do I aim at converting you. I only wish you to act uprightly and steadily, avoiding that duplicity, which in Hutchinson, adds contempt to indignation. If you can promote the prosperity of your people, and leave them happier than you found them, whatever your political principles are, your memory will be honoured.

I have written two pieces here lately for the *Public Advertiser,* on American affairs, designed to expose the conduct of this country towards the colonies in a short, comprehensive, and striking view, and stated, therefore, in out-of-the-way forms, as most likely to take the general attention. The first was called *Rules by which a Great Empire may be reduced to a small one;* the second, *An Edict of the King of Prussia.* I sent you one of the first, but could not get enough of the second to spare you one, though my clerk went the next morning to the printer's, and wherever they were sold. They were all gone but two. In my own mind I preferred the first, as a composition for the quantity and variety of the matter contained, and a kind of spirited ending of each paragraph. But I find that others here generally prefer the second.

I am not suspected as the author, except by one or two friends; and have heard the latter spoken of in the highest terms, as the keenest and severest piece that has appeared here for a long time. Lord Mansfield, I hear, said of it, that it *was very* Able *and very* Artful *indeed;* and would do mischief by giving here a bad impression of the measures of government; and in the colonies, by encouraging them in their **contumacy.** It is re-printed in the *Chronicle,* where you will see it, but stripped of all the capitaling and italicing, that intimate the allusions and mark the emphasis of written discourses, to bring them as near as possible to those spoken: printing such a piece all in one even small charac-ter, seems to me like repeating one of Whitefield's sermons in the monotony of a schoolboy.

> **contumacy:** stubborn resistance to authority

What made it the more noticed here was, that people in reading it were, as the phrase is, *taken in,* till they had got half through it, and imagined it a real edict, to which mis-take I suppose the King of Prussia's *character* must have contributed. I was down at Lord Le Despencer's, when the post brought that day's papers. Mr. Whitehead was there, too, (Paul Whitehead, the author of "Manners,") who runs early through all the papers, and tells the company what he finds remarkable. He had them in another room, and we were chatting in the breakfast parlour, when he came running in to us, out of breath, with the paper in his hand. Here! says he, here's news for ye! *Here's the King of Prussia, claiming a right to this kingdom!* All stared, and I as much as anybody; and he went on to read it. When he had read two or three paragraphs, a gentleman present said, *Damn his impudence, I dare say, we shall hear by next post that he is upon his march with one hundred thousand men to back this.* Whitehead, who is very shrewd, soon after began to smoke it, and looking in my face said, *I'll be hanged if this is not some of your American jokes upon us."* The reading went on, and ended with abundance of laughing, and a general verdict that it was a fair hit: and the piece was cut out of the paper and preserved in my Lord's collection.

I do not wonder that Hutchinson should be dejected. It must be an uncomfortable thing to live among people who he is conscious universally detest him. Yet I fancy he will not have leave to come home, both because they know not well what to do with him, and because they do not very well like his conduct. I am ever your affectionate father, B. Franklin.

Source: Smyth, Albert Henry, ed. *The Writings of Benjamin Franklin.* Vol. VI. London: MacMillan & Company, 1906, pp. 144–147.

AFTERMATH

Benjamin Franklin returned to Philadelphia in 1775 and was quickly chosen to repre-sent Pennsylvania in the Second CONTINENTAL CONGRESS. In 1776 the Congress appointed him as one of three commissioners sent to France to negotiate a treaty. He remained in France until 1785. While there, he worked to increase French aid for the American cause and also helped negotiate the peace treaty with Great Britain that ended the Revolution and recognized American independence. His last public service to the new nation came in 1787 when he served in the CONSTITUTIONAL CONVENTION, thus lending his famous name in support of the new form of government. Benjamin Franklin died in 1790 at the age of 84.

Franklin's son William did not fare so well. He diligently tried to carry out the respon-sibilities of his office as royal governor of New Jersey and thus angered the colonial leaders who led the opposition against Great Britain. On June 15, 1776, the Provincial Congress of New Jersey declared him to be "an enemy to the liberties of this country" and ordered his arrest. He spent two years as a prisoner but was exchanged in 1778. He soon returned to England and spent the rest of his life there as a pensioner of the royal government. He and his father partially reconciled by letter in 1784, but they never saw each other again.

ASK YOURSELF

1. Both Benjamin and William Franklin owed much of their political success to ties between the American colonies and Great Britain. Why do you think Benjamin Franklin turned against Great Britain while William Franklin continued to support the mother country?
2. Benjamin Franklin stated that his son William was "a thorough government man." But Benjamin Franklin still tried to explain and defend his ideas of opposition to the mother country. Why do you think that was so?

TOPICS AND ACTIVITIES TO CONSIDER

- Political differences can often lead to family disagreements such as the division between Benjamin and William Franklin. Investigate more recent political divisions that might have produced other examples of family disagreements.
- In the 18th century, a document published in a newspaper often appeared under a pseudonym, or assumed name, rather than the author's actual name. Benjamin Franklin discussed that he had written some essays for publication, but he was not "suspected as the author." Investigate how, when, and why this practice changed so that newspaper editorials and essays are now signed.

Further Reading

Franklin, Benjamin. *The Autobiography of Benjamin Franklin.* Ed. Leonard W. Labaree. New Haven, CT: Yale University Press, 1964.

Isaacson, Walter. *Benjamin Franklin: An American Life.* New York: Simon & Shuster, 2003.

Morgan, Edmund S. *Benjamin Franklin.* New Haven, CT: Yale University Press, 2002.

Randall, Willard Sterne. *A Little Revenge: Benjamin Franklin and His Son.* Boston: Little, Brown, and Company, 1984.

Skemp, Sheila L. *William Franklin: Son of a Patriot, Servant of a King.* New York: Oxford University Press, 1990.

Wood, Gordon S. *The Americanization of Benjamin Franklin.* New York: Penguin Press, 2002.

Film and Television

Benjamin Franklin, television mini-series, 1974.
Benjamin Franklin, PBS, 2002.
Biography: Benjamin Franklin: Citizen of the World, PBS, 2006.

Web Sites

The Autobiography of Benjamin Franklin: http://www.earlyamerica.com/lives/franklin
Benjamin Franklin: Glimpses of the Man: http://www.pbs.org/benfranklin
The Electric Benjamin Franklin: http://www.ushistory.org/franklin/index.htm

26. Managing the Family Business: Abigail and John Adams (1776–1778, 1783)

INTRODUCTION

The American Revolution had a big impact on families that often resulted in family members taking on new and different responsibilities. This proved particularly true for wives. When husbands went off to fight in the war or serve in a government post such as in the CONTINENTAL CONGRESS, wives were left with having to run the family business and take care of family matters at home. For many women, this was a somewhat new experience. Traditionally, wives had helped their husbands with family businesses, but they had never been in control in such a way that they had to make major decisions on their own. The Revolution changed this for many people because husbands were absent for long periods of time or, in the worst cases, killed in battle, and wives had to take on new responsibilities.

A good example of this sort of development can be found in the changes that occurred in the family of John and ABIGAIL ADAMS. Although JOHN ADAMS earned his living primarily as a lawyer, he also owned a farm that provided a good supplement to the family income. From 1774 until 1783, John was gone from home in Massachusetts for long periods of time. During this period, Abigail assumed the management of the family farm. Both John and Abigail wrote hundreds of letters to each other whenever they were separated during their 54 years of marriage. They discussed a variety of subjects in their correspondence, but the focus during the Revolution often revolved around Abigail's management of the family farm and the decisions she made concerning it.

KEEP IN MIND WHEN YOU READ

1. John and Abigail Adams had been married for 10 years when the Revolution began.
2. Married women had no legal identity of their own at this time and thus could not carry out any legal actions of any kind without the approval of their husbands.
3. Communications traveled very slowly during this period. Although a postal service had been established, all mail was carried from town to town by riders on horseback or in carriages. Thus, the weather and the fighting during the Revolution could slow down delivery of letters.

Document 1: Letter from Abigail Adams to John Adams (May 14, 1776)

I set down to write you a Letter wholy Domestick without one word of politicks or any thing of the Kind, and tho you may have matters of infinately more importance before you, yet let it come as a relaxation to you. Know then that we have had a very cold backward Spring, till about ten days past when every thing looks finely. We have had fine Spring rains which makes the Husbandary promise fair—but the great difficulty has been to procure Labourers. There is such a demand of Men from the publick and such a price given that the farmer who Hires must be greatly out of pocket. A man will not talk with you who is worth hireing under 24 **pounds** per year. Col. Quincy and Thayer give that price, and some give more. Isaac insisted upon my giving him 20 pounds or he would leave me. He is no mower and I found

> **Pence, pounds, shillings:** forms of British money: 20 shillings equal 1 pound

very unfit to take the lead upon the Farm, having no forethought or any contrivance to plan his Buisness, tho in the Execution faithfull. I found I wanted somebody of Spirit who was wiser than myself, to conduct my Buisness. I went about and my Friends inquired but every Labourer who was active was gone and going into the Service. I asked advice of my Friends and Neighbours [and] they all adviced me to let Isaac go, rather than give that price. I setled with him and we parted. Mr. Belcher is now with me and has undertaken to conduct the Buisness, which he has hitherto done with Spirit and activity. I know his virtues I know his faults. Hithertoo I give him 2 **Shillings** per day, and Daniel Nightingale works with him at the same lay. I would have hired him for the season but he was engaged to look after a place or two for people who are gone into the Army. I am still in quest of a Man by the year, but whether I shall effect it, I know not. I have done the best I could. We are just now ready to plant, the barly looks charmingly, I shall be quite a Farmeriss an other year.

You made no perticulir agreement with Isaac so he insisted upon my paying him 13. 6 8. I paid him 12 pounds 18 & 8 **pence,** and thought it sufficient.

When Bass returnd he brought me some Money from you. After the deduction of his account and the horse hire there remain 15 pounds. I have Received 12 from Mr. Thaxter which with one note of 20 pounds which I exchanged and some small matters of interest which I received and a little Hay &c. I have discharged the following debts—To my Father for his Horse twice 12 pounds (he would not have any thing for the last time). To Bracket, 13. 6s. 8d. To Isaac 12. 18. 8. To Mr. Hunt for the House 26. 15. 4. and the Rates of two years 1774, 4 14s. 8d. and for 1775: 7. 11s. 11d. Besides this have supported the family which is no small one you know and paid all little charges which have occurd in the farming way. I hardly know how I have got thro these thing's, but it gives me great pleasure to say they are done because I know it will be an Ease to your mind which amid all other cares which surround you will some times advert to your own Little Farm and to your Family. There remains due to Mr. Hunt about 42 pounds. I determine if it lays in my power to discharge the bond, and I have some prospect of it....

Adieu—Yours,

Hermitta

Source: Letter from Abigail to John Adams, May 14, 1776 [electronic edition]. *Adams Family Papers: An Electronic Archive.* Massachusetts Historical Society: http://www.massh ist.org/digitaladams

Document 2: Letter from John Adams to Abigail Adams (May 27, 1776)

I have three of your Favours, before me—one of May 7, another of May 9, and a third of May 14th. The last has given me Relief from many Anxieties. It relates wholly to private Affairs, and contains such an Account of wise and prudent Management, as makes me very happy. I begin to be jealous, that our Neighbours will think Affairs more discreetly conducted in my Absence than at any other Time....

I think you shine as a Stateswoman, of late as well as a Farmeress. Pray where do you get your Maxims of State, they are very apropos....

I am, with constant Wishes and Prayers for your Health, and Prosperity, forever yours.

Source: Letter from John to Abigail Adams, May 27, 1776 [electronic edition]. *Adams Family Papers: An Electronic Archive.* Massachusetts Historical Society: http://www.massh ist.org/digitaladams

Document 3: Letter from Abigail Adams to John Adams (June 8, 1777)

I generally endeavour to write you once a week, if my Letters do not reach you, tis oweing to the neglect of the post. I generally get Letters from you once a week, but seldom in a fortnight after they are wrote. I am sorry to find that your Health fails. I should greatly rejoice to see you, I know of no earthly blessing which would make me happier, but I cannot wish it upon the terms of ill Health. No seperation was ever more painfull to me than the last, may the joy of meeting again be eaquel to the pain of seperation; I regret that I am in a Situation to wish away one of the most precious Blessings of life, yet as the months pass off, I count them up with pleasure and reckon upon tomorrow as the 5th which has passd since your absence. I have some times melancholly reflections, and immagine these seperations as preparatory to a still more painfull one in which even hope the anchor of the Soul is lost, but whilst that remains no Temperary absence can ever wean or abate the ardor of my affection. Bound together by many tender ties, there scarcly wanted an addition, yet I feel that there soon will be an additionall one. Many many are the tender sentiments I have felt for the parent on this occasion. I doubt not they are reciprocal, but I often feel the want of his presence and the soothing tenderness of his affection. Is this weakness or is it not?

I am happy in a daughter who is both a companion and an assistant in my Family affairs and who I think has a prudence and steadiness beyond her years.

You express a longing after the enjoyments of your little Farm. I do not wonder at it, that also wants the care and attention of its master—all that the mistress can do is to see that it does not go to ruin. She would take pleasure in improvements, and study them with assiduity if she was possessd with a sufficency to accomplish them. The season promises plenty at present and the english grass never lookd better.

You inquire after the Asparagrass. It performs very well this year and produces us a great plenty. I long to send you a Barrell of cider, but find it impracticable, as no vessels can pass

Tyranicide: name of a British naval vessel—the term refers to the act of killing a tyrant or the killer of a tyrant

from this State to yours. I rejoice at the good way our affairs seem to be in and Hope your Herculian Labours will be crownd with more success this year than the last. Every thing wears a better aspect, we have already taken two Transports of theirs with Hessians on board, and this week a prize was carried into Salem taken by the **Tyranicide** with 4000 Blankets and other valuable articles on board....

Good Night tis so dark that I cannot see to add more than that I am with the utmost tenderness Yours ever Yours.

Source: Letter from Abigail to John Adams, June 8, 1777 [electronic edition]. *Adams Family Papers: An Electronic Archive.* Massachusetts Historical Society: http://www.massh ist.org/digitaladams

---

Document 4: Letter from Abigail Adams to John Adams, Boston (August 22, 1777)

My dearest Friend

.... The late call of Men from us will distress us in our Husbandry. I am a great sufferer as the High Bounty one hundred dollors, has tempted of my Negro Head, and left me just in the midst of our Hay. The **english** and **fresh** indeed we have finishd, but the **salt** is just comeing on, and How to turn my self, or what to do I know not. His going away would not worry me so much if it was not for the rapid depretiation of our money. We can scarcly get a days work done for money and if money is paid tis at such a rate that tis almost imposible to live. I live as I never did before, but I am not agoing to complain. Heaven has blessd us with fine crops. I hope to have 200 hundred Bushels of corn and a hundred & 50 weight of flax. English Hay we have more than we had last year, notwithstanding your ground wants manure. We are like to have a plenty of sause. I shall fat Beaf and pork enough, make butter and cheesse enough. If I have neither Sugar, molasses, coffe nor Tea I have no right to complain. I can live without any of them and if what I enjoy I can share with my partner and with Liberty,

english, fresh, salt: types of hay
Home spun: cloth made out of yarn made at home. Homespun was very popular during the Revolution because wearing it was seen as a patriotic action, and women were encouraged to make it so that everyone could wear it instead of continuing to import cloth and clothes from Europe.

I can sing o be joyfull and sit down content.

"Man wants but little here below.

Nor wants that little long."

As to cloathing I have heithertoo procured materials sufficent to cloath my children and servants which I have done wholy in **Home Spun**. I have contracted no debts that I have not discharg'd, and one of our Labourers Prince I have paid seven months wages to since you left me. Besides that I have paid Bracket near all we owed him which was to the amount of 15 pounds lawfull money, set up a cider press &c., besides procuring and repairing many other articles in the Husbandery way, which you know are constantly wanted. I should do exceeding well if we could but keep the money good, but at the rate we go on I know not what will become of us.

But I must bid you adieu or the post will go of without my Letter. Dearest Friend, adieu. Words cannot convey to you the tenderness of my affection.

Portia

Source: Letter from Abigail to John Adams, August 22, 1777 [electronic edition]. *Adams Family Papers: An Electronic Archive.* Massachusetts Historical Society: http://www.masshist. org/digitaladams

---

Document 5: Letter from Abigail Adams to John Adams, Braintree (ca. July 15, 1778)

Dearest of Friends

By Mr. Tailor, who has promised me to deliver this with his own hand to you, or distroy it if necessary, I take the liberty of writing rather more freely than I should otherways venture to do. I cannot think but with pain of being debared this privilidge, the only one left me for my consolation in the many solitary and I may add melancholy hours which pass. I promised myself a negative kind of happiness whenever I could hear of your safe arrival but alass I find a craveing void left akeing in my Breast, and I find myself some days especially more unhappy than I would even wish an Enemy to be. In vain do I strive to divert my attention, my Heart, like a poor bird hunted from her nest, is still returning to the place of its affections, and fastens upon the object where all its cares and tenderness are centered. I must not expect, I ought not indeed for the sake of your repose to wish to be thus frequently, and thus fondly the subject of your meditation, but may I not believe that you employ a few moments every day from the Buisness and pleasures which surround you in thinking of her who wishes not her existance to survive your affection, who never recollects the cruel hour of seperation but with tears. From whence shall I gather firmness of mind bereft of the amicable prop upon which it used to rest and acquire fortitude? The subject is too tender to persue. I see it touches your Heart. I will quit it at the midnight hour, and rise in the morning suppressing these too tender sensibilities....

If I was sure this would reach you I should say many things which I dare not venture to. I stand corrected if I have said any thing already which I ought not to. I feel myself embaresse'd whilst my Heart overflows, and longs to give utterance to my pen. Many domestick affairs I wish to consult upon. I have studied for a method of defraying the necessary expences of my family. In no one Instance is a hundred pound L M better than thirteen pounds Six and Eight pence used to be, in foreign Articles no ways eaquel, in taxes but a fourth part as good. Day Labour at 24 shillings per day. What then can you think my situation must be? I will tell you after much embaresment in endeavouring to procure faithfull hands I concluded to put out the Farm and reduce my family as much as posible. I sit about removing the Tenants from the House, which with much difficulty I effected, but not till I had paid a Quarters Rent in an other House for them. I then with the kind assistance of Dr. [Tufts] procured two young Men Brothers newly married and placed them as Tenants to the halves retaining in my own Hands only one Horse and two Cows with pasturage for my Horse in summer, and [Quincy] medow for **fodder** in winter. At present I have no reason to repent of my situation, my family consists at present of only myself, two children and two Domesticks. Our daughter is at School in Boston, and I wait only to know how I shall be able to discharge my schooling for Master Charles to place him at Haverhill. Debts are my abhorrance. I never will borrow if any other method can be devised. I have thought of this which I wish you to assent to, to order some saleable articles which I will mention to be sent to

> **fodder:** feed for animals that is generally stored so that they can be adequately fed during bad weather

the care of my unkle [Smith] a small trunk at a time, containing ten or 15 pounds Sterling, from which I may supply my family with such things as I need, and the rest place in the hands of Dr. [Tufts] Son who has lately come into Trade, and would sell them for me, by which means if I must pay extravagant prices I shall be more upon an eaquel footing with my Neighbours.

I have been obliged to make fence this year to the amount of 100 & 50 Dollors. I have occasion for only a pair of cart wheels for which I must give 60 pounds Lawfull money. I only mention these few articles to serve as a specimen of the rest. I inquired the price of a new carrage the other day and found it to be no *more* than 300 pounds Lawfull money—at this rate I never will ask for a supply of this *light commodity* from any Body let my situation be what it will. The Season has been fine for grass but for about 3 weeks past we have had a sharp and severe Drouth which has greatly injured our grain and a blast upon english grain with a scarcity for flower so that a loaf which once sold for 4 pence is 4 shillings. Tis rumourd that the French fleet to the amount of 18ten have arrived of Chesepeak. The Enemy have left Philidelphia, but for politicks I refer you to the publick Letters which will accompany this.—Mr. Tailor promises to bring Letters from you whenever he returns. I am in daily expectation of hearing from you. I lament that you lay so far from the sea ports that you must omit some opportunities of writing. I will not suppose that with more leisure you have less inclination to write to your affectionate and Lonely Friend.

Portia

Source: Letter from Abigail to John Adams, July 15, 1778 [electronic edition]. *Adams Family Papers: An Electronic Archive.* Massachusetts Historical Society: http://www.massh ist.org/digitaladams

---

Document 6: Letter from Abigail Adams to John Adams, Braintree (June 20, 1783)

My Dearest Friend

. . . . Our two sons are placed under the care, and in the family of Mr. Shaw. They have been near 3 months absent from me. This week with my daughter and Mr. Smith to accompany us I go to see them. My dear John, where is he? I long to see him. I have been very anxious about him. Such a winter journey. I hope he is with you. I want to receive a Letter from him. If you should continue abroad untill fall I should be glad you would make me a small remittance, goods will not answer. We are glutted with them. I do not wish for any thing more,

> **Russian sheeting:** light, but very strong, linen fabric that is often used similarly to canvas

than I want for my family use. In this way a few peices of Irish linnen and a peice of **Russia sheeting** together with 2 green silk umbrellas I should be glad of as soon as convenient. If you should have an opportunity from France to send me 3 Marsels cotton and silk quilts I should be very glad; they are like the jacket patterns you sent me by Charles. I want a white, a Blew and a pink. Mr. Dana sent 3 to Mrs. Dana; I think she said Mr. Bonfeild procured them. I mentiond in a former Letter a few other articles. I am going to marry one of my family to a young fellow whom you liberated from jail, a son of Capt. Newcombs, to the Jane Glover who has lived 7 years with me and as she never would receive any wages from me I think myself obligated to find her necessaries for house keeping. I have been buying land, and my last adventure came to so poor a market, that I am quite broke. My letter is an unreasonable long one, yet I may take an other sheet of paper—not to night however. I will bid you good Night. I seal this least Mr. Smith should sail before I return. Mean to write more. Have a Letter for Mr. T [Thaxter].

Source: Letter from Abigail to John Adams, June 20, 1783 [electronic edition]. *Adams Family Papers: An Electronic Archive.* Massachusetts Historical Society: http://www.massh ist.org/digitaladams

---

Document 7: Letter from John Adams to Abigail Adams, Paris (August 14, 1783)

My dearest Friend

I have received your two favours of 7 May and 20 June. I had received no Letter from you for so long an Interval that these were really inestimable. I always learn more of Politicks from your Letters, than any others....

Your Purchase of Land tho of only the Value of 200 Dollars gives me more Pleasure than you are aware. I wish you had described it. I Suppose it to be that fine Grove which I have loved and admired from my Cradle. If it is, I would not part with it, for Gold. If you know of any Woodland or salt Marsh to be sold, purchase them and draw upon me for the Money. Your Bills shall be paid upon Sight. Direct the Bills to be presented if I should be returned home, to Messrs. Wilhem and Jan Willink Merchants Amsterdam, who will accept and pay them for the Honour of the Drawer. Pray dont let a Single Tree be cutt upon that Spot. I expect, very soon, to be a private Man, and to have no other Resource for my Family but my Farm, and therefore it is my Intention when I come home to sell my House in Boston and to collect together all the Debts due to me and all other little Things that I can convert into Money and lay it out in Lands in the Neighbourhood of our **Chaumiere**. The whole will make but a Small Farm, Yet it will be large enough for my Desires if my Children are content. You Speak of a high Offices In Gods Name, banish every Idea of such a Thing. It is the Place of the Greatest slavery

Chaumiere: French word that means cottage or bower

and Drudgery in the World. It would only introduce me to endless Squabbles and Disputes, and expose me to eternal obloquy and Envy. I wish that all Parties would unite in the present one who has the Hearts of that People and will keep them. The Opposition will only weaken and distress his Administration, and if another were chosen in his Place, the Administration of that other would be weakened and distressed by a Similar Opposition. I have not health to go through the Business, nor have I Patience to endure the Smart. I beg that neither You nor yours would ever encourage in yourselves or others such a Thought. If after my Return home, the state should think proper to send me to Congress and you will go with me, I will go, for a short time, but not a long one. After that if I should be chosen into the senate or House, I should be willing to contribute my Mite, to the publick service in that Way. At home, upon my Farm and among my Books assisting in the Education of my Children, and endeavouring to introduce them into Business to get their Bread and do some service in the World, I wish to pass the feeble Remnant of my Days. But I am too much hurt, by those

Exertions to which the Times have called me, to wish or to be capable of any great active Employment whatsoever. You know not how much your Friend is altered. The Fever burnt up half his Memory and more than half his Spirits, and has left him, with scorbutic Disorders about him that are very troublesome. Without Repose, if with it, he can never hope to get the better of them. This is said to you my friend in Confidence and is to be communicated to no one else. After having seen so many of my friends, thro Life fall Victims to the great Contest, I think my self very happy to have got through it, in no worse a Condition.

Adieu.

Source: Letter from John to Abigail Adams, August 14, 1783 [electronic edition]. *Adams Family Papers: An Electronic Archive.* Massachusetts Historical Society: http://www.masshist. org/digitaladams

AFTERMATH

Abigail had hoped that John would return to Massachusetts for good once the Revolution ended, but that did not happen. He had served in the Continental Congress from 1774 to 1777. In November 1777, he was appointed commissioner to France. He went to France in early 1778 and spent most of the next 10 years in Europe. While there, he helped negotiate treaties with France and Holland as well as the Treaty of Paris of 1783 that ended the American Revolution. Following the end of the Revolution, Adams was appointed ambassador to Great Britain. He returned to the United States in 1788 and was soon elected as the first vice president under the new CONSTITUTION that was ratified in 1789. He would later be elected president in 1796 and would serve one term.

For the first six years that John served in Europe, Abigail continued to run the farm. In the summer of 1784, she joined him in Europe and remained with him until he returned home. She continued to support his political career, but they chose to put the farm in the hands of a manager following the Revolution so that she could spend more time with her husband wherever he was serving. They both retired to the farm following his loss in the election of 1800. Abigail died on October 28, 1818, and John died on July 4, 1826.

ASK YOURSELF

1. How did Abigail present her decisions and actions about the farm to John? Did her methods of presentation change over time? Did she become more independent in her actions?
2. How did John react to Abigail's decisions and actions about the farm? Did his reaction to what she did change over time? Did he express surprise at her actions?
3. How do their discussions about Abigail's management of the farm show changes in attitudes about the role of women at the time?

TOPICS AND ACTIVITIES TO CONSIDER

- ≈ Abigail Adams is one of the most famous women of this era, but her experiences because of John's absence were not that unusual. Investigate how 18th-century society viewed the role of women and how those views have changed over time.
- ≈ John and Abigail Adams are famous for their written exchange in which Abigail, in a letter written on March 31, 1776, urged John to "remember the ladies." Why do

you think this is the discussion from their letters that is most remembered? Investigate what later events encouraged this development.

Further Reading

Akers, Charles W. *Abigail Adams: An American Woman.* Boston: Little, Brown, 1980.
Bowen, Catherine Drinker. *John Adams and the American Revolution.* Boston: Little, Brown, 1950.
Gelles, Edith B. *Portia: The World of Abigail Adams.* Bloomington: Indiana University Press, 1992.
Levin, Phyllis Lee. *Abigail Adams: A Biography.* New York: St. Martin's Press, 1987.
McCullough, David. *John Adams.* New York: Simon & Schuster, 2001.
Withey, Lynne. *Dearest Friend: A Life of Abigail Adams.* New York: Free Press, 1981.

Film and Television

The Adams Chronicles, television mini-series, 1976.
American Experience: John and Abigail Adams, PBS, 2005.
Biography: John and Abigail Adams, PBS, 2005.
John Adams, television mini-series, 2008.

Web Sites

Abigail Adams Biography: http://www.firstladies.org/biographies/firstladies.aspx?biography=2
Adams Resources at the Massachusetts Historical Society: http:/www.masshist.org/adams/
John Adams: http://www.hbo.com/john-adams

27. Moving as the Armies Move: Baroness von Riedesel's Journal (November 1778–February 1779)

INTRODUCTION

Fighting in the American Revolution proved disruptive to people's daily lives in many ways. Families often had to flee from home in order to avoid being caught up in a battle, or they had to move because the men in their families belonged to the losing side in a particular battle. The latter situation often happened to the wives and children of officers who had chosen to travel to be near their husbands and fathers. This sort of travel was common practice in the 18th century, and a good number of British and Hessian families traveled to America to be near their husbands and fathers, who were officers in the Royal Army. One good example of this can be found in the experiences of the Baroness Frederika Charlotte Riedesel, wife of General FRIEDRICH ADOLPH RIEDESEL.

Frederika Charlotte Riedesel had been born in Brandenburg in 1746, the daughter of a lieutenant general in the Prussian army. She had traveled with the army as a child and knew what it was like to be a camp follower. She married Friedrich Adolph Riedesel in 1762. Her husband sailed for North America in 1776 as commander of the army from Brunswick that would support Great Britain in its effort to suppress the American rebellion. Frederika and her three daughters followed him to America in 1777. They were in New York during the conflicts leading up to the Battle of Saratoga. As a result, the family was caught up in the aftermath when the soldiers who had surrendered were kept as prisoners for the next four years. Originally moved to Boston, the soldiers and their camp followers were moved to Virginia in late 1778. Baroness Riedesel described the difficulties of this trip in her journal.

KEEP IN MIND WHILE YOU READ

1. Baroness Riedesel was part of the aristocracy in Europe and was used to people treating her and her family with respect wherever they went.
2. The areas through which the baroness and her family traveled had already experienced fighting and the property destruction that came with it.

Document: Excerpt from Baroness Riedesel's Journal (November 1778–February 1779)

We reached one day a pretty little town; but our waggon remaining behind, we were very hungry. Seeing much fresh meat in the house where we stopped, I begged the landlady to sell me some. "I have," quoth she, "several sorts of meat: beef, mutton and lamb." Enraptured with this answer, I told her, "Let me have some, I will pay you liberally." But, snapping her fingers, she replied," You shall not have a morsel of it: why have you left your country to slay us and rob us of our property? now that you are our prisoners, it is our turn to vex you." "But," rejoined I, "see these poor children; they are dying of hunger." She remained still unmoved; but, when at length my youngest child, Caroline, who was then about two years and a half old, went to her, seized her hands, and told her in English," Good woman, I am indeed very hungry," she could no longer resist, and carrying the child to her room, she gave her an egg. "But," replied the dear little one, "I have two sisters." Deeply affected by that remark, the hostess gave her three eggs, saying, "I am loth to be so weak, but I cannot refuse the child." By-and-by, she softened, and offered me bread and butter. I made tea, and the hostess looked at our tea-pot with a longing eye, for the Americans are very fond of that beverage; yet they had stoutly resolved not to drink any more, the tax on tea, as is well known, having been the immediate cause of the contest with Great Britain. I offered her, however, a cup, and presented her with a paper case full of tea. This drove away all clouds between us; she begged me to go with her into the kitchen, and there I found her husband eating a piece of pork. The woman went into the cellar to bring me a basket of potatoes. When she returned into the kitchen, the husband offered her some of his dainty food; she tasted it, and returned to him what remained. I was disagreeably struck with this partnership and common enjoyment; but the man probably thought I was envious of it, on account of the hunger I had manifested, and presented me with the little which both had left. What could I do? I feared, that by refusing, I should offend them, and lose the potatoes. I accepted, therefore, the morsel, and having kept up the appearance as if I eat it, I threw it secretly into the fire. We were now in perfect amity; with the potatoes and some butter, I made a good supper, and we had to ourselves three neat rooms, with very good beds....

After our arrival in Virginia, and when we were a day's journey distant from the place of our destination, we had, for our last meal, tea, and a piece of bread and butter for each.

> **guineas:** English gold coins equal to 21 shillings

This was the end of our little stock, and we could here procure nothing, either for our present or future wants, except some fruits, which a peasant gave us for our journey. At noon, we reached a house, where we begged for some dinner; but all assistance was denied us, with many imprecations against the royalists. Seeing some maize, I begged our hostess to give me some of it, to make a little bread. She replied, "That she needed it for her black people: they work for us," she added, "and you come to kill us." Captain Edmonstone offered to pay her one or two **guineas** for a little wheat. But she returned, "You shall not have it even for hundreds of guineas; and it will be so much the better if you all die." The captain became so enraged at these words, that he was about to take the maize; but I prevented him from doing it, thinking that we should soon meet with more charitable people. But in this I was much mistaken, for we did not see even a solitary hut. The roads were execrable, and the horses could hardly move. My children, starving from hunger, grew pale, and for the first time lost their spirits. Captain Edmonstone, deeply affected at this, went about asking something for the children, and received, at last, from one of the waggoners who transported our baggage, a piece of stale bread, of three ounces weight, upon which many a tooth had already exercised its strength. Yet to my children, it was, at this time, a delicious morsel. I broke it into pieces, and was about giving the first piece to the youngest; but she said, "No, mama; my sisters are more in want of it than I am." The two eldest girls, with no less generosity, thought that little Caroline was to have the first piece. I then endeavoured to distribute to each her small portion. Tears ran down my cheeks, and had I ever refused to the poor a piece of bread, I should have thought that retributive justice had overtaken me now. Captain Edmonstone, who was much affected, presented the generous waggoner who had given us his last morsel, with a guinea, and when we were arrived at our place of destination, we provided him, besides, with bread for a part of his journey homeward.

Source: Riedesel, Frederika Charlotte. *Letters and Memoirs Relating to the War of American Independence, and the Capture of the German Troops at Saratoga.* New York: G. & C. Carvill, 1827, pp. 204–206, 211–213.

AFTERMATH

The American Revolution, like any other war, produced great tension between people on various sides of the conflict. As shown in Baroness Riedesel's journal, the local people in the areas they traveled through had grown to hate the British and anyone associated with them in the ongoing fighting. Many of these people sought to punish the enemy by denying them the basics needed for survival. Baroness Riedesel and her children suffered a lack of enough food and proper shelter on their journey as a result of this attitude. She personally struggled with how to handle such an attitude and often begged for food for her children. Baroness Riedesel was not the only person to experience such attitudes and behaviors. Such reactions on both sides were common during the Revolution and added to the suffering that occurred because of the war.

For Baroness Riedesel and her children, the suffering eventually ended. The family moved to New York in late 1779 and then were allowed to go to Canada in July 1781. They left for Germany in 1783. General Riedesel continued to serve in the Brunswick army, fighting in a campaign in the Netherlands from 1788 to 1793. The Riedesels had nine children, six of whom lived past infancy. General Riedesel died in 1800, and Baroness Riedesel died in 1808. Her journals from her experiences in America have provided much information about what it was like for the Hessians who served with the British Army in the Revolution.

ASK YOURSELF

1. Why do you think the Baroness chose to follow her husband? Is this a common practice for military spouses today? What has changed in society since the 18th century that helps explain the changes in the behavior of military spouses?
2. Why did the various women the baroness met originally refuse to give her and her family any food? Why did they eventually relent?

TOPICS AND ACTIVITIES TO CONSIDER

- ⮞ Other officers' wives, such as Martha Washington, traveled with the armies during the American Revolution. Investigate the lives of such women, and compare and contrast what they experienced while they lived with the armies.
- ⮞ The wives of enlisted men also traveled with the armies, often serving as cooks and nurses. Investigate the experiences of these women and compare those with the experiences of the officers' wives. How were they similar, and how were they different? What explains the differences?

Further Reading

Atwood, Rodney. *The Hessians: Mercenaries from Hesse-Kassel in the American Revolution.* New York: Cambridge University Press, 1980.

Berkin, Carol. *Revolutionary Mothers: Women in the Struggle for America's Independence.* New York: Alfred A. Knopf, 2005.

Calhoon, Robert M. *The Loyalists in Revolutionary America, 1760–1781.* New York: Harcourt Brace Jovanovich, 1973.

Cuneo, John R. *The Battles of Saratoga: The Turning of the Tide.* New York: Macmillan, 1967.

Ellet, Elizabeth Fries. *Revolutionary Women in the War for American Independence: A One-Volume Revised Edition.* Westport, CT: Greenwood Publishing Group, 1998.

Evans, Elizabeth. *Weathering the Storm: Women of the American Revolution.* New York: Paragon House, 1975.

Fleming, Thomas. *The Battle of Yorktown.* New York: American Heritage Publications, 1968.

Furneaux, Rupert. *The Battle of Saratoga.* New York: Stern and Day, 1971.

Kerber, Linda K. *Women of the Republic: Intellect and Ideology in Revolutionary America.* Chapel Hill: Published for the Institute of Early American History and Culture by the University of North Carolina Press, 1980.

Lowell. Edward J. *The Hessians and the Other German Auxiliaries of Great Britain in the Revolutionary War.* Williamstown, MA: Corner House, 1970; reprint 1884 ed.

Nelson, William H. *The American Tory.* Oxford: Clarendon Press, 1961.

Norton, Mary Beth. *Liberty's Daughters: The Revolutionary Experience of American Women, 1750–1800.* Boston: Little, Brown and Company, 1980.

Film and Television

Liberty's Kids, television series, 2002–2003.

28. War Splits Families: Letter from Timothy Pickering Jr., to His Father (February 23, 1778)

INTRODUCTION

Although the American Revolution produced many disagreements in many families, it did not always produce divisions that could not be overcome in some way. For some families, the splits produced by the Revolution proved almost impossible to overcome, while others found a way to remain close even when they disagreed politically.

A good example of this sort of accommodation can be found in the family of Timothy Pickering, Jr., of Salem, Massachusetts. Pickering became an ardent supporter of the Patriot cause while his father, Timothy Pickering, Sr., remained a staunch supporter of Great Britain. The son, who became interested in military history and tactics during the 1760s, helped organize the Massachusetts militia once fighting broke out in 1775. He joined the Continental Army and participated in the winter campaign of 1776–1777 in New York and New Jersey. He served as adjutant general from 1777 to 1780 and as quartermaster general from 1780 until after the war ended.

In February 1778, Pickering received word that his father was dying, and he wrote the following letter of farewell at that time. Although he and his father strongly disagreed about politics, his love and respect for his father can clearly be seen in this letter.

KEEP IN MIND WHILE YOU READ

1. The Pickering family had lived in the Salem area since the first years of settlement, so they were well known and potentially influential at the time of the Revolution.
2. Because of his responsibilities as adjutant general in the Continental Army, Timothy Pickering, Jr., could not just go home to Massachusetts to say goodbye to his father.
3. Timothy Pickering, Jr., was stationed at Yorktown, Virginia, while his father lived in Salem, Massachusetts. The British army lay in between these two places, and so the possibility existed that this letter might be seized before it reached its destination.

Document: Letter from Timothy Pickering, Jr. to His Father (February 23, 1778)

Timothy Pickering, Jr. to Timothy Pickering, Sr.

York Town February 23. 1778.

My Honored Father,

With much grief I received the account of your indisposition; but at the same time was happy to find you rather growing better, & that there was a prospect of your recovery. Not that I deemed you anxious to live; I supposed the contrary:—but whether to live or die, I know you are perfectly resigned to the will of Heaven.—But for the sake of your family & friends, I wished you to live yet many years: that I too might again see you, & manifest that filial duty which I feel, & would cheerfully pay, to your latest breath.

When I look back on past time, I regret our difference of sentiment in great as well as (sometimes) in little politics; as it was a deduction from the happiness otherwise to have been enjoyed. Yet you had always too much regard to freedom in thinking & the rights of conscience, to lay upon me any injunctions which could interfere with my own opinion of what was my duty. In all things I have endeavoured to keep a good conscience, void of offence towards God and man. Often have I thanked my Maker for the greatest blessing of my life—your example & instructions in all the duties I owe to God, and my neighbour. They have not been lost upon me; tho' I am aware that in many things I have offended, & come short of my duty. For these things I am grieved; but not as those who have no hope.

I am deeply indebted too for your care in my education; I only regret that I improved my time no better.

But altho' the line of action I have pursued has not always been such as you would have chosen; yet (but I boast not) in regard to religion and morality, I hope you have never repented that I was your son. By God's grace I will in my future life aim at higher attainments in those all-essential points; not only from a sense of duty to my Creator—from a regard to my own happiness here and beyond the grave—but that I may never wound the breast of a parent to whom I am under so many and so great obligations.

My love and duty to you and my mother,

conclude me your obedient son,

Timothy Pickering junr:

Source: Pickering, Octavius, and Charles Wentworth Upham. *The Life of Timothy Pickering by His Son, Octavius Pickering.* Vol. 1. Boston: Little, Brown, and Company, 1867), pp. 209–210.

AFTERMATH

As far as we know, Timothy Pickering's letter of farewell reached his father prior to his death in June 1778. Pickering served ably in the Continental Army until the end of the war. Following the adoption of the new form of government under the CONSTITUTION, he became involved in politics on the national level. He first served as postmaster general and later as secretary of war under GEORGE WASHINGTON. He also became secretary of state when EDMUND RANDOLPH was forced to resign. Pickering continued in this post under JOHN ADAMS, but he was forced out in 1800 because of his strong opposition to U.S. neutrality in the war between France and Great Britain. He served in the U.S. Senate from 1803 to

1811 and in the House of Representatives from 1813 to 1817. During the latter service, he strongly opposed the War of 1812 because he feared it would result in the dissolution of the United States. Following his service in Congress, he retired and spent the rest of his life farming. He died in Salem, Massachusetts, in 1829.

ASK YOURSELF

1. How did Pickering address the disagreement he had had with his father concerning politics? Could he have approached it in a different manner?
2. Pickering thanked his father for setting a good example as he was growing up. What do you think he meant by this statement?

TOPICS AND ACTIVITIES TO CONSIDER

- Timothy Pickering's military service is often overshadowed by his later political service. Investigate other examples of military leaders who later got involved in politics. Investigate how their military service impacted their political experience, and why some were more successful in politics than others.
- Wars often produce family divisions as people end up on different sides of the fight. For those in the United States, the war most often thought of in this way is the Civil War of the 1860s, but it has happened with other wars as well. Investigate family divisions produced by various wars in American history. Investigate how the divisions produced by war have been similar from conflict to conflict, and how they have differed depending on the specific circumstances of each war under consideration.

Further Reading

Clarfield, Gerard H. *Timothy Pickering and American Diplomacy, 1795–1800.* Columbia: University of Missouri Press, 1969.

McLean, David. *Timothy Pickering and the Age of the American Revolution.* New York: Arno Press, 1982.

Pickering, Octavius, and Charles Wentworth Upham. *The Life of Timothy Pickering by His Son, Octavius Pickering.* 4 vols. Boston: Little, Brown, and Company, 1867–1873.

Web Sites

Timothy Pickering as Quartermaster General: http://www.qmfound.com/COL_Timothy_Pickering.htm

Timothy Pickering as Secretary of State: http://history.state.gov/departmenthistory/people/pickering-timothy

29. Raising Children: Letters between Thomas Jefferson and His Daughter Martha (1783, 1787)

INTRODUCTION

Whether a country is at peace or involved in a war, parents hope that their children can gain the sort of education they need for the future. This proved true during the American Revolution as education efforts continued as much as possible even during the midst of conflict. The amount of education available varied greatly depending on location, gender, and social class. The educational system was better in the northern and middle colonies and children who came from wealthy families were more likely to receive a good education. Generally, wealthy children in the South studied with private tutors because few schools were available. The focus for boys tended to revolve around acquiring the skills and knowledge to be successful in business and public life, while the focus for girls revolved around gaining the skills necessary to be a good wife.

A good example of this sort of educational focus can be seen in the family of THOMAS JEFFERSON. Jefferson's wife, Martha, died in September 1782, and he thereafter sought to ensure that his two daughters had all the advantages they needed for success in the life he expected them to live in the future. In the year following his wife's death, Jefferson wrote to his daughter Martha urging her to study hard. These sorts of encouragements continued for a number of years as Martha continued her education in a more formal manner by attending schools in Philadelphia and France. In 1787 Martha responded to these encouragements by describing what she had been doing and stating that she was studying harder and hoped that her father would be satisfied with the results. Although Jefferson encouraged Martha to read a variety of materials, much of the focus of his educational plan for her revolved around her learning art, music, dancing, and a foreign language, all skills that would help her attract a good husband, the primary goal of education for women at this time.

KEEP IN MIND WHILE YOU READ

1. Thomas Jefferson loved to read all sorts of books and was probably one of the most intellectual men living during the Revolution.
2. Women had no major public role to play at this time, so knowledge of politics and government was not seen as necessary.

3. Thomas Jefferson was very involved in the public arena during the Revolution and thus was separated from his family for months at a time.

Document 1: Letter from Thomas Jefferson to His Daughter Martha (November 28, 1783)

TO MARTHA JEFFERSON:

MY DEAR PATSY Annapolis, Nov. 28, 1783.

After four days journey I arrived here without any accident and in as good health as when I left Philadelphia. The conviction that you would be more improved in the situation I have placed you than if still with me, has solaced me on my parting with you, which my love for you has rendered a difficult thing. The acquirements which I hope you will make under the tutors I have provided for you will render you more worthy of my love, and if they cannot increase it they will prevent it's diminution. Consider the good lady who has taken you under her roof, who has undertaken to see that you perform all your exercises, and to admonish you in all those wanderings from what is right or what is clever to which your inexperience would expose you, consider her I say as your mother, as the only person to whom, since the loss with which heaven has been pleased to afflict you, you can now look up; and that her displeasure or disapprobation on any occasion will be an immense misfortune which should you be so unhappy as to incur by any unguarded act, think no concession too much to regain her good will. With respect to the distribution of your time the following is what I should approve.

from 8. to 10 o'clock practise music.
from 10. to 1. dance one day and draw another
from 1. to 2. draw on the day you dance, and write a letter the next day.
from 3. to 4. read French.
from 4. to 5. exercise yourself in music.
from 5. till bedtime read English, write &c.

Communicate this plan to Mrs. Hopkinson and if she approves of it pursue it. As long as Mrs. Trist remains in Philadelphia cultivate her affections. She has been a valuable friend to you and her good sense and good heart make her valued by all who know her and by nobody on earth more than by me. I expect you will write to me by every post. Inform me what books you read, what tunes you learn, and inclose me your best copy of every lesson in drawing. Write also one letter every week either to your aunt Eppes, your aunt Skipwith, your aunt Carr, or the little lady from whom I now inclose a letter, and always put the letter you so write under cover to me. Take care that you never spell a word wrong. Always before you write a word consider how it is spelt, and if you do not remember it, turn to a dictionary. It produces great praise to a lady to spell well. I have placed my happiness on seeing you good and accomplished, and no distress which this world can now bring on me could equal that of your disappointing my hopes. If you love me then, strive to be good under every situation and to all living creatures, and to acquire those accomplishments which I have put in your power, and which will go far towards ensuring you the warmest love of your affectionate father,

TH: JEFFERSON

P. S. Keep my letters and read them at times that you may always have present in your mind those things which will endear you to me.

Source: Ford, Paul Leicester, ed. *The Writings of Thomas Jefferson*. Vol. 3. New York: G. P. Putnam's Sons, 1894, pp. 344–346.

Document 2: Letter from Martha Jefferson to Her Father (April 9, 1787)

FROM MARTHA JEFFERSON:
MY DEAR PAPA Panthemont, April 9th, 1787.
I am very glad that the beginning of your voyage has been so pleasing, and I hope that the rest will not be less so, as it is a great consolation for me, being deprived of the pleasure of seeing you, to know at least that you are happy. I hope your resolution of returning in the end of April is always the same. I do not doubt but what Mr. Short has written you word that my sister sets off with Fulwar Skipwith in the month of May, and she will be here in July. Then, indeed, shall I be the happiest of mortals; united to what I have the dearest in the world, nothing more will be requisite to render my happiness complete. I am not so industrious as you or I would wish, but I hope that in taking pains I very soon shall be. I have already begun to study more. I have not heard any news of my harpsichord; it will be really very disagreeable if it is not here before your arrival. I am learning a very pretty thing now, but it is very hard. I have drawn several little flowers, all alone, that the master even has not seen; indeed, he advised me to draw as much alone as possible, for that is of more use than all I could do with him. I shall take up my Livy, as you desire it. I shall begin it again, as I have lost the thread of the history. As for the **hysterics,** you may be quiet on that head, as I am not lazy enough to fear them. Mrs. Barett has wanted me out, but Mr. Short told her that you had forgotten to tell Madame L'Abbesse to let me go out with her. There was a gentleman, a few

> **hysterics:** fit of uncontrollable laughter or crying

days ago, that killed himself because he thought that his wife did not love him. They had been married ten years. I believe that if every husband in Paris was to do as much, there would be nothing but widows left. I shall speak to Madame Thaubeneu about dining at the Abbess's table. As for needlework, the only kind that I could learn here would be embroidery, indeed netting also; but I could not do much of those in America, because of the impossibility of having proper silks; however, they will not be totally useless. You say your expectations for me are high, yet not higher than I can attain. Then be assured, my dear papa, that you shall be satisfied in that, as well as in any thing else that lies in my power; for what I hold most previous is your satisfaction, indeed I should be miserable without it. You wrote me a long letter, as I asked you; however, it would have been much more so without so wide a margin. Adieu, my dear papa. Be assured of the tenderest affection of your loving daughter,
M. JEFFERSON
Pray answer me very soon—a long letter, without a margin. I will try to follow the advice they contain with the most scrupulous exactitude.

HARPSICHORD

A harpsichord is a musical instrument that looks very similar to a piano. It is played by means of a keyboard just like a piano, but there the similarities cease. A piano makes a sound because a felt-covered hammer hits the string when a key is played, but a harpsichord produces sound by plucking a string when a key is played. Harpsichords were very popular and widely used from the 1500s until the mid-1800s. Composers of the Baroque era (1600–1750) used the harpsichord as a primary instrument in many of their compositions. But by the late 18th century, the harpsichord was being replaced by the piano, so it was a bit unusual that the Jeffersons chose to purchase a harpsichord instead of the increasingly popular piano. Harpsichords continued to exist, and they experienced a bit of revival in the late 20th century as composers once more used them in the music they wrote.

Source: Randolph, Sarah N. *The Domestic Life of Thomas Jefferson.* New York: Harper & Brothers, 1871, pp. 117–118.

AFTERMATH

Thomas Jefferson remained involved in the public arena following the Revolution. He served as ambassador to France from 1785 until 1789. During that period, his daughter Martha was also in France; his daughter Mary joined them in 1787. Following his return to the United States, Jefferson served as the first secretary of state under President GEORGE WASHINGTON. Jefferson was elected vice president in 1796 and president in 1800. While president, he oversaw the Louisiana Purchase, which set the stage for future American westward expansion. When Jefferson left the office of president in 1809, he retired to his home at Monticello in Virginia. He seldom ventured very far from home, and spent most of his time writing letters to friends and engaging in various experiments on his farm. He died on July 4, 1826, the fiftieth anniversary of the adoption of the DECLARATION OF INDEPENDENCE, the public action for which Jefferson was most famous.

Jefferson apparently believed that his educational regimen for his daughter succeeded because he was happy with her marriage and the life she came to live following the Revolution. In 1790 Martha married her cousin THOMAS MANN RANDOLPH. During the years 1802–1803 and 1805–1806, she served as "First Lady" during her father's presidency. Otherwise, she lived a relatively quiet life, out of the public spotlight. She focused much of her attention on making sure her 12 children had a good education. She established a school at Edgehill, the family plantation, where she educated her children in mathematics, history, literature, music, and languages. Martha Jefferson Randolph died on October 10, 1836.

ASK YOURSELF

1. Why did Jefferson encourage Martha to organize her studies in the manner he suggests? What did he hope would be the results?
2. Why was it so important for Martha to gain skills in music and art? Why was it important for her to learn French?

3. Why do you think Jefferson decided that leaving Martha with Mrs. Hopkinson was the best thing he could do for her at the time? What do you think that reflects about relationships between fathers and daughters as well as ideas about the education of girls in the 18th century?

TOPICS AND ACTIVITIES TO CONSIDER

- Ideas about education have changed over the years. Investigate what was thought important for boys and girls to learn during the Revolutionary era and compare that to what was considered important in the 19th and 20th centuries.
- Popular musical instruments have changed over time. Today, the piano would probably be one of the most popular instruments for children to learn to play. Martha Jefferson, however, focused on the harpsichord. Investigate what instruments have been popular for children to learn to play during the history of the United States and consider why these instruments have changed over time.

Further Reading

Cremin, Lawrence. *American Education: The Colonial Experience, 1607–1783.* New York: Harper & Row, 1970.

Criss, Mildred. *Jefferson's Daughter.* New York: Dodd, Mead, 1948.

Glenn, Thomas Allen. *Some Colonial Mansions and Those Who Lived in Them, Second Series.* Philadelphia: Henry T. Coates & Company, 1900, pp. 199–242.

Kukla, Jon. *Mr. Jefferson's Women.* New York: Alfred A. Knopf, 2007.

Langhorne, Elizabeth. *Monticello: A Family Story.* Chapel Hill, NC: Algonquin Books, 1987.

Malone, Dumas. *Jefferson and His Time.* 6 vols. Boston: Little, Brown, and Company, 1948–1981.

Peterson, Merrill D. *Thomas Jefferson and the New Nation: A Biography.* New York: Oxford University Press, 1970.

Simmons, Dawn Langley. *Mr. Jefferson's Ladies.* Boston: Beacon Press, 1966.

Wayson, Billy L. *Martha Jefferson Randolph: The Education of a Republican Daughter and Plantation Mistress,* 1782–1809. PhD dissertation, University of Virginia Press, 2008.

Film and Television

Thomas Jefferson: A Film by Ken Burns, television mini-series, 1996.

Web Sites

Thomas Jefferson Digital Archives: http://etext.virginia.edu/jefferson

The Thomas Jefferson Papers at the Library of Congress: http://memory.loc.gov/ammem/collections/jefferson_papers

Thomas Jefferson's Monticello: http://www.monticello.org

RELIGION

30. DIFFERENT CULTURES: NATIVE AMERICAN CHRISTIANITY, NICHOLAS CRESSWELL'S DIARY (1775)

INTRODUCTION

From the point of first contact between Europeans and Native Americans, there were tensions related to religion and culture. Europeans perceived the Native Americans as less than civilized, if not outright savage, while those native to the land did not understand why Europeans acted as they did. Europeans sought to convert Native Americans to Christianity, assuming this would help civilize them. Many Europeans did not believe that this effort really worked, and the tensions between the two groups continued and often degenerated into fighting and war.

But some Europeans found their experiences with Native Americans to be very different from what they had been told to expect, and those differences often revolved around the practice of religion after Christianity had been introduced. Nicholas Cresswell, an Englishman, had come to America in 1774 to seek adventure and, hopefully, his fortune. In 1775 he journeyed to the Ohio Valley to explore and engage in trade. While on this trip, he witnessed a Native American religious service. In his diary, he recorded his surprise at what he saw.

KEEP IN MIND WHILE YOU READ

1. Cresswell was from England and had little experience of people different from himself prior to this trip to the American colonies.
2. Cresswell was a Methodist and had little direct experience of the Moravians, so the service might have seemed strange to him in many ways.

Document: Excerpt from The Journal of Nicholas Cresswell (1775)

Saturday, August 26th, 1775. Set out early this morning, travelled very hard till noon, when we passed through the largest Plum Tree Thicket I ever saw. I believe it was a mile long, nothing but the Plum and Cherry Trees. Killed a Rattlesnake. Just as the Sun went down we stopped to get our Supper on some Dewberries (a small berry something like a Gooseberry). Mr. Anderson had gone before me and said he would ride on about two miles to a small run where he intended to camp, as soon as I had got sufficient. I mounted my Horse and followed him till I came to a place where the road forked. I took the path that I supposed he had gone and rode till it began to be dark, when I imagined myself to be wrong, and there was not a possibility of me finding my way back in the night. Determined to stay where I was till morning, I had no sooner alighted from my horse, but I discovered the glimmering of a fire about four hundred yards from me. This rejoiced me exceedingly, supposing it was Mr. Anderson.

When I got there, to my great disappointment and surprise found three Indian women and a little boy. I believe they were as much surprised as I was. None of them could speak English and I could not speak Indian. I alighted and marked the path I had come and that I had left, on the ground with the end of my stick, made a small channel in the earth which I poured full of water, laid some fire by the side of it, and then laid myself down by the side of the fire, repeating the name of Anderson which I soon understood they knew. . . .

Sunday, August 27th, 1775. . . . In about an hour she brought me to Mr. Anderson's camp, who had been very uneasy at my absence and employed an Indian to seek me. I gave my **Dulcinea** a **match coat**, with which she seemed very well pleased. Proceeded on our journey and about noon got to an Indian Town called Wale-hack-tap-poke, or the Town with a good Spring, on the Banks of the Muskingham and inhabited by Dellawar Indians. Christianized under the **Moravian Sect**, it is a pretty town consisting of about sixty houses, and is built of logs and covered with Clapboards. It is regularly laid out in three spacious streets which meet in the centre, where there is a large meeting house built of logs sixty foot square covered with Shingles, Glass in the windows and a Bell, a good plank floor with two rows of forms. Adorned with some few pieces of Scripture painting, but very indifferently executed. All about the meeting house is kept very clean.

> **Dulcinea:** beloved of Don Quixote often used as slang for sweetheart
> **match coat:** coat of coarse wool
> **Moravian Sect:** Christian denomination that traces its origins back to Central Europe and the teachings of 15th-century reformer John Hus.

In the evening went to the meeting. But never was I more astonished in my life. I expected to have seen nothing but anarchy and confusion, as I have been taught to look upon these beings with contempt. Instead of that, here is the greatest regularity, order, and decorum, I ever saw in any place of Worship, in my life. With that solemnity of behaviour and modest, religious deportment would do honour to the first religious society on earth, and put a bigot or enthusiast out of countenance. The parson was a Dutchman, but preached in English. He had an Indian interpreter, who explained it to the Indians by sentences. They sung in the Indian language. The men sit on one row of forms and the women on the other with the children in the front. Each sex comes in and goes out of their own side of the house. The old men sit on each side the parson. Treated with Tea, Coffee, and Boiled Bacon at supper. The Sugar they make themselves out of the sap of a certain tree. Lodged at Whiteman's house, married to an Indian woman. . . .

Sunday, October 1st, 1775. Took leave of most of my acquaintances in town. Mr. Douglas gave me an Indian Tobacco pouch made of a Mink Skin adorned with porcupine quills. He is desirous of keeping a correspondence with me, which in all probability will be for the interest of us both. I have conceived a great regard for the Indians and really feel a most sensible regret in parting from them, however contemptible opinion others may entertain of these honest poor creatures. If we take an impartial view of an Indian's general conduct with all the disadvantages they labour under, at the same time divest ourselves of prejudice, I believe every honest man's sentiments would be in favour of them.

Source: Cresswell, Nicholas. *The Journal of Nicholas Cresswell, 1774–1777*. New York: The Dial Press, 1924, pp. 104–107, 116–117.

AFTERMATH

Cresswell returned to Virginia where he hoped to buy land in order to profit from his trip to the American colonies. The growing conflict with Great Britain prevented success in that venture, and he returned home to England in 1777. He married and settled down, never to return to the United States. His reaction to Native Americans proved to be unusual because few people of European descent came to believe that Native Americans were anything but uncivilized savages who should be moved out of the way in order to allow European civilization to expand. Throughout the course of the late 1700s and the 1800s, U.S. authorities pushed Native Americans into the more desolate and remote areas of the central part of the North American continent. By the beginning of the 20th century, most Native Americans had been forced to move to reservations either in Oklahoma or the Dakotas. Fairly successful efforts to convert them to Christianity continued throughout all of these conflicts. Today, Christianity remains a strong part of Native American culture in many parts of the United States.

ASK YOURSELF

1. What sorts of stories about Native Americans do you think Cresswell had heard that would explain his reaction to what he saw on this trip?
2. Why do you think Cresswell did not work harder to make sure that he did not get separated from Mr. Anderson? Do you think Mr. Anderson and he believed he could navigate in the woods better than he actually could?

TOPICS AND ACTIVITIES TO CONSIDER

- ❧ Europeans often reacted strongly when describing Native Americans they met on early trips to the North American continent. Investigate these descriptions and compare them to what Cresswell describes.
- ❧ Christian missionaries have worked among Native Americans almost from the point Christopher Columbus first landed in the New World. Investigate these various efforts, and compare and contrast the efforts of different denominations and different European countries.
- ❧ A number of people from the 1500s to the 1700s condemned the actions of Europeans while defending Native Americans. Investigate people who took such stands. Compare and contrast what they said and what happened to them.

Further Reading

Calloway, Colin G. *The American Revolution in Indian Country: Crisis and Diversity in Native American Communities*. Cambridge: Cambridge University Press, 1999.

Heckewelder, John Gottlieb Ernestus. *A Narrative of the Mission of the United Brethren among the Delaware and Mohegan Indians from Its Commencement in the Year 1740 to the Close of the Year 1808.* New York: Arno Press, 1971 (1820).

Hurt, R. Douglas. *The Ohio Frontier: Crucible of the Old Northwest, 1720–1830.* Bloomington: Indiana University Press, 1996.

Van Every, Dale. *A Company of Heroes: The American Frontier, 1775–1783.* New York: Morrow, 1962.

Web Site

History of the Moravian Church: http://www.moravian.org/history

31. Religion Influences Action: The Schwenkfelders' Declaration against Service in the Militia (1777)

INTRODUCTION

One of the areas in which the American Revolution produced strains came in the area of religion. A person's religious beliefs can impact the side a person takes in a conflict. Taking a side can be particularly difficult for people whose religious beliefs dictate that all wars are wrong. The QUAKERS are the most famous of the religious groups that oppose all wars, but there were other such groups in the American colonies at the time of the Revolution, and they all tried to be neutral. Among these other groups was the Schwenkfelders.

The Schwenkfelders were followers of CASPAR SCHWENKFELD VON OSSIG, a Protestant Reformer who lived in Germany in the 16th century and emphasized inner spirituality over outward form. The Schwenkfelders often suffered persecution in Europe, and many chose to immigrate to the American colonies in the 1700s. The first group arrived in Philadelphia in 1731, and other groups came over the next several years. They held strong pacifist beliefs and could not bring themselves to serve in the colonial MILITIA. On May 1, 1777, the sect issued the following declaration on military service.

KEEP IN MIND WHILE YOU READ

1. According to colonial law, all adult men had to serve in the militia. So, opposing such service meant to break the law.
2. Because Pennsylvania had been founded by Quakers under the leadership of William Penn, the colony provided freedom of conscience to its residents.

Document: The Schwenkfelders' Declaration against Service in the Militia (1777)

We who are known by the name Schwenkfelders hereby confess and declare that for conscience's sake it is impossible for us to take up arms and kill our fellowmen; we also believe that so far as knowledge of us goes this fact is well known concerning us.

We have hitherto been allowed by our lawmakers to enjoy this liberty of conscience.

We have felt assured of the same freedom of conscience for the future by virtue of the public resolution of Congress and our assembly.

We will with our fellow citizens gladly and willingly bear our due share of the common civil taxes and burdens excepting the bearing of arms and weapons.

We cannot in consequence of this take part in the existing militia arrangements, though we would not withdraw ourselves from any other demands of the government.

Whereas, at present, through contempt of the manifested divine goodness and through other sins, heavy burdens, extensive disturbances by war, and diverse military regulations are brought forth and continued;

Whereas, we on the first of this month made a candid declaration concerning present military arrangements to the effect that we cannot on account of conscience take part in said military affairs; and

Whereas, it seems indeed probable that military service will be enacted from many of our people and that on refusal to render such service heavy fines will be imposed;

Therefore, the undersigned who adhere to the apostolic doctrines of the sainted Casper Schwenkfeld and who seek to maintain the same by public services and by instruction of the young have mutually agreed, and herewith united themselves to this end that they will mutually with each other bear such fines as may be imposed on account of refusal for conscience's sake to render military service in case deadly weapons are carried and used. Those on whom such burdens may fall will render a strict account to the managers of the Charity Fund in order that steps may be taken to a proper adjustment.

Source: Kiebel, Howard Weigner. *The Schwenkfelders in Pennsylvania, a Historical Sketch.* Vol. XIII, Pt. XII. Lancaster, PA: Pennsylvania German Society Publications, 1904, pp. 152–153.

AFTERMATH

The Schwenkfelders, along with the other pacifist groups, faced much persecution for their refusal to serve in the military in time of war. Neither the PATRIOTS, who supported independence, nor the LOYALISTS, who wanted to stay part of the British Empire, could understand the religious groups who opposed war. But these groups faced the persecution; they remained faithful to their beliefs and refused to fight in the Revolution. The Schwenkfelders continued to live in the Philadelphia area. They formally organized as a church in 1909. At present, there are five congregations within a 50-mile radius of Philadelphia.

ASK YOURSELF

1. Why do you think the Schwenkfelders were willing to face further persecution by issuing this pacifist statement?
2. What sort of impact do you think such pacifist statements had on recruitment for the military during the American Revolution?

TOPICS AND ACTIVITIES TO CONSIDER

> ☙ In every war, there have been people who have held pacifist views and opposed military service. Investigate groups that have held such views in wars other than the American Revolution and compare them to the Schwenkfelders.

❧ The Schwenkfelders were only one of a number of small religious groups that immigrated to Pennsylvania during the 18th century. Investigate other groups such as the Amish and the Mennonites, and compare how their religious beliefs were similar and how they were different.

Further Reading

Dollin, Norman. *The Schwenkfelders in Eighteenth-Century America.* PhD dissertation, Columbia University, 1971.

Piepkorn, Arthur Carl. *Profiles in Belief: The Religious Bodies of the United States and Canada.* 4 vols. New York: Harper & Row, 1977–1979.

Schultz, Selina Gerhard. "The Schwenkfelders of Pennsylvania." *Pennsylvania History* 24 (October 1957): 293–320.

Web Sites

Central Schwenkfelder Church: http://www.centralschwenkfelder.com

Kriebel, Martha B. The Schwenkfelders: http://www.ucc.org/about-us/hidden-histories/the-schwenkfelders.html

Schwenkfelder Library and Heritage Center: http://www.schwenkfelder.com

32. The Issue of Religious Freedom: Boston Supports Religion for the Sake of Order in Its Response to the Massachusetts Declaration of Rights of 1780 (May 12, 1780)

INTRODUCTION

Debates over the public support of organized religion had taken place almost from the moment the American colonies were settled in the early 1600s. Massachusetts had been founded by the Pilgrims and Puritans, religious groups seeking to establish their own churches. In the 17th century, most people believed that communal order was only possible when everyone in a community belonged to the same church. The Pilgrims and Puritans left England so they could establish the kind of church they wanted to attend in the New World. They originally did not allow other denominations in their towns. By the time of the Revolution, however, it was often common to have more than one church or one denomination in a community. The Massachusetts government still generally required public support for churches, regardless of denomination.

With the outbreak of the Revolution, all the colonies had to create new governments as a result of the breakdown of the British system. Leaders in Massachusetts debated what to do for several years. Finally, in 1780, they proposed a new state constitution that included a declaration of rights. The Massachusetts Declaration of Rights provided for personal freedom of religion, but it still required all citizens of Massachusetts to financially support a church in their community. The citizens of Boston thought this was a good idea and publicly supported the proposal because they thought it would promote public order.

KEEP IN MIND WHILE YOU READ

1. The belief that a common church was necessary for public order had existed in one form or another since the days of the Roman Empire.
2. People who did not endorse government support of organized religion could not live in Massachusetts prior to the Revolution.

Document: Boston's Response to the Massachusetts Declaration of Rights of 1780 (May 12, 1780)

The Return of Boston:

The only Article now to be attended to is the third in the Decleration of Rights, which Asserts that Piety, Religion and morality are essential to the happiness, Peace and Good order of a People and that these Principles are diffused by the Publick Worship of God, and by Publick Instructions &c—and in Consequence makes provision for their support. The alterations proposed here which you will Lay before the Convention were designed to Secure the Reights of Consience and to give the fullest Scope to religious Liberty In support of the proposition it urged that if Publick Worship and Publick teaching, did certainly (as was allowed) defuse a general Sence of Duty & moral Obligations, and, so secured the safety of our Persons and Properties, we ought chearfully to pay those from whose agency we derived such Advantages. But we are Attempting to support (it is said) the Kingdom of Christ; It may as well be said we are supporting the Kingdom of God, by institution of a Civil Government, which Declared to be an Ordinance to the Deity, and so refuse to pay the civil magistrate. What will be the consequence of such refusal—The greatest disorders, if not a Dissolution of Society. Suspend all provision for the inculation of Morality, religion and Piety, and confusion & every evil work may be justly dreaded; for it is found that with all the Restraints of religion induced by the Preaching of Ministers, and with all the Restraints of Goverment inforced by civil Law, the World is far from being as quiet an abode as might be wished. Remove the former by ceasing to support Morality, religion and Piety and it will be soon felt that human Laws were feble barriers opposed to the uninformed lusts of Passions of Mankind. But though we are not supporting the kingdom of Christ may we not be permitted to Assist civil society by an addoption, and by the teaching of the best set of Morals that were ever offered to the World. To Object to these Morrals, or even to the Piety and Religion we aim to inculcate, because they are drawn from the Gospel, must appear very singular to an Assembly generally professing themselves Christians. Were this really our intention, no Objection ought to be made to it provided, as in fact the case that equal Liberty is granted to every religious Sect and Denomination Whatever, and it is only required that every Man should pay to the support of Publick Worship In his own way. But should any be so Conscientious that they cannot pay to the support of any of the various denominations among us they may then alott their Money to the support of the Poor.

Source: *A Report of the Record Commissioners of the City of Boston, Containing the Boston Town Records of 1778–1783.* Boston: Rockwell and Churchill, City Printers, 1895, 129–135.

AFTERMATH

The attitude expressed by the citizens of Boston reflected the dominant view in the state of Massachusetts in 1780. The constitution was approved with the Declaration of Rights included. Massachusetts was one of the last states to adopt a new constitution. Part of the reason it took so long was because of the debate over the Declaration of Rights and its requirement for public support of religion. Massachusetts had an official church and required public support of organized religion until 1833, when the state finally ended public support of an official state church.

ASK YOURSELF

1. Why do you think the citizens of Boston would think that requiring public support of organized religion would be a good idea?
2. Why do you think people thought that a community could only have peace and order if everyone belonged to the same church?

TOPICS AND ACTIVITIES TO CONSIDER

- Most of the churches in Massachusetts in 1780 were Congregational. Investigate their ideas about the role of organized religion in society.
- The CONGREGATIONAL CHURCHES developed out of the beliefs of the Pilgrims and Puritans. Investigate these groups to see how their ideas were similar and how they were different. Also, consider how these beliefs changed from the time of settlement in the early 1600s to the outbreak of the American Revolution in 1775.

Further Reading

Allison, Robert J. *A Short History of Boston*. Beverly, MA: Commonwealth Editions, 2004.

Brown, Richard D. *Massachusetts: A Bicentennial History*. New York: W. W. Norton, 1978.

Cooper, James F. *Tenacious of Their Liberties: The Congregationalists in Colonial Massachusetts*. New York: Oxford University Press, 1999.

Curry, Thomas J. *The First Freedoms: Church and State in America to the Passage of the First Amendment*. New York: Oxford University Press, 1986.

Petlis, Ronald M. *The Massachusetts Constitution of 1780: A Social Contract*. Amherst: University of Massachusetts Press, 1978.

Walker, Williston. *A History of the Congregational Churches in the United States*. New York: The Christian Literature Company, 1894.

Web Site

Religion and the Founding of the American Republic: Religion and the American Revolution: http://www.loc.gov/exhibits/religion/rel03.html

33. THE QUESTION OF PUBLIC SUPPORT FOR ORGANIZED RELIGION: ASHBY, MASSACHUSETTS, OPPOSES ENFORCED PUBLIC SUPPORT IN ITS RESPONSE TO THE MASSACHUSETTS DECLARATION OF RIGHTS OF 1780 (JUNE 2, 1780)

INTRODUCTION

One might think that the citizens of other towns in Massachusetts would follow the example set by Boston and endorse the requirement in the proposed Declaration of Rights of 1780 that all citizens be required to belong to a church and to financially support that church. But that did not prove to be true. A number of communities responded to the proposal by stating that they believed that such requirements interfered with a person's individual beliefs, and that the government should not force a person to support an institution against their will. Also, the CONGREGATIONAL CHURCH would have benefitted the most from such requirements because it was the largest denomination, so the result would have been a de facto state church even if the intention was to allow some individual flexibility. The town of Ashby expressed these concerns clearly in its response to the proposed Declaration of Rights.

KEEP IN MIND WHILE YOU READ

1. The belief that a common church was necessary for public order had existed in one form or another since the days of the Roman Empire.
2. The fact that the citizens of Ashby felt it was all right to object to the proposal in the state Constitution shows that the ideas about the public support of religion had begun to change.

Document: The Town of Ashby's Response to the Massachusetts Declaration of Rights of 1780 (June 2, 1780)

The Return of Ashby:
We Object against Those words in the second Article; (the publick piece)—

We also Object against the Whole of the third Article;—The reasons for our exceptions against those words—(the publick piece) in the second, and for our rejection of the whole of the third Article, are as follows.—

Reason the 1st that all the Liberty and security which any religeous Society can resonably desire, is granted by the Legeslature, in the second Article, without the words (the publick piece) which are there incerted, that said second Article stands clear and intelageble without these words—(the publick piece)—

Reason 2 The third Article is inconsistant with the second for the second Article alows of no restraint upon any one as to their persons, Liberty, or Estates, except in them words, objected to as above—

The third Article lays a restraint: for those who cannot Concientiously or Convenantly attend upon any publick teachers are under restraint as to their Estates & so injurd as to their Liberty and property—

Reason 3. Religeous Societys as such have no voice in Chusing the Legeslature, the Legeslature therefore have no right to make Law binding on them as such; every religeous Society, as such, is intirely independant on any body politick, the Legeslature therefore have no more right to make Laws Binding on them, as such, then the Court of Great Britton have to make Laws binding on the Independant states of America—

Reason 4 as religeous Societys and bodys politick, are bodys distinct and independant of each other, they have not aright therefore to make Laws binding on each other; how amaising absurd it would be for a number of persons in a Town to form into a religeous Society and in that Capacity make Laws or authorise others to make Laws binding on the Town as a body politick—

Reason 5 that which is of greatest importance ought not to be subordinated to that which is least the well being and prosperity of religeous Society as such, is of greater importance, then that of politick bodys as such, the reason therefore which is given in the third Article for investing the Legeslature with authority to make Laws binding on religeous Societys as such is inconsistant and against the piece and welfare of the State—

Reason 6th. The Rivers of blood which has ran from the Veins of Marters! and all the torment which they have indured in the flames! was ocationed by the authority of Legeslature over religeous Society in consequence of the authority of the Legeslature or the authority arising from the authority of the Legeslature, the Feet of Paul & Silas where made fast in the stocks, the three Children Cast into the Furnace of fire, Daniel into the Lions Den, and many other such instances might be inumerated—

Reason 7th. the third Article says the people of this common wealth have a right to invest their Legeslature with power to make Laws that are binding on religeous Society as (as we understand them) which is as much as to say we will not have Christ to reign over us that the Laws of this Kingdom are not sufficient to govern us, that the prosperity of his Kingdom is not eaqualy important with the Kingdoms of this world and that the Ark of God stands in need of Uzza's band to keep it from falling to the ground, butt lett us attend sereously to this important Truth that I will build my Church upon this Rock, and the Gates of Hell shall not prevail against it, now where resides this power in Christ only? or in the Legeslature?—it may be Objected against the Reasons here given that it leaves people two Louse and does not ingadge them to there duty & therby all religion will fall to the ground and this Objection indeed is very plausible because it may flow from an outward zeal for a form of Godliness without the power butt is it not founded upon this Supposition that men are not sufficiently ingadged to the practice of their Duty unless they doe somthing that God never required of them—

He that made us reasonable Creatures and Conferd upon us as the Blessing of the Gospell has by this frame and situation laid us under the strongest Obligation to the practice of Piety, Religeon, and Morality that can posibly be conceived, & if this wont impress our minds to doe our Duty nothing will.

Source: "The Return of Ashby (Middlesex County), 1780." *Massachusetts Archives.* CCLXXVII. Boston: Commonwealth of Massachusetts, Archives Division, 1970, p. 3.

AFTERMATH

The citizens of Ashby failed in their efforts to change the proposed Massachusetts Declaration of Rights of 1780. It was approved along with the rest of the new Constitution for the state. But the debate continued over whether people should be required to support organized religion, both at the state and national levels. In 1791 the First Amendment to the U.S. CONSTITUTION was ratified, which prohibited the federal government from establishing an official church for the country. But it also forbade the national government from interfering with state official churches. These continued to exist in a number of states. Massachusetts finally ended its official support of the Congregational Church in 1833.

ASK YOURSELF

1. Why do you think the citizens of Ashby did not agree with other communities that thought that it was important to have public support of organized religion?
2. The citizens of Ashby gave a long list of reasons why they thought this requirement was a mistake. Which do you think was the most important reason for them? Why?

TOPICS AND ACTIVITIES TO CONSIDER

- Investigate the history of the town of Ashby, Massachusetts. Consider what in its history prior to 1780 might explain its stance regarding the Declaration of Rights.
- Investigate the discussions of support for organized religion in other states during the Revolution. Consider how these discussions differed from state to state and investigate what in the states' histories might explain the differences.

Further Reading

Brown, Richard D. *Massachusetts: A Bicentennial History.* New York: W. W. Norton, 1978.
Cooper, James F. *Tenacious of Their Liberties: The Congregationalists in Colonial Massachusetts.* New York: Oxford University Press, 1999.
Curry, Thomas J. *The First Freedoms: Church and State in America to the Passage of the First Amendment.* New York: Oxford University Press, 1986.
Petlis, Ronald M. *The Massachusetts Constitution of 1780: A Social Contract.* Amherst: University of Massachusetts Press, 1978.

Walker, Williston. *A History of the Congregational Churches in the United States.* New York: The Christian Literature Company, 1894.

Whitney, Andrew. *Ashby, Springfield, and Fitchburg, Massachusetts.* Fitchburg: H. M. Downs Printing Company, 1912.

Web Site

Religion and the Founding of the American Republic: Religion and the American Revolution: http://www.loc.gov/exhibits/religion/rel03.html

34. The Revolt against Great Britain Is a Bad Idea: Jonathan Boucher Preaches a Sermon in Opposition to Revolution (1775)

INTRODUCTION

As the arguments between Great Britain and the colonies increased from the end of the French and Indian War in 1763 to the outbreak of actual fighting at Lexington and Concord in 1775, all sorts of community leaders and public figures spoke out in support of one side or the other. Even pastors and other religious leaders made such statements, often using the pulpit as a platform to urge their parishioners to take a particular side. During the colonial era, pastors filled a community leadership role by urging people to be good citizens. Particularly in New England, church leaders often provided local support to public officials because of the historically close ties between church and state. But pastors throughout the colonies supported government authorities in very public ways.

The Revolution changed much of this practice because people increasingly moved to separate church and state in order to reduce the influence of pastors and other church leaders. Much of this change resulted from anger aimed at pastors who were LOYALISTS and had urged their parishioners not to oppose the British government. A good example of this type of pastor is Jonathan Boucher. Born in Cumberland, England, in 1738, Boucher had come to Port Royal, Virginia, in 1759 to serve as a tutor. He returned to England in 1762 and took orders in the Church of England. Upon his return to the colonies in 1763, he pastored several churches in Virginia and Maryland and ran a school for boys. Among his students was JOHN PARKE CUSTIS, stepson of GEORGE WASHINGTON. Throughout the 1760s and 1770s, Boucher often used his pulpit to urge the members of his church to respect government authority and remain loyal to Great Britain.

KEEP IN MIND WHILE YOU READ

1. Boucher had grown up in England and still had family there, so his ties to both Great Britain and the colonies were strong.
2. As a minister of the Church of England, Boucher's ultimate superiors in the church resided in Britain.
3. This sermon was preached in 1775, but Boucher had been criticizing the opposition to the British government by the colonies since the mid-1760s.

Document: Jonathan Boucher's Sermon (1775)

Stand fast, therefore, in the liberty wherewith Christ hath made us free. (Galatians 5:1).

....To have become noted either as a political writer or preacher, as some (who at least are unacquainted with my preaching) are pleased to tell you I now am, is a circumstance that gives me no pleasure. I was sorry to hear the observation; not (I thank God!) from any consciousness of my having ever written or preached any thing of which (at least in point of principle) I have reason to be ashamed; but because it is painful to reflect, that it should have fallen to my lot to live in times, and in a country, in which such subjects demand the attention of every man. Convinced in my judgment that it is my duty to take the part which I have taken, though I cannot but lament it's not having produced all the beneficial consequences which I fondly flattered myself it might, I dare not allow myself to discontinue it. The time, I know, has been, when addresses of this sort from English pulpits were much more frequent than they now are. Even now, however, they are not wholly discontinued; sermons on political topics, on certain stated days, are still preached, and with the authority of Government. This is mentioned to obviate a charge, that I am singular in continuing the practice; as it proves that such preaching is not yet proscribed from our pulpits....

As the liberty here spoken of [in the passage] respected the Jews, it denoted an exemption from the burthensome services of the ceremonial law; as it respected the Gentiles, it meant a manumission from bondage under the *weak and beggarly elements of the world,* and an admission into the covenant of grace: and as it respected both in common, it meant a freedom from the servitude of sin. Every sinner is, literally, a slave; for, *his servants ye are to whom ye obey:*—and the only true liberty is the liberty of being the servants of God; for, *his service in perfect freedom.* The passage cannot, without infinite perversion and torture, be made to refer to any other kind of liberty; much less to that liberty of which every man now talks, though few understand it....

....The word *liberty,* as meaning civil liberty, does not, I believe, occur in all the Scriptures. With the aid of a **concordance,** I find only two or three passages, in two apocryphal writers, that look at all like it....I entreat your indulgence, whilst, without too nicely scrutinizing the propriety of deducing from a text a doctrine which it clearly does not suggest, I once more adopt a plan already chalked out for me, and deliver to you what occurs to me as proper for a Christian audience to attend to on the subject of Liberty.

It has just been observed, that the liberty inculcated in the Scriptures, (and which alone the Apostle had in view in this text,) is wholly of the spiritual or religious kind. This liberty was the natural result of the new religion in which mankind were then instructed; which certainly gave them no new civil privileges. They remained subject to the governments under which they lived, just as they had been before they became Christians; and just as others were who never became Christians, with this difference only, that the duty of submission and obedience to Government was enjoined on the converts to Christianity with new and stronger sanctions. The doctrines of the Gospel make no manner of alteration in the nature or form of Civil Government; but enforce afresh, upon all Christians, that obedience which is due to the respective Constitutions of every nation in which they may happen to live....

....Obedience to Government is every man's duty, because it is every man's interest; but it is particularly incumbent on Christians, because (in addition to it's moral fitness) it

> **concordance:** alphabetical index showing the places the words occur in the Bible

is enjoined by the positive commands of God: and therefore, when Christians are disobedient to human ordinances, they are also disobedient to God. If the form of government under which the good providence of God has been pleased to place us be mild and free, it is our duty to enjoy it with gratitude and with thankfulness; and, in particular, to be careful not to abuse it by licentiousness. If it be less indulgent and less liberal than in reason it ought to be, still it is our duty not to disturb and destroy the peace of the community, by becoming refractory and rebellious subjects, and *resisting the ordinances of God.* However humiliating such acquiescence may seem to men of warm and eager minds, the wisdom of God in having made it our duty is manifest. For, as it is the natural temper and bias of the human mind to be impatient under restraint, it was wise and merciful in the blessed Author of our religion not to add any new impulse to the natural force of this prevailing propensity, but, with the whole weight of his authority, altogether to discountenance every tendency to disobedience.

If it were necessary to vindicate the Scriptures for this their total unconcern about a principle which for many other writings seem to regard as the first of all human considerations, it might be observed, that, avoiding the vague and declamatory manner of such writings, and avoiding also the useless and impracticable subtleties of metaphysical definitions, these Scriptures have better consulted the great general interests of mankind, by summarily recommending and enjoining a conscientious reverence for law whether human or divine. To respect the laws, is to respect liberty in the only rational sense in which the term can be used; for liberty consists in a subserviency to law. "Where there is no law," says Mr. Locke, "there is no freedom." The mere man of nature (if such an one there ever was) has no freedom: *all his lifetime he is subject to bondage.* It is by being included within the pale of civil polity and government that he takes his rank in society as a free man....

...."And, therefore, the love of liberty which does not produce this effect, the love of liberty which is not a real principle of dutiful behaviour towards authority, is as hypocritical as the religion which is not productive of a good life. Licentiousness is, in truth, such an excess of liberty as is of the same nature with tyranny. For, what is the difference betwixt them, but that one is lawless power exercised under pretence of authority, or by persons vested with it; the other, lawless power exercised under pretence of liberty, or without any pretence at all? A people, then, must always be less free in proportion as they are more licentious; licentiousness being not only different from liberty, but directly contrary to it—a direct breach upon it."

True liberty, then, is a liberty to do every thing that is right, and the being restrained from doing any thing that is wrong. So far from our having a right to do everything that we please, under a notion of liberty, liberty itself is limited and confined—but limited and confined only by laws which are at the same time both it's foundation and it's support. It can, however, hardly be necessary to inform you, that ideas and notions respecting liberty, very different from these, are daily suggested in the speeches and the writings of the times; and also that some opinions on the subject of government at large, which appear to me to be particularly loose and dangerous, are advanced in the sermon now under consideration; and that, therefore, you will acknowledge the propriety of my bestowing some farther notice on them both.

It is laid down in this sermon, as a settled maxim, that the end of government is "the common good of mankind." I am not sure that the position itself is indisputable; but, if it were, it would by no means follow that, "this common good being matter of common feeling, government must therefore have been instituted by common consent." There is an appearance of logical accuracy and precision in this statement; but it is only an appearance.

The position is vague and loose; and the assertion is made without an attempt to prove it. If by men's "common feelings" we are to understand that principle in the human mind called common sense, the assertion is either unmeaning and insignificant, or it is false. In no instance have mankind ever yet agreed as to what is, or is not, "the common good." A form or mode of government cannot be named, which these "common feelings" and "common consent," the sole arbiters, as it seems, of "common good," have not, at one time or another, set up and established, and again pulled down and reprobated. What one people in one age have concurred in establishing as the "common good," another in another age have voted to be mischievous and big with ruin. The premises, therefore, that "the common good is matter of common feeling," being false, the consequence drawn from it, viz., that government was instituted by "common consent," is of course equally false.

This popular notion, that government was originally formed by the consent or by a compact of the people, rests on, and is supported by, another similar notion, not less popular, nor better founded. This other notion is, that the whole human race is born equal; and that no man is naturally inferior, or, in any respect, subjected to another; and that he can be made subject to another only by his own consent. The position is equally ill-founded and false both in it's premises and conclusions. In hardly any sense that can be imagined is the position strictly true; but, as applied to the case under consideration, it is demonstrably not true. Man differs from man in every thing that can be supposed to lead to supremacy and subjection, *as one star differs from another star in glory.* It was the purpose of the Creator, that man should be social: but, without government, there can be no society; nor, without some relative inferiority and superiority, can there be any government. A musical instrument composed of chords, keys, or pipes, all perfectly equal in size and power, might as well be expected to produce harmony, as a society composed of members all perfectly equal to be productive of order and peace....

....Mr. Locke indeed says, that, "by consenting with others to make one body-politic under government, a man puts himself under an obligation to every one of that society to submit to the determination of the majority, and to be concluded by it." For the sake of the peace of society, it is undoubtedly reasonable and necessary that this should be the case: but, on the principles of the system now under consideration, before Mr. Locke or any of his followers can have authority to say that it actually is the case, it must be stated and proved that every individual man, on entering into the social compact, did first consent, and declare his consent, to be concluded and bound in all cases by the vote of the majority. In making such a declaration, he would certainly consult both his interest and his duty; but at the same time he would also completely relinquish the principle of equality, and eventually subject himself to the possibility of being governed by ignorant and corrupt tyrants. Mr. Locke himself afterwards disproves his own position respecting this supposed obligation to submit to the "determination of the majority," when he argues that a right of resistance still exists in the governed: for, what is resistance but a recalling and resuming the consent heretofore supposed to have been given, and in fact refusing to submit to the "determination of the majority?" It does not clearly appear what Mr. Locke exactly meant by what he calls "the determination of the majority:" but the only rational and practical public manner of declaring "the determination of the majority," is by law: the laws, therefore, in all countries, even in those that are despotically governed, are to be regarded as the declared "determination of a majority" of the members of that community; because, in such cases, even acquiescence only must be looked upon as equivalent to a declaration. A right of resistance, therefore, for which Mr. Locke contends, is incompatible with the duty of submitting to the determination of "the majority," for which he also contends.

It is indeed impossible to carry into effect any government which, even by compact, might be framed with this reserved right of resistance. Accordingly there is no record that any such government ever was so formed. If there had, it must have carried the seeds of it's decay in it's very constitution. For, as those men who make a government (certain that they have the power) can have no hesitation to vote that they also have the right to unmake it; and as the people, in all circumstances, but more especially when trained to make and unmake governments, are at least as well disposed to do the latter as the former, it is morally impossible that there should be anything like permanency or stability in a government so formed. Such a system, therefore, can produce only perpetual dissensions and contests, and bring back mankind to a supposed state of nature; arming every man's hand, like Ishmael's, against every man, and rendering the world an *aceldama,* or field of blood.—Such theories of government seem to give something like plausibility to the notions of those other modern theorists, who regard all governments as invasions of the natural rights of men, usurpations, and tyranny. On this principle it would follow, and could not be denied, that government was indeed fundamentally, as our people are sedulously taught it still is, an evil. Yet it is to government that mankind owe their having, after their fall and corruption, been again reclaimed, from a state of barbarity and war, to the conveniency and the safety of the social state: and it is by means of government that society is still preserved, the weak protected from the strong, and the artless and innocent from the wrongs of proud oppressors. It was not without reason, then, that Mr. Locke asserted that a greater wrong cannot be done to prince and people, than is done by "propagating wrong notions concerning government"....

.... Kings and princes (which are only other words for supreme magistrates) were doubtless created and appointed, not so much for their own sakes, as for the sake of the people committed to their charge: yet are they not, therefore, the creatures of the people. So far from deriving their authority from any supposed consent or suffrage of men, they receive their commission from Heaven; they receive it from God, the source and original of all power. However obsolete, therefore, either the sentiment or the language may now be deemed, it is with the most perfect propriety that the supreme magistrate, whether consisting of one or of many, and whether denominated an emperor, a king, an archon, a dictator, a consul, or a senate, is to be regarded and venerated as the **viceregent** of God....

> **viceregent:** deputy or assistant to a governor or other ruler

This long inquiry concerning the divine origin and authority of government might perhaps have been deemed rather curious than useful, were it not of acknowledged moment, that some dangerous inferences which are usually drawn from the contrary opinion should be obviated. One of these dangerous inferences it seems to have been the aim of the sermon now before me to inculcate. Government being assumed to be a mere human ordinance, it is thence inferred, that "rulers are the servants of the public:" and, if they be, no doubt it necessarily follows, that they may (in the coarse phrase of the times) be *cashiered* or continued in pay, be reverenced or resisted, according to the mere whim or caprice of those over whom they are appointed to rule. Hence the author of this sermon also takes occasion to enter his protest against "passive obedience and nonresistance"....

.... No government upon earth can rightfully compel any one of it's subjects to an active compliance with any thing that is, or that appears to his conscience to be, inconsistent with, or contradictory to, the known laws of God: because every man is under a prior and superior obligation to *obey God in all things.* When such cases of incompatible demands of duty occur, every well-informed person knows what he is to do; and every well-principled person will do what he ought, viz. he will submit to the ordinances of God, rather than comply with the commandments of men. In thus acting he cannot err: and this alone is "passive obedience;" which I entreat you to observe is so far from being "unlimited obedience," (as it's enemies willfully persist to miscall it,) that it is the direct contrary. Resolute not to disobey God, a man of good principles determines, in case of competition, as the lesser evil, to disobey man: but he knows that he should also disobey God, were he not, at the same time, patiently to submit to any penalties incurred by his disobedience to man....

.... Mr. Locke, like many inferior writers, when defending resistance, falls into inconsistencies and is at variance with himself. "Rebellion being," as he says, "an opposition not to persons, but to authority, which is founded only in the constitution and laws of the government, those, whoever they be, who by force break through, and by force justify their violation of them, are truly and properly rebels." To this argument no one can object: but it should be attended to, that, in political consideration, it is hardly possible to dissociate the ideas of authority in the abstract from persons vested with authority. To resist a person legally vested with authority, is, I conceive, to all intents and purposes, the same thing as to resist authority. Nothing but it's success, could have rescued the revolution from this foul imputation, had it not been for the abdication. Accordingly this great event has always hung like a mill-stone on the necks of those who must protest against rebellions; whilst yet their system of politics requires that they should approve of resistance, and the revolution....

.... "[T]he Divine Author of our existence" has beyond all question given to "one part of the human race" to hold over another. Without some paramount and irresistible power, there can be no government. In our Constitution, this supremacy is vested in the King and the Parliament; and, subordinate to them, in our Provincial Legislatures. If you were now released from this constitutional power, you must differ from all others "of the human race," if you did not soon find yourselves under a necessity of submitting to a power no less absolute, though vested in other persons, and a government differently constituted. And much does it import you to consider, whether those who are now so ready to promise to make *the grievous yoke of your fathers lighter,* may not themselves verify Rehoboam's assertion, and make you feel that *their little fingers are thicker than your father's loins.*

Be it (for the sake of argument) admitted, that the government under which till now you have lived happily is, most unaccountably, all at once become *oppressive and severe;* did you, of yourselves, make the discovery? No: I affirm, without any apprehension of being contradicted, that you are acquainted with these oppressions only from the report of others. For what, then, (admitting you have a right to resist in any case,) are you now urged to resist and rise against those whom you have hitherto always regarded (and certainly not without reason) as your *nursing fathers and nursing mothers?* Often as you have already heard it repeated without expressing any disapprobation, I assure myself it will afford you no pleasure to be reminded, that it is on account of an insignificant duty on tea, imposed by the British Parliament; and which, for aught we know, may or may not be constitutionally imposed; but which, we well know, two-thirds of the people of America can never be called on to pay. Is it the part of an *understanding people,* of loyal subjects, or of good Christians, instantly to resist and rebel for a cause so trivial? O my brethren, consult your own hearts, and follow your own judgments! and learn not your "measures of obedience" from men who weakly or wickedly imagine there can be liberty unconnected with law—and whose aim it is to drive you on, step by step, to a resistance which will terminate, if it does not begin, in rebellion! On all such trying occasions, learn the line of conduct which it is your duty and interest to observe, from our Constitution itself: which, in this particular, is a fair transcript or exemplification of the ordinance of God. Both the one and the other warn you against resistance: but you are not forbidden either to remonstrate or to petition. And can it be humiliating to any man, or any number of men, to ask, when we have but to *ask and it shall be given?*...

If we, and our fellow-subjects, have been conscientiously faithful in the discharge of our duty, we can have no reason to doubt that our delegates will be equally faithful in the discharge of theirs. Our Provincial Assemblies, it is true, are but one part of our Colonial Legislature: they form, however, that part which is the most efficient. If the present general topic of complaint be, in their estimation, well founded, and a real and great grievance, what reason have you to imagine that all the Assemblies on the Continent will not concur and be unanimous in so representing it? And if they should all concur so to represent it, it is hardly within the reach of supposition that all due attention will not be paid to their united remonstrances. So many and such large concessions have often been made, at the instance only of individual assemblies, that we are warranted in relying, that nothing which is reasonable and proper will ever be withheld from us, provided only it be asked for with decency, and that we do not previously forfeit our title to attention by becoming refractory and rebellious.

Let it be supposed, however, that even the worst may happen, which can happen; that our remonstrances are disregarded, our petitions rejected, and our grievances unredressed: what, you will naturally ask—what, in such a case, would I advise you to do?—Advice, alas! is all I have to give; which, however, though you may condescend to ask and to regard it, will neither be asked, nor accepted, by those who alone can give it great effect. Yet, circumscribed as our sphere of influence is, and, therefore, even in our humble department, we have some duties to perform. To your question, therefore, I hesitate not to answer, that I wish and advise you to act the part of reasonable men and of Christians. You will be pleased to observe, however, that I am far from thinking that your virtue will ever be brought to so severe a test and trial. The question, I am aware, was an ensnaring one, suggested to you by those who are as little solicitous about your peace, as they are for my safety: the answer which, in condescension to your wishes, I have given to it, is direct and plain; and not more applicable to you, than it is to all the people of America. If you think the duty of threepence a pound upon tea, laid on by the British Parliament, a grievance, it is your duty to instruct your members to take all the constitutional means in their power to obtain redress: if those means fail of success, you cannot but be sorry and grieved; but you will better bear your disappointment, by being able to reflect that it was not owing to any misconduct of your own. And, what is the whole history of human life, public or private, but a series of disappointments? It might be hoped that Christians would not think it grievous to be doomed to submit to disappointments and calamities, as their Master submitted, even if they were as innocent. His disciples and first followers shrunk from no trials nor dangers. Treading in the steps of him who, *when he was reviled, blessed, and when he was persecuted, suffered it,* they willingly laid down their lives, rather than resist some of the worst tyrants that ever disgraced the annals of history. Those persons are as little acquainted with general history, as they are with the particular doctrines of Christianity, who represent such submission as abject and servile. I affirm, with great authority, that "there can be no better way of asserting the people's lawful rights, than the disowning unlawful commands, by thus patiently suffering." When this doctrine was more generally embraced, our holy religion gained as much by submission, as it is now in a fair way of losing for want of it.

Having, then, my brethren, thus long been *tossed to and fro* in a wearisome circle of *uncertain traditions,* or in speculations and projects still more uncertain, concerning government, what better can you do than, following the Apostle's advice, *to submit yourselves*

JOHN LOCKE

John Locke was an English philosopher and political theorist who lived during the 17th century. His writings had a major influence on people in the American colonies during the Revolutionary era. Locke grew up during the English Civil War of the 1640s and entered public service in 1665 as the secretary to the English ambassador to the Brandenburg court in modern-day Germany. He continued in public service until he fled to Holland in 1683 along with his employer, the Earl of Shaftesbury, who had strong disagreements with King Charles II of England. Locke lived in exile until the Glorious Revolution in 1689 allowed him to return to England, where he continued in public service until his retirement in 1700. While in exile, Locke composed most of his important writings. Included in this group was *Two Treatises of Government*. In this piece, Locke considered the proper role of a government and declared that a people can be justified to revolt if the government fails to represent their interests properly. Locke stated that the majority of the people in a country should determine its direction, and that the people had to be represented in some way in the government. These ideas appealed greatly to the colonial revolutionaries who fought against what they perceived to be British tyranny in the shape of unapproved taxes and lack of representation.

to every ordinance of man, for the Lord's sake; whether it be to the King as supreme, or unto GOVERNORS, as unto them that are SENT by him for the punishment of evil-doers, and for the praise of them that do well? For, so is the will of God, that with well-doing ye may put to silence the ignorance of foolish men: as free, and not using your liberty for a cloke of maliciousness, but as the servants of God. Honour all men: love the brotherhood: fear God: honour the king.

Source: Boucher, Jonathan. *A View of the Causes and Consequences of the American Revolution, with an Historical Preface.* London: G. G. and J. Robinson, 1797, pp. 495, 496–497, 504, 505–506, 507–509, 510–515, 516–519, 534, 544, 546, 552, 553–555, 556–560.

AFTERMATH

In 1775 Jonathan Boucher pastored Queen Anne's Parish in Prince George's County, Maryland. His sermons against the growing colonial opposition received the attention of local PATRIOT leaders in Maryland, particularly after fighting broke out in Massachusetts in April 1775. The local committee of safety put him under constant surveillance, and crowds burned him in effigy. He started preaching with loaded pistols on the pulpit in case of trouble. Fearing the worst, Boucher and his wife, Eleanor, fled to Britain in September 1775. Boucher never returned to Maryland, and he never recovered his property there. He did receive some compensation from the British government when they allotted money for the Loyalists who had fled the colonies during the Revolution. He pastored several churches in England and died there in 1804.

ASK YOURSELF

1. Why do you think Boucher was so opposed to the growing revolutionary movement in the colonies?
2. Why did Boucher's sermons produce such a strong reaction from local leaders? Do you think they really thought he could sway people's opinions, or did they just want to present a united front to leaders back in England?

TOPICS AND ACTIVITIES TO CONSIDER

- ❧ Investigate the role of church leaders during times of crisis such as the American Revolution, the Civil War, World War I, and World War II. Has the role changed over time? If so, why do you think that has happened? If not, why not?
- ❧ Investigate the Loyalists during the American Revolution. Where did most of them come from? Why did they oppose the Revolution? What happened to most of them?

Further Reading

Boucher, Jonathan. *Reminiscences of an American Loyalist, 1738–1789*. Port Washington, NY: Kennikat Press, 1967(1925).

Calhoon, Robert M. *The Loyalists in Revolutionary America, 1760–1781*. New York: Harcourt Brace Jovanovich, 1973.

Nelson, William H. *The American Tory*. Oxford: Clarendon Press, 1961.

Rhoden, Nancy L. *Revolutionary Anglicanism: The Colonial Church of England Clergy during the American Revolution*. New York: New York University Press, 1999.

Zimmer, Anne Y. *Jonathan Boucher, Loyalist in Exile*. Detroit: Wayne State University Press, 1978.

Web Sites

American Loyalists: http://www.redcoat.me.uk

The On-Line Institute for Advanced Loyalist Studies: http://www.royalprovincial.com

United Empire Loyalists' Association of Canada: http://www.uelac.org

35. The Revolt against Great Britain Is a Good Idea: Abraham Keteltas Preaches a Sermon in Support of Revolution (1777)

INTRODUCTION

Although some pastors like Jonathan Boucher preached sermons opposing revolution and urging people to remain loyal to the king, others used their sermons to express support for the revolt. It is difficult to figure out exactly how many clergy members supported and how many opposed the Revolution, but many who opposed the Revolution left the country as Boucher did in 1775. So, most of the preachers who remained in the United States during the Revolution either supported the Revolution or had no strong feelings either way, at least that they expressed publicly.

A representative example of a pastor who supported the revolt against Great Britain was Abraham Keteltas. Born in New York City in 1732, Keteltas attended Yale and graduated in 1752. He was licensed as a minister in 1756 and served as pastor to the Presbyterian Church in Elizabethtown, New Jersey, from 1756 to 1760. He was dismissed at that time and left the Presbyterian Church in 1765. He then served as an itinerant preacher among the Dutch and French parishes in Jamaica and Long Island, New York, because he understood both languages. He fled to Newburyport, Massachusetts, when the British occupied Long Island in 1776. He preached the following sermon in Newburyport in 1777.

KEEP IN MIND WHILE YOU READ

1. Keteltas preached this sermon in Massachusetts (a colony settled by the Puritans from England), but he was from New York (a colony settled first by Dutch and then English and French Protestants). These religious differences could produce tensions between colonies.
2. The British withdrew from Massachusetts in March 1776 and went to New York City. So, Keteltas had fled from where the British army was to where it had been previously.

Document: *Abraham Keteltas' Sermon in Support of the Revolution (1777)*

Psalm 74, Verse 22.

Arise O God! Plead thine own Cause.

.... In all ages of the world, God has raised up men who have by their writings and public speeches, pled his people's cause. How many able advocates in both houses of parliament, have warmly pled and espoused the cause of this much injured country. How many learned, sensible, and excellent pamphlets have been written, both in England and America, to vindicate our rights and liberties, and prevent our destruction and blessed be God, that all true christians, in every part of the world, who plead the cause of truth, liberty, and virtue, are in effect interceeding for us. How many fervent prayers are continually ascending from millions of sanctified and benevolent hearts in our behalf, to the throne of grace; and what is more important than all these, we are deeply interested in the all-powerful and all-prevailing intercession of Jesus our merciful High Priest. We have an infinitely important friend at the court of Heaven, a friend who so loved us, as to die for us; a friend who has all power in Heaven and upon earth, and who is omnipotent to quell the rage, and subdue all the efforts of earth and hell.....

[W]e have reason to conclude, that the cause of this American Continent, against the measures of a cruel, bloody, and vindictive ministry, is the cause of God. We are contending for the rights of mankind, for the welfare of millions now living, and for the happiness of millions yet unborn. If it is the indisputed duty of mankind, to do good to all as they have opportunity, especially to those who are of the houshold of faith, if they are bound by the commandments of the supreme law-giver, to love their neighbor as themselves, and do to others as they would that others should do unto them; then the war carried on against us, is unjust and unwarrantable, and our cause is not only righteous, but most important: It is God's own cause: It is the grand cause of the whole human race, and what can be more interesting and glorious. If the principles on which the present civil war is carried on by the American colonies, against the British arms, were universally adopted and practiced upon by mankind, they would turn a vale of tears, into a paradise of God: whereas opposite principles, and a conduct, founded upon them, has filled the world with blood and stupor, with rapine and violence, with cruelty and injustice, with wretchedness, poverty, horror, desolation, and despair: We cannot therefore doubt, that the cause of liberty, united with that of truth & righteousness, is the cause of God. This is the glorious cause in which Great-Britain herself, has frequently and strenuously contended against tyrants and oppressors. Not to mention preceding struggles for liberty, when Charles the first invaded the rights of his people, the Lords and Commons, aided by their adherents, rose up in arms, and waged a war against him, which terminated in the loss of his crown and life: and when his infatuated son, James the second; imitating his father's fatal example, endeavoured to introduce popery and arbitrary power into his kingdom; the people of England, invited the prince of Orange to vindicate their liberties, who expel'd the tyrant from his throne, and was placed on it himself, by the votes of a free parliament. For the sake of liberty and the protestant religion, during the reign of this glorious and auspicious king, the Pretender was excluded from the throne, and the succession to it, was settled in the royal house of Hanover. Great-Britain cannot in justice blame us, for imitating her in those noble thoughts for liberty, which have been her greatest glory—she cannot condemn us, without condemning the conduct of her greatest patriots and heroes, without denying her king's right to his crown, and declaring her opposition to the spirit and interest of her own excellent constitution. I am bold to affirm, that all the surpassing glory, by which she has eclipsed other nations, has been owing to this admirable form of government, so favorable to the rights of mankind. She never has been more illustrious at home or abroad, never more remarkable for her internal glory or external splendor, her peace, plenty and prosperity at home, or her victories, atchievments, & conquests abroad, than when her liberties flourished, and a patriot king sway'd the sceptre; as she never has been poorer, more miserable and inglorious, never been more impotent in herself, or made a meaner figure in the eyes of her neighbors, than when her liberties were violated, and a tyrant sat upon the throne....

....O England! thou once beloved, happy, and glorious country! Thou land of freedom and delight! How is thy gold become dim, and thy fine gold changed! It was full of judgment; righteousness lodged in it, but now murderers. Thy rulers are companions of thieves, every one loveth gifts, and followeth after rewards: they judge not the fatherless, neither doth the cause of the widow come unto them.

You see my brethren, from the preceding observations, the unspeakable advantages of liberty, to Great-Britain, and how fatal to her have been the invasion and decline of this inestimable blessing. How absurd then! how inglorious! how cruel and unjust is her conduct, in carrying on this bloody war, to ruin and enslave us—Liberty is the grand fountain, under God, of every temporal blessing, and what is infinitely more important, it is favorable to the propagation of unadulterated christianity. Liberty is the parent of truth, justice, virtue, patriotism, benevolence, and every generous and noble purpose of the soul. Under the influence of liberty, the arts and sciences, trade, commerce, and husbandry flourish and the wilderness blossoms like the rose....

Under the auspicious smiles of Liberty, riches increase, industry strains every nerve, secure of property, and joy and plenty smile on every side. How inestimable a blessing then must liberty be, and how inconceivably great its loss!

But if liberty is thus friendly to the happiness of mankind, and is the cause of the kind parent of the universe; certainly tyranny & oppression are the cause of the devil, the cause which God's soul hates. The holy scriptures abound with instances and prophecies of his judgments against tyrants and oppressors; and not only sacred, but prophane history, prove the fulfilment of those prophecies....

Thus has God, in the most lively characters, written his hatred and detestation of tyranny and oppression, upon the bodies of those who have been guilty of those heaven daring offences—thus hath he shewn how much he detests, and how severely he will punish cruelty and injustice, the murder of the innocent, and the invasion of their rights and property. And now are there any who call themselves christians, who dare avow, espouse and support, the invasion of liberty, and the murder of those who rise up in its vindication? Yes, to the disgrace of human nature be it spoken, there are such inveterate foes to mankind: and who are They? they are the military and parliament of Great-Britain, with their adherents and abettors. The ground work of their present destructive measures, is this most iniquitous decree—That the parliament of Great-Britain, hath power, and of right ought to have power, to make laws and statutes to bind these colonies in all cases whatsoever. This decree is contrary to the laws of God and man, to the British constitution, **Magna Charta,** and bill of rights, the Charters of the Colonies, and even the express stipulations of preceding kings and their representatives; and as the cause is iniquitous in itself, so the war to support it, has been carried on, in the most inhuman, cruel, and injurious manner. The houses and possessions of

> **Magna Charta (Magna Carta):** charter of rights granted by King John on June 15, 1215

the friends to the country, have been seiz'd and plundered, rich and valuable furniture has been wantonly destroyed, or meanly seized and carried away: Our negroes, who have been nourished and brought up by us, and the savages of the wilderness, for whose temporal and eternal welfare we have labored, have been instigated to mangle, scalp, and murder us. Every engine has been employed to ruin our commerce, trade, husbandry and religion: Every method has been contrived and executed, to deprive us of the necessaries of life, and cause us to perish for the want of food, cloathing, and the means of defence. Our ships have been seized and confiscated, our poor brethren, taken in them, compelled to fight against us: our prisoners starved to death; our wives and daughters have been ravished: numerous families of little ones compelled to leave their own habitations and provisions, wander about in a strange land, beg their bread, and expose themselves to all the severity of the season.

We have this further consolation to support us under our present affliction; that all our assemblies on the continent, and the Congress at two several times, have endeavored, by the most humble and earnest petitions to the throne, to prevent the fatal war, which now rages and desolates our land. Every expedient, that human sagacity could dictate, to divert the gathering storm, has been tried: both houses of parliament, and the people of England and Ireland, have been most affectionately addressed and supplicated, to pity and relieve us, and suffer us to enjoy our ancient privileges; and it was not until every pacific measure failed, and our petitions were scornfully treated, and rejected, and a powerful fleet and army had actually invaded us and shed our blood; that we took up arms, in behalf of our lives and liberties. Our cause therefore, my dear brethren, is not only good, but it has been prudently conducted: Be therefore of good courage; it is a glorious cause: It is the cause of truth, against error and falsehood; the cause of righteousness against iniquity; the cause of the oppressed against the oppressor; the cause of pure and undefiled religion, against bigotry, superstition, & human inventions. It is the cause of the reformation, against popery; of liberty, against arbitrary power; of benevolence, against barbarity, and of virtue against vice. It is the cause of justice and integrity, against bribery, venality, and corruption. In short, it is the cause of heaven against hell—of the kind Parent of the universe, against the prince of darkness, and the destroyer of the human race. It is the cause, for which heroes have fought, patriots have bled, prophets, apostles, martyrs, confessors, and righteous men have died. Nay, it is a cause, for which the Son of God came down from his celestial throne, and expired on a cross—it is a cause, for the sake of which, your pious ancestors forsook all the delights and enjoyments of England, that land of wealth and plenty, and came to this once howling wilderness, destitute of houses, cultivation, fields, the comforts and conveniencies of life. This is a cause, for the prosperity of which, millions of fathers are praying, and our gracious High Priest is interceding: it is a cause, which thousands, and ten thousands of our friends in England and Ireland, are patronizing, and for which, even the consciences of our very enemies are pleading: therefore do not despond, my dear brethren, at the present gloomy prospects.

The cause of God—his own cause, must prosper, in spite of earth and hell—God will effectually plead it; he will plead it by his almighty word, his all conquering spirit, and his over ruling providence. No weapon formed against Zion, shall prosper: every tongue that riseth up against her, shall be condemned: God is in the midst of her, she shall not be moved: God will help her, and that right early: Trust ye therefore in the Lord Jehovah, for in the Lord Jehovah there is everlasting strength. Cast all your burdens and cares upon the Lord, and he will sustain you—he will never suffer the righteous to be moved. Eminent Divines & celebrated poets, have given it as their opinion, that America will be a glorious land of freedom, knowledge, and religion,—an asylum for distressed, oppressed, and persecuted virtue. Let this exhilarating thought, fill your souls, and give new ardor and encouragement to your hopes—you contend not only for your own happiness, for your dear relations; for the happiness of the present inhabitants of America; but you contend for the happiness of millions yet unborn. Exert therefore, your utmost efforts, strain every nerve, do all you can to promote this cause—plead earnestly with God, in its behalf, by continual prayer and supplication, by repentance and reformation, by forsaking every vice, & the practice of universal virtue. Be ready to fight for it, and maintain it to the last drop of your blood. *Herein was the love of God manifested, that he laid down his life for us, and we ought to lay down our lives for the brethren.* Pray for the happy period when tyranny, oppression, and wretchedness shall be banished from the earth; when universal love and liberty, peace & righteousness, shall prevail; when angry contentions shall be no more, and wars shall cease, even unto the ends of the earth. When the Jews shall be brought into the christian church, with the fulness of the Gentiles, and all Israel shall be saved. When the celestial country and the heaven of heavens shall resound with joyful acclamations, because the kingdoms of this world, are become the kingdoms of our Lord and of our Christ. *Hasten this blessed, this long wish'd for period, O Father of mercies, for thy dear Son's sake.* AMEN, and AMEN.

Source: Keteltas, Abraham. *God Arising and Pleading His People's Cause; or the American War in Favor of Liberty, Against the Measures and Arms of Great Britain, Shewn to be the Cause of God.* Newburyport, MA: John Mycall, 1777, pp. 13–14, 19–25, 29–32.

AFTERMATH

Such sermons as this one preached by Abraham Keteltas became more common as the Revolution continued. As the war dragged on, many pastors urged their parishioners to keep fighting until victory was achieved. They described the Revolution as a war ordained by God, and cast the fighting of the war as obeying God's call. Such calls helped rally the people and keep them committed to the cause, and thus probably helped achieve ultimate victory against Great Britain.

CONFLICTS IN BRITISH HISTORY: THE ENGLISH CIVIL WAR AND THE GLORIOUS REVOLUTION

The "preceding struggles for liberty" to which Keteltas referred were the English Civil War and the Glorious Revolution. Following the death of Elizabeth I in 1603, the Stuarts of Scotland also became kings of England. Throughout the 1600s, increasing tensions between the king and the members of Parliament produced armed conflicts at times as the two parties fought over money and religion. In the 1640s, civil war broke out as the supporters of Parliament fought the supporters of the king. The end result was the execution of Charles I and the creation of a Commonwealth government under the leadership of Oliver Cromwell for a time. The monarchy was restored in 1660 with the return of Charles II, but problems continued. In 1685 James II, a Roman Catholic, became king and sparked further conflicts as Protestants feared he would seek to reconvert Britain back to Roman Catholicism. In 1688 the leaders of Parliament forced James II to flee and replaced him with his closest Protestant relative, William of Orange, the husband of James's daughter Mary. These conflicts established the legal reality that the monarch of England must be a Protestant, and that he or she cannot govern without the consent of Parliament.

Abraham Keteltas was an ardent supporter of the Revolution. He had served in the New York Provincial Congress in 1776 prior to fleeing Long Island. From 1776 to 1782 he preached in a number of Presbyterian churches in Connecticut and Massachusetts. Following the end of the war, he retired and returned to his home in Jamaica, New York, where he died in 1798.

ASK YOURSELF

1. Why do you think Abraham Keteltas supported independence so strongly? Does his background, or do his religious beliefs, help explain his support?
2. How do you think you would have reacted had you been present to hear this sermon? Do you think members of the clergy should urge their parishioners to become involved in public events? Why or why not?

TOPICS AND ACTIVITIES TO CONSIDER

- Investigate 18th-century ideas about what sort of public role people expected pastors and other church leaders to fill. How do those ideas compare to today's expectations? What has changed in the two centuries since the Revolution occurred to change these ideas?
- Investigate the Dutch- and French-speaking people who lived in New York and surrounding areas at the time of the Revolution. What was their opinion of the fight between Great Britain and her colonies? Who did they want to see win? Why?

Further Reading

Bailyn, Bernard. *The Ideological Origins of the American Revolution.* Cambridge, MA: The Belknap Press of Harvard University Press, 1967.

Bridenbaugh, Carl. *Mitre and Sceptre: Transatlantic Faiths, Ideas, Personalities, and Politics: 1689–1775.* New York: Oxford University Press, 1962.

Fortson, S. Donald. *The Presbyterian Creed: A Confessional Tradition in America, 1729–1870.* Eugene, OR: Wipf and Stock, 2009.

Heimert, Alan. *Religion and the American Mind: From the Great Awakening to the Revolution.* Cambridge, MA: Harvard University Press, 1966.

Hoffman, Ronald, Mechal Sobel, and Fredrika J. Teute. *Through a Glass Darkly: Reflections on Personal Identity in Early America.* Chapel Hill: Published for the Institute of Early American History and Culture by the University of North Carolina Press, 1977.

Noll, Mark A. *America's God: From Jonathan Edwards to Abraham Lincoln.* New York: Oxford University Press, 2002.

Noll, Mark A. *Christians in the American Revolution.* Washington, DC: Christian University Press, 1977.

SLAVERY

36. Growing Opposition to Slavery: Petition Seeking Freedom (1777)

INTRODUCTION

Following the adoption of the DECLARATION OF INDEPENDENCE and its statement that "all men are created equal," increasing numbers of people debated whether slavery should still continue to exist in the former British colonies. In the northern states, some slaves even petitioned for their freedom. In Massachusetts, some slaves had earlier asked the colonial legislature to free them, arguing that the practice was immoral and un-Christian. Once the colonies had declared independence from Great Britain, other slaves in Massachusetts used the ideas of liberty and freedom expressed in the Declaration of Independence to argue against their enslavement. In this petition of 1777, the slaves used all three arguments in their effort to convince the legislators that they should be freed.

KEEP IN MIND WHILE YOU READ

1. Although slavery existed in Massachusetts, it was not a major part of the local economy.
2. Most slaves were illiterate at the time because many people believed it was dangerous to teach slaves to read and write.

Document: Slaves in Massachusetts Petition for Their Freedom (1777)

To the Honourable Counsel & House of Representatives for the State of Massachusetts Bay in General Court assembled, January 13, 1777.

The petition of A Great Number of Blackes detained in a State of slavery in the Bowels of a free & christian Country Humbly shuwith that your Petitioners Apprehend that thay have in Common with all other men a Natural and Unaliable Right to that freedom which the Grat Parent of the Unavese hath Bestowed equalley on all menkind and which they have

Never forfuted by Any Compact or Agreement whatever—but thay wher Unjustly Dragged by the hand of cruel Power from their Derest frinds and sum of them Even torn from the Embraces of their tender Parents—from A populous Plasant And plentiful cuntry And in Violation of Laws of Nature and off Nations And in defiance of all the tender feelings of humanity Brough hear Either to Be sold Like Beast of Burthen & Like them Condemnd to Slavery for Life—among A People Profesing the Religion of Jesus A people Not Insensible of the Secrets of Rationable Being Nor without spirit to Resent the unjust endeavours of others to Reduce them to A state of Bondage and Subjection your honouer Need not to be informed that A Life of Slavery Like that of your Petioners Deprived of Every social Priviledge of Every thing Requiset to Render Life Tolable is far worse then Nonexistance.

In imitation of the Lawdable Example of the Good People of these States your Petitionoers have Long and Patiently waited the Evnt of petition after petition By them presented to the Legislative Body of this state And cannot but with Grief Reflect that their Sucess hath ben but too similar they Cannot but express their Astonisments that It has Never Bin Consirdered that Every Principle from which Amarica has Acted in the Cours of their unhappy Dificultes with Great Briton Pleads Stronger than A thousand arguments in favowrs of Your petioners thay therfor humble Beseech your Honours to give this petion its due weight and consideration & cause an act of the Legislatur to be past Wherby they may Be Restored to the Enjoyments of that Which is the Naturel Right of all men—and their Children who wher Born in this Land of Liberty may not be heald as Slaves after they arive at the age of Twenty one years so may the Inhabitance of thes State No longer chargeable with the inconsistancey of acting themselves the part which they condem and oppose in Others Be prospered in their present Glorious Struggle for Liberty and have those Blessing to them, &c.

Source: "Negro Petitions for Freedom." *Collections, Massachusetts Historical Society.* 5th series, III. Boston, 1877, pp. 436–437.

AFTERMATH

Such petitions as this one became more common in Massachusetts and the other northern states following the Revolution, but they did not always prove successful. Greater numbers of people in the northern states thought slavery was a bad institution, but they hesitated to interfere with it legally. Much of the debate revolved around whether slaves were human beings or property. Throughout most of the colonial era, slaves were regarded as property. By the end of the Revolution, the state of Massachusetts had started to recognize slaves legally as both property and persons. This change in legal outlook in Massachusetts helped set the stage for the end of slavery in that state and provided encouragement for others to push for its abolition elsewhere.

ASK YOURSELF

1. What do you think the reactions of the members of the Massachusetts legislature would have been to this petition? Would reactions be different today than they were in 1777?
2. Which argument (immoral, un-Christian, denying liberty) in favor of granting freedom to the petioners do you think was the strongest one for slaves and others to make at the time? Why? Which argument do you personally think is the strongest one? Why?

TOPICS AND ACTIVITIES TO CONSIDER

- ↝ Throughout human history, slavery has been described as both a moral and an immoral institution. Investigate and compare and contrast the historical arguments about the morality of slavery.
- ↝ Historically, those in the United States have used petitions to ask their government officials to make changes. Investigate the various issues that have been addressed through petitions, paying attention to which efforts succeeded and which failed.

Further Reading

Berlin, Ira, and Ronald Hoffman. *Slavery and Freedom in the Age of the American Revolution.* Charlottesville: University of Virginia Press, 1983.

Brown, Richard D. *Massachusetts: A Bicentennial History.* New York: W. W. Norton, 1978.

Davis, David Brion. *The Problem of Slavery in the Age of Revolution.* Ithaca, NY: Cornell University Press, 1975.

MacLeod, Duncan J. *Slavery, Race, and the American Revolution.* Cambridge: Cambridge University Press, 1975.

Morgan, Edmund S. *American Slavery, American Freedom.* New York: Oxford University Press, 1975.

Nash, Gary B. *Freedom and Revolution.* Madison: University of Wisconsin Press, 1991.

Quarles, Benjamin. *The Negro in the American Revolution.* Chapel Hill: University of North Carolina Press, 1961.

Zilversmit, Arthur. *The First Emancipation: The Abolition of Slavery in the North.* Chicago: University of Chicago Press, 1967.

Web Sites

African American Experience: http://www.history.org/Almanack/people/african

African Americans and the End of Slavery in Massachusetts: http://www.masshist.org/endofslavery

37. GROWING OPPOSITION TO SLAVERY: LEGAL ARGUMENTS AGAINST THE INSTITUTION IN MASSACHUSETTS (1780, 1783)

INTRODUCTION

As the Revolution continued, people raised more questions about the legality of slavery and the treatment of former slaves after they were freed. In Massachusetts, both slaves and former slaves increasingly sought redress for grievances through a variety of legal means. They declared that they had the same rights as the people who protested British infringements on freedom and liberty, and they urged authorities to respect those rights. In 1780 a group of freedmen led by Paul Cuffe petitioned the Massachusetts state legislature, asking that they either be given the right to vote or be free from taxation. Although they did not use the phrase "no taxation without representation," they clearly intended to remind the legislators of that slogan. Three years later, another slave, Quock Walker, declared that he had been promised freedom by his previous owner and filed assault charges for efforts to re-enslave him. Massachusetts Chief Justice WILLIAM CUSHING instructed the jury that slavery was illegal under Massachusetts law, and the jury ruled in Walker's favor. Both efforts used legal arguments based on the ideas behind the American Revolution to justify their positions.

KEEP IN MIND WHILE YOU READ

1. Massachusetts had been one of the first colonies to protest against British taxes, arguing strongly that people could only be taxed by their own representatives.
2. Although people sometimes criticized the efforts of slave catchers and others who sought to return people to slavery, such practices were generally not considered illegal.

Document 1: Freed Slaves Petition Massachusetts for Civil Rights (1780)

To the Honorable Council and House of Representatives, in General Court Assembled for the State of Masschusetts Bay, in New England:

The petition of several poor negroes & mulattoes, who are inhabitants of the town of Dartmouth, humbly showeth:

That we being chiefly of the African extract and by reason of long bondage and hard slavery, we have been deprived of enjoying the profits of our labor or the advantage of inheriting estates from our parents, as our neighbors the white people do, having some of us not long enjoyed our own freedom; yet of late, contrary to the invariable custom and practice of the country, we have been, and now are, taxed both in our polls and that small pittance of estate which, through much hard labor and industry, we have got together to sustain ourselves and families withall. We apprehend it, therefore, to be hard usage, and will doubtless (if continued) reduce us to a state of beggary, whereby we shall become a burthen to others, if not timely prevented by the interposition of your justice and power.

Your petitioners further show, that we apprehand ourselves to be aggrieved, in that, while we are not allowed the privilege of freemen of the State, having no vote or influence in the election of those that tax us, yet many of our color (as is well known) have cheerfully entered the field of battle in the defence of the common cause, and that (as we conceive) against a similar exertion of power (in regard to taxation) too well known to need a recital in this place.

We most humbly request, therefore, that you would take our unhappy Case into your serious consideration, and, in your wisdom and power, grant us relief from taxation, while under our present depressed circumstances; and your poor petitioners, as in duty bound, shall ever pray &c.

Source: Williams, George W. *History of the Negro Race in America.* Vol. 2, New York: G. P. Putnam's Sons, 1883, p. 126.

Document 2: Commonwealth v. Jennison: *Charge of Chief Justice Cushing (1783)*

AS TO THE DOCTRINE OF SLAVERY and the right of Christians to hold Africans in perpetual servitude, and sell and treat them as we do our horses and cattle, that (if it true) had been heretofore countenanced by the province laws formerly, but nowhere is it expressly enacted or established. It has been a usage—a usage which took its origin from the practice of some of the European nations, and the regulations of British government respecting the then colonies, for the benefit of trade and wealth. But whatever sentiments have formerly prevailed in this particular or slid in upon us by the example of others, a different idea has taken place with the people of America, more favorable to the natural rights of mankind, and to that natural, innate desire of liberty, which with heaven (without regard to color, complexion, or shape of noses)...has inspired all the human race. And upon this ground our constitution of government, by which the people of this commonwealth have solemnly bound themselves, sets out with declaring that all men are born free and equal—and that every subject is entitled to liberty, and to have it guarded by the laws, as well as life and property—and in short is totally repugnant to the idea of being born slaves. This being the case, I think the idea of slavery is inconsistent with our own conduct and constitution; and there can be no such thing as perpetual servitude of a rational creature, unless his liberty is forfeited by some criminal conduct or given up by personal consent or contract....

Verdict Guilty.

Source: *Commonwealth v. Jennison. Massachusetts Historical Society Papers.* Vol. 13. Boston: Massachusetts Historical Society, 1873, p. 294.

AFTERMATH

Both cases played a role in the abolition of slavery in Massachusetts. The petitioners from 1780 did not succeed at that time, but their effort helped lay the groundwork for legislation adopted in 1783 that did give legal rights and privileges to African Americans. Paul Cuffe prospered as an owner of several ships. A devout QUAKER, Cuffe also became involved in efforts to move former slaves to Sierra Leone in Africa. Quock Walker's case is often described as the legal end of slavery in Massachusetts because he was able to hold on to his freedom. The case was never actually set down in the law reports of the time, but Walker's success reflected the changing attitudes toward slavery in Massachusetts following the end of the Revolutionary War. And this changing outlook spread throughout most of the northern states in the decades immediately after the Revolution. Every state north of Maryland adopted an act for the gradual abolition of slavery, although it would take well into the 1800s for all slaves in northern states to gain their freedom.

ASK YOURSELF

1. How do you think the legislators in Massachusetts reacted when they were accused of doing the same thing the British had done back in the 1760s? Do you think the petitioners against the taxes were correct in their charges against the state of Massachusetts? Why or why not?
2. It might have been possible for Justice Cushing to deal with the assault charge without directly attacking slavery. Why do you think he chose to speak out against it so strongly?

TOPICS AND ACTIVITIES TO CONSIDER

- The Declaration of Independence has been a standard for judging whether laws or practices by the government are good or not ever since it was adopted. Investigate the various ways the Declaration of Independence has been used since its adoption to encourage changes in law or practice on the part of the United States and other countries as well.
- Various legal efforts have been undertaken by people to attack the institution of slavery. Investigate court cases such as the Quock Walker case or the *Amistad* case to explore the arguments made against slavery and learn about the results of the cases.

Further Reading

Berlin, Ira, and Ronald Hoffman. *Slavery and Freedom in the Age of the American Revolution.* Charlottesville: University of Virginia Press, 1983.

Davis, David Brion. *The Problem of Slavery in the Age of Revolution.* Ithaca, NY: Cornell University Press, 1975.

MacLeod, Duncan J. *Slavery, Race, and the American Revolution.* Cambridge: Cambridge University Press, 1975.

Morgan, Edmund S. *American Slavery, American Freedom.* New York: Oxford University Press, 1975.

Nash, Gary B. *Freedom and Revolution.* Madison: University of Wisconsin Press, 1991.

Quarles, Benjamin. *The Negro in the American Revolution.* Chapel Hill: University of North Carolina Press, 1961.

Sherwood, H. N. "Paul Cuffe." *Journal of Negro History* VIII (April 1923):153–232.

Zilversmit, Arthur. *The First Emancipation: The Abolition of Slavery in the North.* Chicago: University of Chicago Press, 1967.

Web Sites

African American Experience: http://www.history.org/Almanack/people/african

African Americans and the End of Slavery in Massachusetts: http://www.masshist.org/endofslavery

Quock Walker Case—Africans in America: http://www.pbs.org/wgbh/aia/part2/2h38.html

38. ADVERTISEMENTS FOR RUNAWAY APPRENTICES AND SLAVES (1775–1780)

INTRODUCTION

In the 18th century, large numbers of people worked in settings where their daily lives were regimented and under the control of their bosses. Some people had been apprenticed to artisans in order to learn specific trades, and others had been sold into slavery. Clearly, these people would experience differences in the future because the apprentices would become independent once they had worked out their indentures, but the slaves faced lives with no freedom. However, the day-to-day experiences of these people could often be very similar because neither group had many legal rights that would have provided protection from bosses who overworked them or treated them cruelly. As a result, both apprentices and slaves often ran away in order to escape the situations in which they lived. In an effort to regain their laborers, the people they worked for often took out advertisements in the local newspapers in an effort to get the runaways back. Although these advertisements indicated whether the runaway was an apprentice or a slave, that often was the only real difference between the two because their bosses wanted both back and offered rewards for their return.

KEEP IN MIND WHILE YOU READ

1. The runaway slaves would have been African Americans while the apprentices would probably have been Caucasian.
2. Because running away was illegal for both slaves and apprentices, anyone could have forcibly taken the runaways and returned them to their masters without any fear of being criticized by others.

Document 1: Advertisements for Runaway Apprentices (1775–1780)

Connecticut Courant (Hartford), January 9, 1775

Last night run away from the subscriber an apprentice boy, named Benjamin Taylor, about 19 years old, 5 feet 10 inches high, by trade a shoemaker and **tanner,** has light

> **tanner:** one whose work is making leather by soaking animal hides in acid

colour'd hair, had on a brown cloth colour'd coat and jacket a pair of buck skin breeches, a pair of blue duffle trowsers, took with him one suit of cloths more of a brownish colour, and sundry other articles of wearing apparel. Whoever shall return him shall have two dollars reward and charges paid by ALEXANDER McNEEL. All masters of vessels are forbid carrying him off.

Maryland Gazette (Annapolis), September 12, 1775

RAN AWAY last night from the subscribers [the undersigned], an English servant man named John Scott, a square well made fellow, about five feet four inches high, a good complexion, something sunburnt, wears his own brown straight hair; took with him a blue cloth coat with a red plush cape, a good scarlet knit jacket with calimanco back, old buckskin breeches, a pair of double channelled pumps capped at each toe, but may change his cloaths, as he stole a very good dark claret coloured coat with yellow buttons; he is a very artful scoundrel. Also a white woman, something taller than the fellow, of a very dark complexion, a ring-worm on her upper lip, a small scar on one cheek; she has left behind a mulatto bastard, for having which she is bound to appear next in court; It is probable they will pass for man and wife. TWENTY SHILLINGS Reward for each if taken in the county, and FORTY SHILLINGS each if taken fifty miles from home, will be paid by

WILLIAM BOARDLEY, and
WOOLMAN GIBSON the 3rd.

Connecticut Courant (Hartford), April 25, 1780

RUN AWAY from the subscriber, on the evening of the 23d instant, an apprentice boy; named PAUL SAYRE, a native of Long Island, by trade a goldsmith, about nineteen years of age, about five feet, seven or eight inches high, a thick set fellow, thick lips, flat nose, light eyes, somewhat pitted with the small pox, has short, straight, dark hair. Had on and carried with him, a broadcloth blue coat, jacket and breeches, a light brown short coat, with open sleeves, a jacket about the same colour, a blue great coat, a pair of brown broadcloth breeches; a large castor hat, almost new, two pairs of shoes, a pair of open work silver shoe buckles, and sundry other articles of cloathing. Whoever will take up said apprentice and return him to his master, or confine him so that he shall get him again, shall have One Hundred Dollars Continental Money Reward, and all necessary charges paid by JAMES TILEY.

N. B. It is supposed that he will endeavour to go on to Long Island. All masters of vessels and others are forbid carrying him off, or harbouring or concealing him at their peril.

Document 2: Advertisements for Runaway Slaves (1775–1780)

Connecticut Courant (Hartford), January 9, 1775

> **dussil:** type of heavy cloth

Run away from the Subscriber at Goshun, on the 24th day of November past, a Negro man named York, upwards of fifty years of age, about five feet eight inches high, had on when he went away a black jacket, brown coat, leather breeches, and **dussil** great coat, whoever will take up said fellow and deliver him to me, shall have Two Dollars Reward, and all necessary Charges paid by JOSIAH WILLINGBY.

Virginia Gazette (Pinckney–Williamsburg), January 6, 1776

FOURTEEN POUNDS REWARD

RUN away from the subscriber, the 26th of November last, 4 negro men, **viz.** HARRY, Virginia born, 5 feet 8 or 9 inches high, 30 years of age, a dark mulatto, with long bushy hair; he is of the Indian breed, straight and well made, dresses neat, and has a variety of clothes with him, amongst others, a blue **fearnought** great coat. He has worked several years at the carpenter's and wheelwright's trade, and can glaize and paint. LEWIS, an outlandish, short, thick fellow, remarkably bow-legged, an excellent wheelwright and waggon maker, and a very good blacksmith. He carried with him, amongst other clothes, a blue suit. AARON, a likely Virginia born fellow, of the middle size, stoops a little, has a hoarse voice, and had on the usual clotheing of negroes. MATTHEW, a Virginia born, dark mulatto, 18 years of age, 5 feet 8 or 9 inches high, stammers a little, and speaks quick, when surprized, and is close-kneed. These 4 went off in a **yawl** with two others, who have been since committed to the public gaol. As one of them was taken in the yawl **without the cape,** I conclude the other 4 are in Lord Dunmore's service. I will give FIVE POUNDS each for securing the two first, and FORTY SHILLINGS each for the other two, besides what they law allows. They are all outlawed.

EDMUND RUFFIN

Pennsylvania Gazette (Philadelphia), August 7, 1776

IN MENS CLOTHES

RUN away the 30th of July last, from the Jerseys to Philadelphia or New-York, a MULATTOE Woman Slave, named *Maria;* had on a white or red and white jacket, white **ticken** breeches, white stockings, old mens shoes, and an old beaver hat; she is hardly discernable from a white woman, is rather thinish visage, middle size, thick legs, long black hair, and about 35 years old; she hath left behind her three young children, a good master and mistress, and is going towards New-York after a married white man, who is a soldier in the Connecticut service there. Whoever secures the said Mulattoe in goal, and will immediately advertise the same in this paper, shall have FOUR DOLLARS reward.

> **fearnought:** thick woolen cloth
> **ticken:** another version of ticking (tightly woven fabric of cotton or linen)
> **viz.:** namely
> **without the cape:** outside the mouth of Chesapeake Bay
> **yawl:** small sailing ship

AFTERMATH

Sometimes, the Revolution made runaways more common and more difficult to apprehend. The British governor of Virginia, John Murray, Lord Dunmore, encouraged slaves to run away and join the British fight against the rebels. He promised them freedom if they did so. Apprentices often ran away and joined the army, believing that it would be a better life than what they were currently experiencing. And the fighting made it difficult for people to hunt them down in order to force them back home. Apprenticeships continued to be the primary way for young free men to learn a trade well into the 19th century. Even today, many people learn specialized skills through apprenticeships. Slavery existed in the United States until it was ended by the adoption of the 13th Amendment in 1865. So, both apprentices and slaves continued to run away well into the 19th century because of the severity of their living conditions. But the 19th century also witnessed a growing abolitionist movement that helped lead to the end of slavery and increasing calls for legislation to regulate apprenticeships. Both of these developments reflected a rising awareness of the need to improve working conditions for everyone. For many reformers in the 19th century, the goal was to make people's lives better by improving the conditions under which they worked. It would be the 20th century before many of these efforts reached fruition.

ASK YOURSELF

1. Why do you think apprentices chose to run away so much when there was going to be a definite end to their service?
2. Why did some runaways choose to go alone while others choose to leave in groups? What difference could it have made?

TOPICS AND ACTIVITIES TO CONSIDER

- ๛ Apprenticeship was a common method of job training from the Middle Ages to the 19th century. Investigate the various types of trades that could be learned through an apprenticeship. Which types were most common in the 18th century?
- ๛ Slavery existed throughout the New World prior to the 19th century. Investigate where it existed and how it differed from place to place.

Further Reading

Derles, Scott, and Tony Smith. *Working Americans, 1770–1869, from the Revolutionary War to the Civil War*. Millerton, NY: Grey House Publishing, 2008.

Franklin, John Hope. *Runaway Slaves: Rebels on the Plantation*. New York: Oxford University Press, 1999.

Herndon, Ruth Wallis, and John E. Murray. *Children Bound to Labor: The Pauper System in Early America*. Ithaca, NY: Cornell University Press, 2009.

Hodges, Graham Russell. *Slavery, Freedom and Culture among Early American Workers*. Armonk, NY: M. E. Sharpe, 1998.

Jernegan, Marcus Wilson. *Laboring and Dependent Classes in Colonial America, 1607–1783*. New York: Ungar, 1960.

Kaplan, Sidney, and Emma Nogrady Kaplan. *The Black Presence in the Era of the American Revolution*. Rev. ed. Amherst: University of Massachusetts Press, 1989.

Pybus, Cassandra. *Epic Journeys of Freedom: Runaway Slaves of the American Revolution and Their Global Quest for Liberty*. Boston: Beacon Press, 2006.

Web Site

African American Experience: http://www.history.org/Almanack/people/african

39. Let's Free the Slaves: Letter from Alexander Hamilton to John Jay (March 14, 1777)

INTRODUCTION

As the debate over slavery's justification continued during the American Revolution, the issue also got caught up in the debates over how to fight the war and the growing need for more troops. As early as 1775, John Murray, Lord Dunmore, royal governor of Virginia, had offered freedom to slaves in the colony if they would join him to fight the American revolutionaries. Throughout the course of the war, some Americans argued that the slaves should be freed and armed so that the CONTINENTAL ARMY would have more men to fight the British. One of the people who urged such a plan was ALEXANDER HAMILTON. Hamilton, born in the British colony of Nevis in the Leeward Islands, had come to New York in 1772 in order to attend King's College (now Columbia University). He got involved in writing essays against the British government in 1774 and joined the Continental Army in 1776. By early 1777, he was serving as aide-de-camp to GEORGE WASHINGTON, a position in which he spent much time organizing and systematizing army operations. He sought to increase the number of troops available to participate, and this goal led him to support the proposal to enlist African Americans to help fight. In the following letter to JOHN JAY, he explained his support for this very radical proposal.

KEEP IN MIND WHILE YOU READ

1. Alexander Hamilton grew up in the sugar-growing colonies of the Caribbean, so he would have been very familiar with slavery and its effects.
2. Slavery was legal in all the states at this time, although it was most heavily concentrated in the southern states.
3. George Washington had originally banned the recruitment of African Americans to fight in the Continental Army, but he changed his mind after Dunmore's proclamation.

Document: Letter from Alexander Hamilton to John Jay (March 14, 1777)

COLONEL LAURENS, who will have the honor of delivering you this letter, is on his way to South Carolina, on a project which I think, in the present situation of affairs there, is a very good one, and deserves every kind of support and encouragement. This is to raise two, three, or four battalions of negroes, with the assistance of the government of that State, by contributions from the owners, in proportion to the number they possess. If you should think proper to enter upon the subject with him, he will give you a detail of his plan. He wishes to have it recommended by Congress to the State; and, as an inducement, that they would engage to take those battalions into continental pay.

It appears to me that an expedient of this kind, in the present state of southern affairs, is the most rational that can be adopted, and promises very important advantages. Indeed, I hardly see how a sufficient force can be collected in that quarter without it; and the enemy's operations there are growing infinitely serious and formidable. I have not the least doubt that the negroes will make very excellent soldiers with proper management; and I will venture to pronounce that they cannot be put into better hands than those of Mr. Laurens. He has all the zeal, intelligence, enterprise, and every other qualification necessary to succeed in such an undertaking. It is a maxim with some great military judges, that with sensible officers, soldiers can hardly be too stupid; and, on this principle, it is thought that the Russians would make the best troops in the world, if they were under other officers than their own. The King of Prussia is among the number who maintain this doctrine, and has a very emphatical saying on the occasion, which I do not exactly recollect. I mention this, because I frequently hear it objected to the scheme of embodying negroes, that they are too stupid to make soldiers. This is so far from appearing to me a valid objection, that I think their want of cultivation (for their natural faculties are probably as good as ours) joined to that habit of subordination, which they acquire from a life of servitude, will make them sooner become soldiers than our white inhabitants. Let officers be men of sense and sentiment, and the nearer the soldiers approach to machines, perhaps the better.

I foresee that this project will have to combat much opposition from prejudice and self-interest. The contempt we have been taught to entertain for the blacks, makes us fancy many things that are founded neither in reason nor experience; and an unwillingness to part with property of so valuable a kind, will furnish a thousand arguments to show the impracticability, or pernicious tendency, of a scheme which requires such a sacrifice. But it should be considered, that if we do not make use of them in this way, the enemy probably will; and that the best way to counteract the temptations they will hold out, will be to offer them ourselves. An essential part of the plan is to give them their freedom with their muskets. This will secure their fidelity, animate their courage, and, I believe, will have a good influence upon those who remain, by opening a door to their emancipation. This circumstance, I confess, has no small weight in inducing me to wish the success of the project; for the dictates of humanity and true policy equally interest me in favor of this unfortunate class of men.

With the truest respect and esteem,

I am, sir, your most obedient servant.

ALEX. HAMILTON

Source: Johnston, Henry P., ed. *The Correspondence and Public Papers of John Jay.* Vol. 1 of 4. New York: G. P. Putnam's Sons, 1890, pp. 191–193.

LORD DUNMORE

John Murray, Lord Dunmore, was the royal governor of Virginia from 1771 until he fled in the face of PATRIOT opposition in June 1776. A strong supporter of British authority, he was willing to use any means in order to keep the colonies under control. On November 15, 1775, he issued a proclamation calling on loyal citizens to join his forces and offering freedom to any slaves belonging to rebels who would fight with him. Dunmore's efforts had a polarizing effect in Virginia and elsewhere as many Americans came to believe that the British intended to stir up slave insurrections throughout the country in an effort to put down the rebellion. Many white people who had been neutral joined the Patriots in response to Dunmore's proclamation. But the proclamation also resulted in many African Americans joining the British. Approximately one thousand slaves ran away and joined Dunmore in the aftermath of his proclamation. Slaves in other parts of America also ran away and joined the British as well, hoping that freedom would be the result of their service. Many of those who survived the war went into exile along with white LOYALISTS who chose not to remain in the United States following the end of the war.

AFTERMATH

Although the need for troops was strong, the proposal to formally free and enlist slaves in South Carolina did not reach fruition. The state of South Carolina actually considered ending the war effort when urged to adopt this plan. But many blacks enlisted and served throughout the course of the Revolution. The states north of Virginia increasingly allowed free blacks to enlist in an effort to meet their recruitment quotas for the Continental Army. States such as New York and Maryland offered bounties to slave owners if they would allow their slaves to enlist. The owners received the money, and the slaves received their freedom—if they survived the war. African Americans, both slave and free, participated in every major battle of the American Revolution and thus helped the colonies win their independence. Such service helped reinforce the slowly growing opposition to the institution of slavery that would eventually lead to the rise of the abolitionist movement in the 1830s.

ASK YOURSELF

1. Why do you think Alexander Hamilton considered it so important to recruit slaves for the Continental Army in South Carolina?
2. At the time Hamilton wrote this letter, John Jay was serving as president of the CONTINENTAL CONGRESS. Do you think Hamilton's letter was aimed just at John Jay or did Hamilton assume his arguments in favor of this proposal would be shared with other members of Congress?
3. Do you think Hamilton would have supported such a proposal if the need for more troops had not been so great? Why or why not?

TOPICS AND ACTIVITIES TO CONSIDER

- A number of people on both sides in the American Revolution argued for freeing and arming the slaves in order to fight the war more efficiently. Investigate some of these arguments and compare the bases for them.

> ❧ Military service proved to be a ticket to freedom for slaves during the American Revolution. Investigate other wars in American history prior to the adoption of the 13th Amendment to see if that was true at other times as well.

Further Reading

Berlin, Ira, and Ronald Hoffman. *Slavery and Freedom in the Age of the American Revolution.* Charlottesville: University of Virginia Press, 1983.

Davis, David Brion. *The Problem of Slavery in the Age of Revolution.* Ithaca, NY: Cornell University Press, 1975.

Kaplan, Sidney, and Emma Nogrady Kaplan. *The Black Presence in the Era of the American Revolution.* Rev. ed. Amherst: University of Massachusetts Press, 1989.

MacLeod, Duncan J. *Slavery, Race, and the American Revolution.* Cambridge: Cambridge University Press, 1975.

McDonald, Forrest. *Alexander Hamilton: A Biography.* New York: W. W. Norton, 1979.

Morgan, Edmund S. *American Slavery, American Freedom.* New York: Oxford University Press, 1975.

Nash, Gary B. *Freedom and Revolution.* Madison: University of Wisconsin Press, 1991.

Quarles, Benjamin. *The Negro in the American Revolution.* Chapel Hill: University of North Carolina Press, 1961.

Randall, Willard Sterne. *Alexander Hamilton: A Life.* New York: Harper Collins, 2003.

Film and Television

Alexander Hamilton, PBS, 2007.

40. Growing Questions about Slavery: Essay by Caesar Sarter (1774)

INTRODUCTION

European settlers in the New World had enslaved Africans since the 16th century, and American colonists, particularly in the southern colonies, had engaged in the practice as a way to gain cheap labor. But by the middle of the 18th century, some people were questioning the legitimacy of slavery as an institution. QUAKERS had first questioned the institution in the late 1600s, and their calls for change increased in the 1700s. They were joined by others who debated whether slavery was a moral institution. Part of what fueled some of these early questions developed out of reform efforts sparked by the First GREAT AWAKENING in the 1740s and 1750s. The Awakening's focus on the responsibility of the individual for the state of his or her soul and personal salvation led some to question their treatment of others, including their slaves. The arguments with Great Britain over the rights of the colonies in the 1760s and 1770s only added to these debates. More people became aware of the potential conflict between colonists fighting for their rights while denying the rights of their slaves. The following essay, written by Caesar Sarter, a former slave, called on people of the time to live up to their ideals by setting the enslaved Africans free.

KEEP IN MIND WHILE YOU READ

1. People throughout the colonies, but particularly in Massachusetts, had been crying out for the British to respect and honor their individual rights since the mid-1760s.
2. Although slavery was not widespread in New England and did not directly constitute a major portion of the economy the way it did in the more southern colonies, many merchants and ship owners engaged in the slave trade in a major way.
3. Part of the debate over slavery revolved around whether Africans were fully human and thus deserving of the rights British colonists claimed for themselves.

Document: Caesar Sarter's "Essay on Slavery" (1774)

Please to give the following Address, *To those who are Advocates for holding the Africans in Slavery,* a place in your next, and you will oblige one, who is a well-wisher to his brethren, who are now in that unhappy state.

As this is a time of great anxiety and distress among you, on account of the infringement not only of your Charter rights; but of the natural rights and privileges of freeborn men; permit a poor, though *freeborn,* African, who, in his youth, was **trapanned** into Slavery and who has born the galling yoke of bondage for more than twenty years; though at last, by the blessing of God, has shaken it off, to tell you, and that from experience, that as

> **trapanned:** entrapped or lured

Slavery is the greatest, and consequently most to be dreaded, of all temporal calamities: So its opposite, *Liberty,* is the greatest temporal good, with which you can be blest! The importance of which, you can clearly evince to the world you are sensible of, by your manly and resolute struggles to preserve it. Your fore fathers, as I have been often informed, left their native country, together with many dear friends, and came into this country, then a howling wilderness inhabited, only, by savages, rather choosing, under the protection of their GOD, to risk their lives, among those merciless wretches, than submit to tyranny at home: While, therefore, this conduct gives you their exalted sense of the worth of *LIBERTY,* at the same time, it shews their utmost abhorrence of that *CURSE OF CURSES, SLAVERY.*—Your Parliament, to their immortal honor be it mentioned, to whom WE feel that gratitude, which so high a favour naturally produces, in an ingenious mind have exerted their utmost abilities, to put a final stop, to so iniquitous a business, as the Slave Trade is: That they have not succeeded in their laudable endeavours was not their fault: But they were defeated by his late Excellency only—Now, if you are sensible, that slavery is in itself, and in it consequences, a great evil; why will you not pity and relieve the poor, distressed, enslaved Africans?—Who, though they are entitled to the same *natural rights of mankind* that you are, are, nevertheless, groaning in bondage! A bondage which will only terminate with life: To them a shocking consideration indeed! Though too little, I fear, thought of by most of you who enjoy the profits of their labour. As the importation of slaves into this Province, is generally laid aside, I shall not pretend a refutation of the arguments, generally brought in support of it; but request you, to let that excellent rule given by our Saviour, *to do to others, as you would, that they should do to you,* have its due weight with you. Though the thought be shocking—for a few minutes, suppose that you were trepanned away.—The husband from the dear wife of his bosom—the wife from her affectionate husband—children from their fond parents—or parents from their tender and beloved offspring, whom, not an hour before, perhaps, they were fondling in their arms, and in whom they were promising themselves much future happiness: Suppose, I say that you were thus ravished from such a blissful situation, and plunged into miserable slavery, in a distant quarter of the globe: Or suppose you were accompanied by your wife and children, parents and brethren, manacled by your side—harrowing thought! And that after having suffered the most amazing hardships, your fetters were knocked from your galled limbs, only to expose you to keener anguish!—Exposed to sale with as little respect to decency, as though you were a brute! And after all this, if you were unwilling to part with all you held dear, even without the privilege of droping a tear over your dear friends, who were clinging round you; equally dreading the cruel separation, which would probably prove an endless one, you must be plied with that conclusive argument, the cat-o'nine tails, to reduce you to what your inhuman masters would call Reason. Now, are you willing all this should befall you? If you can lay your hand on your breast, and solemnly affirm that you should; Why then go on and prosper! For your treatment of the Africans is an exact compliance with the abovementioned rule: But if, on the other hand, your conscience answers in the negative; Why, in the name of Heaven, will you suffer such a gross violation of that rule by which your conduct must be tried, in that day, in which you must be accountable for all your actions, to that impartial Judge, who hears the groans of the oppressed and who will, sooner or later, avenge them of their oppressors! I need not tell you, who are acquainted with the scriptures that this kind of oppression is discountenanced by them. Many passages, to this purpose, might be adduced, but I shall at present, mention but one, Exod chap 20 ver. 16 *"And he that stealeth a man, and selleth him, or if he be found in his hand, he shall surely be put to death."*

Though we are brought from a land of ignorance, it is as certain, that we are brought from a land of comparative innocence—from a land that flows, as it were, with Milk and Honey—and the greater part of us carried, where we are, not only deprived of every comfort of life: But subjected to all the tortures that a most cruel inquisitor could invent, or a capricious tyrant execute, and where we are likely, from the vicious examples before us, to become tenfold more the children of satan, than we should, probably, have been in our native country. Though 'tis true, that some of our wars proceed from petty discourds among ourselves, it is as true, that the greater part of them, and those the most bloody, are occasioned, in consequence of the Slave trade.—Though many think we are happier here, than there, and will not allow us the privilege of judging for ourselves, they are certainly in an error. Every man is the *best* judge of his own happiness, and every heart best knows its own bitterness.—While I feel the loss of my country, and my friends, I can, by sad experience, adopt that expression in Prov. 25th Chap. 20 verse. *As he that taketh away a garment in cold weather, and as vinegar upon nitre, so is he that singeth songs to a heavy heart.* Let me, who have now no less than eleven relatives suffering in bondage beseech you good people, to attend to the request of a poor African, and consider the evil consequences, and gross heinousness of reducing to, and retaining in slavery a free people. Would you desire the preservation of your own liberty? As the first step let the oppressed Africans be liberated; then, and not till then, may you with confidence and consistency of conduct, look to Heaven for a blessing on your endeavours to knock the shackles with which your task masters are hampering you, from your own feet. On the other hand, if you are still determined to harden your hearts, and turn a deaf ear to our complaints, and the calls of God, in your present Calamities; Only be pleased to recollect the miserable end of Pharoah, in Consequence of his refusal to set those at Liberty, whom he had unjustly reduced to cruel servitude. Remember the fate of Miriam for despising an Ethiopean woman, *Numb. 12* chap. *1*st and *10*th. verses. I need not point out the absurdity of your exertions for liberty, while you have slaves in your houses, for one minute's reflection is, methinks, sufficient for that purpose.—You who are deterred from liberating your slaves, by the consideration of the ill consequences to yourselves must remember, that we were not the cause of our being brought here. If the compelling us, against our wills, to come here was a sin; to retain us, without our consent, now we are here, is, I think, equally culpable let ever so great inconvenience arising therefrom, accrue to you. Not to trespass too much on your patience; would you unite in this generous, this noble purpose of granting us liberty; Your honorable assembly, on our humble petition, would, I doubt not, free you from the trouble of us by making us grants in some back part of the country. If in this attempt to serve my countrymen, I have advanced any thing to the purpose, I pray it may not be the less noticed for coming from an African.

Source: *The Essex Journal and Merrimack Packet.* Newburyport, MA: August 17, 1774.

AFTERMATH

Sarter's argument in favor of the end of slavery reflected the slowly growing opposition to the institution in America. The Revolutionary era focus on human rights pushed some people to organize in an effort to end the institution. In 1775, some people in Philadelphia formed the first antislavery organization in America, the PENNSYLVANIA SOCIETY FOR THE ABOLITION OF SLAVERY. As the years passed after the end of the Revolution in 1783, greater numbers of those in the United States came to believe that slavery was an immoral institution. Debates about slavery increased as time passed, eventually helping to produce the Civil War in the 1860s. The United States finally fully ended slavery with the adoption of the THIRTEENTH AMENDMENT in 1865.

ASK YOURSELF

1. Why do you think Sarter decided to come out in such a public manner to urge Americans to end slavery? Do you believe it would have been dangerous for him to do so?
2. Part of Sarter's argument urges Americans to obey the golden rule (do unto others as you would have done unto you). He lived in Massachusetts. Would that sort of argument have been more effective in Massachusetts than elsewhere?
3. Sarter ties the liberty of colonists at the time with the liberty of slaves. Do you think this would be an effective argument in the midst of the growing arguments with Great Britain?

TOPICS AND ACTIVITIES TO CONSIDER

- ➢ Sarter is only one of many former slaves to write urging an end to the institution of slavery. Investigate other former slaves who spoke out against slavery. Compare and contrast their arguments, focusing on what factors made them similar and what factors made them different.
- ➢ Throughout American history, a number of religious groups such as the Quakers spoke out against the institution of slavery. Investigate the various religious groups that criticized slavery, paying particular attention to why they thought the institution was wrong.
- ➢ Some thought that the ideas supporting individual liberty produced by the growing argument with Great Britain in the 1760s and 1770s also supported the end of slavery. Investigate the connection between these two outlooks, both at the time of the American Revolution and in the years following that event.

Further Reading

Berlin, Ira, and Ronald Hoffman. *Slavery and Freedom in the Age of the American Revolution.* Charlottesville: University of Virginia Press, 1983.

Davis, David Brion. *The Problem of Slavery in the Age of Revolution*. Ithaca, NY: Cornell University Press, 1975.

MacLeod, Duncan J. *Slavery, Race, and the American Revolution*. Cambridge: Cambridge University Press, 1975.

Morgan, Edmund S. *American Slavery, American Freedom*. New York: Oxford University Press, 1975.

Nash, Gary B. *Freedom and Revolution*. Madison: University of Wisconsin Press, 1991.

Quarles, Benjamin. *The Negro in the American Revolution*. Chapel Hill: University of North Carolina Press, 1961.

Zilversmit, Arthur. *The First Emancipation: The Abolition of Slavery in the North*. Chicago: University of Chicago Press, 1967.

41. THE CHURCH QUESTIONS THE INSTITUTION OF SLAVERY: ESSAY BY THE REVEREND SAMUEL HOPKINS (1776)

INTRODUCTION

As colonists increasingly called on Great Britain to respect their rights as citizens of the British Empire, some increasingly questioned how people in the North American colonies treated the weak and downtrodden. The most obvious target for such concerns was the enslavement of Africans. Former slaves such as Caesar Sarter and religious groups such as the QUAKERS spoke out against slavery even before the Revolutionary War had begun. But church leaders of most denominations in America said nothing about the issue of slavery. That began to change in 1776 when Samuel Hopkins, pastor of a CONGREGATIONAL CHURCH in Newport, Rhode Island, published *A Dialogue Concerning the Slavery of the Africans*. Hopkins had been well trained as a minister, graduating from Yale in 1741 and working closely with JONATHAN EDWARDS for seven years in the 1750s. Hopkins moved to Newport in 1770. In his essay opposing slavery, Hopkins called on leaders to see the connections between their fight against British infringements on their rights and the failure of colonists to recognize the rights of the Africans they held in slavery.

KEEP IN MIND WHILE YOU READ

1. Newport, Rhode Island, was a major seaport in the 1770s and a center of the slave trade because so many of the local merchants were involved in that industry. So, many of the members of Hopkins' church would have been financially involved in the slave trade.
2. In writing this essay, Hopkins tried to connect political and spiritual arguments against the enslavement of Africans because he thought that would appeal to the most people.

Document: Samuel Hopkins' Essay (1776)

The slavery that now takes place is in a Christian land, and without the express sanction of civil government; and it is all of the same kind and from one original, which is most notoriously unjust, and if it be unrighteous in one instance, it is so in almost every instance; and the unrighteousness of it is most apparent, and most masters have no color of claim to hold their servants in bondage; and this is become a general and crying sin, for which we are under the awful frowns of Heaven. These things, which make the case so different from the slavery which took place in the apostles' days, may be a good reason of a different conduct, and make it duty to oppose and bear testimony, both in public and more privately, against this evil practice, which is so evidently injurious to individuals, and threatens our ruin as a people....

It has always been the way of tyrants to take great pains to keep their vassals in ignorance, especially to hide from them the tyranny and oppression of which they are the subjects; and for this reason they are enemies to the liberty of the press, and are greatly provoked when their conduct is set in a true light before the public, and the unrighteousness they practise properly exposed. The complaint we are now considering seems to be of the same kind with this, and well becomes all those petty tyrants who have slaves in their possession, which they are conscious they cannot vindicate, but the unrighteousness will be detected if free inquiry and freedom of speech cannot be suppressed; and this complaint is of the same kind with the conduct of the masters of slaves in the West Indies in opposing their being taught any thing of Christianity, because they know every gleam of this light carries a discovery of the unrighteousness of the treatment they receive.

The present situation of our public affairs and our struggle for liberty, and the abundant conversation this occasions in all companies, while the poor negroes look on and hear what an aversion we have to slavery and how much liberty is prized, they often hearing it declared publicly and in private, as the voice of all, that slavery is more to be dreaded than death, and we are resolved to live free or die, etc.; this, I say, necessarily leads them to attend to their own wretched situation more than otherwise they could. They see themselves deprived of all liberty and property, and their children after them, to the latest posterity, subject to the will of those who appear to have no feeling for their misery, and are guilty of many instances of hard-heartedness and cruelty towards them, while they think themselves very kind; and therefore, to make the least complaint, would be deemed the height of arrogance and abuse; and often if they have a comparatively good master now, with constant dread they see a young one growing up, who bids fair to rule over them, or their children, with rigor.

They see the slavery the Americans dread as worse than death is lighter than a feather compared to their heavy doom, and may be called liberty and happiness when contrasted with the most abject slavery and unutterable wretchedness to which they are subjected; and in this dark and dreadful situation they look round and find no help—no pity—no hope! And when they observe all this cry and struggle for liberty for ourselves and children, and see themselves and their children wholly overlooked by us, and behold the sons of liberty oppressing and tyrannizing over many thousands of poor blacks who have as good a claim to liberty as themselves, they are shocked with the glaring inconsistence, and wonder they themselves do not see it. You must not, therefore, lay it to the few who are pleading the cause of these friendless, distressed poor, that they are more uneasy than they used to be in a sense of their wretched state and from a desire of liberty: there is a more mighty and irresistible cause than this, viz., all that passes before them in our public struggle for liberty.

And why should the ministers of the gospel hold their peace and not testify against this great and public iniquity, which we have reason to think is one great cause of the public calamities we are now under? How can they refuse to plead the cause of these oppressed poor against the cruel oppressor? They are commanded to lift up their voice, and cry aloud, and show the people their sins. Have we not reason to fear many of them have offended Heaven by their silence, through fear of the masters, who stand ready to make war against any one who attempts to deprive them of their slaves, or because they themselves have slaves which they are not willing to give up?

Might they not fully expose this iniquity, and bear a constant testimony against it, in such a manner as would have no tendency to influence our servants to behave ill in any respect, by giving them, at the same time, proper cautions and directions? . . .

No wonder there are many and great difficulties in reforming an evil practice of this kind, which has got such deep root by length of time and is become so common. But it does not yet appear that they cannot be removed by the united wisdom and strength of the American colonies, without any injury to the slaves or disadvantage to the public. Yea, the contrary is most certain, as the slaves cannot be put into a more wretched situation, ourselves being judges, and the community cannot take a more likely step to escape ruin, and obtain the smiles and protection of Heaven. This matter ought, doubtless, to be attended to by the general assemblies, and continental and provincial congresses; and if they were as much united and engaged in devising ways and means to set at liberty these injured slaves as they are to defend themselves from tyranny, it would soon be effected. . . .

Let this iniquity be viewed in its true magnitude, and in the shocking light in which it has been set in this conversation; let the wretched case of the poor blacks be considered with proper pity and benevolence, together with the probably dreadful consequence to this land of retaining them in bondage, and all objections against liberating them would vanish. . . .

If many thousands of our children were slaves in Algiers, or any parts of the Turkish dominions, and there were but few families in the American colonies that had not some child or near relation in that sad state, without any hope of freedom to them or their children unless there were some very extraordinary exertion of the colonies to effect it, how would the attention of all the country be turned to it! How greatly should we be affected with it! Would it not become the chief topic of conversation? Would any cost or labor be spared, or any difficulty or hazard be too great to go through, in order to obtain their freedom? If there were no greater difficulties than there are in the case before us, yea, if they were ten times greater, would they not be soon surmounted as very inconsiderable? I know you, sir, and every one else, must answer in the affirmative without hesitation. And why are we not as much affected with the slavery of the many thousands of blacks among ourselves whose miserable state is before our eyes? And why should we not be as much engaged to relieve them? The reason is obvious. It is because they are negroes, and fit for nothing but slaves, and we have been used to look on them in a mean, contemptible light, and our education has filled us with strong prejudices against them, and led us to consider them, not as our brethren, or in any degree on a level with us, but as quite another species of animals, made only to serve us and our children, and as happy in bondage as in any other state. This has banished all attention to the injustice that is done them, and any proper sense of their misery or the exercise of benevolence towards them. If we could only divest ourselves of these strong prejudices which have insensibly fixed on our minds, and consider them as by nature and by right on a level with our brethren and children, and those of our neighbors, and that benevolence which loves our neighbor as ourselves, and is agreeable to truth and righteousness, we should begin to feel towards them, in some measure at least, as we should towards our children and neighbors in the case above supposed, and be as much engaged for their relief.

If parents have a son pressed on board a king's ship, how greatly are they affected with it! They are filled with grief and distress, and will cheerfully be at almost any cost and pains to procure his liberty; and we wonder not at it, but think their exercises and engagedness for his deliverance very just, and stand ready to condemn him who has no feeling for them and their son, and is not ready to afford all the assistance in his power in order to recover him. At the same time we behold vast numbers of blacks among us, torn from their native country and all their relations, not to serve on board a man-of-war for a few years, but to be abject, despised slaves for life, and their children after them, and yet have not the least feelings for them or desire of their freedom. These very parents, perhaps, have a number of negro slaves on whom they have not the least pity, and stand ready highly to resent it if any one espouses their cause so much as to propose they should be set at liberty. What reason for this partiality? Ought this so to be? An impartial person, who is not under the prejudices of interest, education, and custom, is shocked with it beyond all expression. The poor negroes have sense enough to see and feel it, but have no friend to speak a word for them, none to whom they may complain....

And if we continue in this evil practice and refuse to let the oppressed go free, under all this light and admonition suited to convince and reform us, and while God is evidently correcting us for it as well as for other sins, have we any reason to expect deliverance from the calamities we are under? May we not rather look for slavery and destruction like that which came upon the obstinate, unreformed Jews? In this light I think it ought to be considered by us; and viewed thus, it affords a most forcible, formidable argument not to put off liberating our slaves to a more convenient time, but to arise, all as one man, and do it with all our might, without delay, since delaying in this case is awfully dangerous as well as unspeakably criminal....

But if we obstinately refuse to reform what we have implicitly declared to be wrong, and engaged to put away the holding the Africans in slavery, which is so particularly pointed out by the evil with which we are threatened, and is such a glaring contradiction to our professed aversion to slavery and struggle for civil liberty, and improve the favor God is showing us as an argument in favor of this iniquity and encouragement to persist in it, as you, sir, have just now done, have we not the greatest reason to fear, yea, may we not with great certainty conclude, God will yet withdraw his kind protection from us, and punish us yet seven times more? This has been God's usual way of dealing with his professing people; and who can say it is not most reasonable and wise? He, then, acts the most friendly part to these colonies and to the masters of slaves, as well as to the slaves themselves, who does his utmost to effect a general emancipation of the Africans among us; and, in this view, I could wish the conversation we have now had on this subject, if nothing better is like to be done, were published and spread through all the colonies, and had the attentive perusal of every American.

Source: Hopkins, Samuel. *The Works of Samuel Hopkins*. 3 vols. Vol. II. Boston: Doctrinal Tract and Book Society, 1852, pp. 569–588.

AFTERMATH

Hopkins showed great bravery in speaking out against slavery, and he was one of the first Congregational ministers to do so. He backed up his words with actions, raising money to free a number of slaves in Newport. He also joined with EZRA STILES in raising money to train black missionaries to send to Africa. Hopkins worked out a plan for a colony of former slaves in Africa, but he was prevented from carrying out his plan because of a lack of financial support for the idea. Although Hopkins did not see the end of slavery in the United States, his ideas influenced others who spoke out against the institution as both a moral evil and as an entity that contradicted the beliefs U.S. citizens supported. Hopkins also wrote numerous works about theology, which had a great influence on the clergy of New England in the 19th century. He served as pastor in Newport for 33 years until his death in 1803.

ASK YOURSELF

1. If slavery and the slave trade were such important parts of the local economy in Newport, why do you think Samuel Hopkins spoke out so strongly against it?
2. Many people supported slavery for Africans because they believed Africans were not fully human. How does Hopkins argue against this idea? Do the attitudes he spoke against still exist today?
3. Samuel Hopkins based his arguments against slavery on both political and spiritual ideas. Which category do you think was the most important to him? Why? Why does he include the other category in his essay?

TOPICS AND ACTIVITIES TO CONSIDER

- Newport, Rhode Island, was a major seaport in the 1770s. Investigate its role in trade in general and more specifically in the international slave trade at the time.
- Samuel Hopkins clearly believed that the arguments used by those in the former colonies against the actions of Great Britain could be turned against them regarding the institution of slavery. Investigate how this might be true, both at the time of the American Revolution and in the years following that event.
- From the time of the American Revolution until the outbreak of the Civil War, more preachers came out in opposition to the institution of slavery. Investigate the church leaders who took such a stand and compare their reasons to those of Samuel Hopkins.

Further Reading

Berlin, Ira, and Ronald Hoffman. *Slavery and Freedom in the Age of the American Revolution.* Charlottesville: University of Virginia Press, 1983.

Conforti, Joseph A. *Samuel Hopkins and the New Divinity Movement: Calvinism, the Congregational Ministry, and Reform in New England between the Great Awakenings.* Grand Rapids, MI: Christian University Press, 1981.

Davis, David Brion. *The Problem of Slavery in the Age of Revolution.* Ithaca, NY: Cornell University Press, 1975.

Lovejoy, David S. *Samuel Hopkins: Religion, Slavery, and the Revolution.* Philadelphia: United Church Press, 1976.

MacLeod, Duncan J. *Slavery, Race, and the American Revolution.* Cambridge: Cambridge University Press, 1975.

Morgan, Edmund S. *American Slavery, American Freedom.* New York: Oxford University Press, 1975.

Nash, Gary B. *Freedom and Revolution.* Madison: University of Wisconsin Press, 1991.

Quarles, Benjamin. *The Negro in the American Revolution.* Chapel Hill: University of North Carolina Press, 1961.

Walker, Williston. *A History of the Congregational Churches in the United States.* New York: The Christian Literature Company, 1894.

Zilversmit, Arthur. *The First Emancipation: The Abolition of Slavery in the North.* Chicago: University of Chicago Press, 1967.

WAR AND LOCAL CONFLICT

42. Conflicts on the Frontier during the War: Indian Attacks (1773–1777)

INTRODUCTION

From the moment Europeans first set foot in the New World, there had been conflicts with the people already living here. In all accounts from the early explorers to the reports back to Europe from early settlers, Europeans and Native Americans fought each other for control of the land. Throughout the 18th century, France and Great Britain fought a series of four wars for control of North America, and both sought to use Native Americans as allies to help win the wars. As colonial settlers moved west into the lands beyond the Appalachian Mountains, they faced attacks from the Natives of the area who were trying to keep control of their territory. The first document describes such an attack in the Ohio Valley in September 1773 from the perspective of the Europeans.

As the conflict between the colonies and Great Britain grew, both sides hoped to develop alliances with Native Americans in an effort to use their fighting abilities and to protect themselves from attacks by other tribes. Overall, the British authorities proved more successful in these efforts because most of Native Americans realized that an American victory in the Revolution would result in further expansion westward into their lands. But neither side proved able to control their Native American allies, and the reaction was one of horror whenever an attack occurred, whether as a formal military engagement or an attack on a frontier settlement. In a letter written in 1777, William Weeks, a paymaster of a New Hampshire regiment, described what Native Americans had done on the frontiers of New York prior to the battle of Saratoga.

KEEP IN MIND WHILE YOU READ

1. Settlers of European descent and Native Americans had been fighting each other for over two hundred years when the events described in the documents occurred.
2. People of European descent believed that land could be individually owned, while Native Americans believed that it belonged to the tribe as a whole.
3. Europeans thought that the Native American way of fighting wars was barbaric.

Document 1: Essex Gazette *(Salem, Massachusetts)*, February 15, 1774: Story from Williamsburg *(December 23, 1773)*

The following inhuman affair, we are informed, from good authority, was transacted on the frontiers of Fincastle, about the latter end of September last:—Capt. William Russell, with several families, and upwards of 30 men, set out with an intention to reconnoitre the country towards the Ohio, and settle in the limits of the expected new government. A few days after they set out, unluckily the party was separated into three detachments; the main body in the front, with the women and children, and their cattle and baggage; in the center Capt. Russell's son, with 5 white men, and two negroes; who, the fatal night before the murder, encamped a few miles short of the front. In the morning, about day break, while asleep in the camp, they were fired upon by a party of Indians, who killed young Mr. Russel, and four other white men, and one negro. Capt. Russel shortly after bringing up the rear, unexpectedly came on the corpse of his son, which was mangled in an inhuman manner, and there was left in him a dart arrow, and a war-club was left beside him. After this unexpected assault, the party, upon getting intelligence, returned to the inhabitants. It appeared that the Indians had pursued young Russel's party some considerable distance the day before, and, upon overtaking them took that defenceless opportunity to perpetrate their barbarity.

Document 2: William Weeks's Description of Indian Behavior on the Frontiers of New York *(1777)*

There is a very good crop in these parts, but soon comes a desolation; wherever we march we keep our horses in the fields among corn and oats, so that the enemy, if they gain the ground, may have poor fare for them and their horses. Tories are very troublesome here—many of them take up arms against us and lurk in the woods with the Indians waiting for a scalp. It is believed the Tories have scalped many of their countrymen, as there is a premium from Burgoyne for scalps. They are daily taken and brought in by our scouts and I believe some of them will swing very soon.

The Indians treat both sexes with the same barbarity, have killed and scalped whole families together—men, women, and children. At one place, as our men were passing, they saw a man, his wife and children scalped (by those savages), gaping and expiring and the hogs rooting their bodies.

A few days ago I rode a little distance from camp where we had a few men stationed to guard the sick. I had just passed the place where a party of Indians happened to lay and stopped at the first house talking with an officer. As I sat upon my horse, out rushed those Indians and fired at some men swimming in the water and chased some as they were passing. I, seeing this, screamed to the guard to pursue them, and rode toward them. They discharged their pieces toward us, and fired one ball into the house not far from the door where I was. Immediately upon our pursuing them they ran into the woods and got off. We were in such haste they had not time to get a scalp. They killed two; one shot in the water, who got out and ran a considerable distance before he fell. Since then they have cut off more of our men—one hundred Indians in the woods do no more harm than 1,000 British troops. They have been the death of many brave fellows—I hope they will meet with their reward for their cursed barbarity.

Source: Weeks, William. *Five Straws Gathered from Revolutionary Fields.* Ed. Hiram Bingham. Cambridge, MA: University Press, 1901, pp. 14–16.

AFTERMATH

Such events occurred throughout the Revolution as both the British and colonists tried to convince Native Americans that they would benefit the most if their side won the war. Some tribes sided with the PATRIOTS, and some tried to be neutral, but the larger tribes (particularly the Iroquois) sided with the British. The British loss in the Revolution meant a loss for Native Americans as well. The United States gained control of all the land between the Atlantic Ocean and the Mississippi River and quickly moved to settle these areas as well as gain more territory from the Mississippi River to the Pacific Ocean. As settlers moved west, they pushed the tribes onto smaller and smaller pieces of land. Native Americans fought back for over a century, but they were not able to stop the westward advance. By the 20th century, most tribes had been confined to reservations either in the Dakotas or Oklahoma, with a few groups managing to hold on to lands in other parts of the country.

ASK YOURSELF

1. Why do you think people like William Russell wanted to move west even when they knew there was a potential threat from the Native Americans who already lived there?
2. Why do you think William Weeks described what he saw in such detail in his letter?
3. Why do you think the British and the colonists wanted alliances with the Native Americans when both sides believed that Natives fought in a barbaric manner?

TOPICS AND ACTIVITIES TO CONSIDER

- ᔰ North American settlers of European descent and Native Americans have fought many wars with each other, both before and after the Revolution. Investigate some of these other wars and compare their major events.
- ᔰ Throughout the course of European exploration and settlement in the New World, numerous treaties were signed with Native Americans. Investigate some of the major treaties, focusing on how they reflect cultural as well as political differences.
- ᔰ There were a number of engagements during the Revolution in which Native Americans were major participants. Investigate some of these events and discuss how the Natives were used by both sides in the war.

Further Reading

Calloway, Colin G. *The American Revolution in Indian Country: Crisis and Diversity in Native American Communities.* Cambridge: Cambridge University Press, 1999.

Graymont, Barbara. *The Iroquois in the American Revolution.* Syracuse, NY: Syracuse University Press, 1972.

Hurt, Douglas R. *The Ohio Frontier: Crucible of the Old Northwest, 1720–1830.* Bloomington: Indiana University Press, 1996.

Taylor, Alan. *The Divided Ground: Indians, Settlers, and the Northern Borderland of the American Revolution.* New York: Alfred A. Knopf, 2006.

Web Site

Washburn, Wilcomb E. Indians and the American Revolution: http://www.americanrevolution.org/ind1.html

43. NAVAL SERVICE DURING WAR: ANDREW SHERBURNE'S MEMOIR (1779)

INTRODUCTION

When the Revolutionary fighting began in 1775, everyone knew that there would be fighting on land and at sea. So the members of the CONTINENTAL CONGRESS sought ways to be successful in both. On October 13, 1775, the Congress passed a resolution providing for the construction of a naval vessel to intercept British supply ships headed for the American colonies. Throughout the course of the war, a number of naval ships would be commissioned for service against the British Royal Navy. Included in this number was the *USS Ranger,* launched on May 10, 1777, in Kittery, Maine. Originally commanded by JOHN PAUL JONES, the *Ranger* came to be commanded by Captain THOMAS SIMPSON following Jones's move to the *Bonhomme Richard* in 1778.

Acquiring men for these new naval vessels was not always easy. Many trained sailors decided to remain on their merchant vessels or join privateers because they thought it was a better way to make money. But others were caught up by the calls for men to fight for American independence and joined the navy to answer that call. Andrew Sherburne was such a person. His memoir about his naval service describes how excited he got about the possibility of serving in the colonial navy and fighting the British. In the document below, he recounts how he came to join the navy and embarked on his first tour of duty on the *Ranger* in 1779.

KEEP IN MIND WHILE YOU READ

1. In the 18th century, the age of 14 was often seen as adulthood in many ways. Children had often gone to work as apprentices or were in the family business by that age, so it was not that unusual for a lad such as Andrew Sherburne to go off to sea by age 14.
2. The British Royal Navy was the best navy in the world at the time of the American Revolution. Defeating a British ship at sea was considered to be a great naval achievement at this time.

Document: Excerpt from Memoirs of Andrew Sherburne *(1779)*

I was about nine years of age when Gen. Gage, with a land and naval force, took possession of Boston, which has been termed the "cradle of American independence." The seizure of Boston exasperated the feelings of the colonists in every section of our country. I distinctly recollect the period when the farmers of Londonderry could scarcely settle themselves to their work. They felt that their rights were invaded. Many persons of talents or influence were friendly to the measures pursued by the British parliament; they were termed "Tories." Another class, which remonstrated against those measures, received the name of "Whigs." My uncle with whom I resided was a decided Whig. Having formed acquaintances in Boston, where he had served his time at the cabinet-maker's business, he felt a deep interest in the events which occurred there. He took the newspapers; (there were comparatively few published at that day,) his neighbors assembled about him, and the fire-side conversation turned on the rights of the people, the injustice of parliament, the detection of Tories, &c. The conflicts at Lexington and Bunker's hill, and the burning of Charleston, roused the Irish "Yankies" of Londonderry. The young men posted off to the battle ground, prompted by their sires, who followed them with their horses laden with provisions. My ears were open to all the passing news. I wished myself old enough to take an active part in this contest. Little did I realize at that time the horrors of war. I had not yet heard the clash of arms, the groans of the dying, and the shouts of the victors. Nor did I imagine at this period, when I so much abhorred swearing, that the time would arrive when I should become a profane sailor. What is man? "At his best estate he is altogether vanity."

In Londonderry the influence of Doct. Matthew Thornton, one of the signers of the declaration of independence, was exerted with great effect on the side of liberty.—When I was about eleven years of age, my uncle removed from Londonderry to Epsom. Here another distinguished patriot had resided, Capt. Mc'Leary. He fell with General Warren, on Bunker's Hill. I recollect the four following lines of a dirge, commemorative of the deaths of Warren and Mc'Leary, and their companions.

"My trembling hand and aching heart,
O how it throbs this day;
Their loss is felt in every part
Of North America."

> **manual exercise:** prescribed movements in the handling of a weapon or other military item during a drill or ceremony

These lines indicate the spirit of the times, rather than the poetic talent of their author. A martial spirit was diffused through the little circle of my acquaintances.—As the men were frequently called together for military discipline, their example was not lost upon the boys.—Lads from seven years old and upwards, were formed into companies, and being properly officered, armed with wooden guns and adorned with plumes, they would go through the **manual exercise** with as much regularity as the men. If two or three boys met, their martial ardor showed itself in exercising with sticks instead of muskets. Many a bitter sigh and broken heart, however, testified in the end the result of this military excitement.

Parents saw with pain their sons advancing from childhood to youth. My reader can but faintly imagine the feelings of an aged father, or an affectionate mother, perhaps a widow, when news arrived that a son had fallen in the field of battle, or had languished and died in an hospital, or still remained a prisoner in the hands of a foe, whose tender mercies were cruel. Danger however did not deter our young men from pressing forward to the battle ground, or sailing to meet the foe upon the ocean.

....Soon after this I returned to my parents in Portsmouth. An abundance of new objects was here presented to my view. Ships were building, prizes taken from the enemy unloading, privateers fitting out, **standards** waved on the forts and **batteries,** the exercising of soldiers, the roar of cannon, the sound of martial music and the call for volunteers so infatuated me, that I was filled with anxiety to become an actor in the scenes of war. My eldest brother, Thomas, had recently returned from a cruise on board the General Mifflin, of Boston, Capt. Mc'Neal. This ship had captured thirteen **prizes,** some of which, however, being of little value, were burnt, some were sold in France, others reached Boston, and their cargoes were divided among the crew of that ship. On my brother's return I became more eager to try my fortune at sea. My father, though a high Whig, disapproved the practice of privateering. Merchant vessels, at this period, which ran safe, made great gains, seamen's wages were consequently very high. Through my fathers influence Thomas was induced to enter the merchants' service. Though not yet fourteen years of age, like other boys, I imagined myself almost a man. I had intimated to my sister, that if my father would not consent that I should go to sea, I would run away, and go on board a **privateer.** My mind became so infatuated with the subject, that I talked of it in my sleep, and was overheard by my mother. She communicated what she had heard to my father.—My parents were apprehensive that I might wander off and go on board some vessel without their consent. At this period it was not an uncommon thing for lads to come out of the country, step on board a privateer, make a cruise and return home, their friends remaining in entire ignorance of their fate, until they heard it from themselves. Others would pack up their clothes, take a cheese and a loaf of bread and steer off for the army. There was a disposition in commanders of privateers and recruiting officers to encourage this spirit of enterprise in young men and boys. Though these rash young adventurers did not count the cost, or think of looking at the dark side of the picture, yet this spirit, amidst the despondency of many, enabled our country to maintain a successful struggle and finally achieve her independence.

The continental ship of war, Ranger of eighteen guns, commanded by Thomas Simpson, Esq. was at this time shipping a crew in Portsmouth. This ship had been ordered to join the Boston and Providence, **frigates** and the Queen of France of twenty guns, upon an expedition directed by Congress. My father having consented that I should go to sea, preferred the service of Congress to privateering. He was acquainted with Capt. Simpson.—On board this ship were my two half uncles, Timothy and James Weymouth. Accompanied by my father, I visited the rendezvous of the Ranger and shipped as one of her crew. There were probably thirty boys on board this ship. As most of our principal officers belonged to the town, parents preferred this ship as a station for their sons who were about to enter the naval service. Hence most of these boys were from Portsmouth. As privateering was the order of the day, vessels of every description were employed in the business. Men were not wanting who

batteries: emplacements where artillery is mounted

frigates: fast, medium-sized sailing warships of the 18th and early 19th century

privateer: privately owned ship commissioned in war to capture enemy ships

prizes: something, especially a warship, taken by force

standards: flags, banners, etc. as emblems of military units

would hazard themselves in vessels of twenty tons or less, manned by ten or fifteen hands. Placing much dependence on the protection of my uncles, I was much elated with my supposed good fortune, which had at last made me a sailor.

I was not yet fourteen years of age. I had received some little moral and religious instruction, and was far from being accustomed to the habits of town boys, or the maxims or dialect of sailors. The town boys thought themselves vastly superior to country lads; and indeed in those days the distinction was much greater than at present. My diffidence and aversion to swearing, rendered me an object of ridicule to those little profane chaps. I was insulted, and frequently obliged to fight. In this I was sometimes victorious. My uncles, and others, prompted me to defend my rights. I soon began to improve in boxing, and to indulge in swearing. At first this practice occasioned some remorse of conscience.—I however endeavored to persuade myself that there was a necessity for it. I at length became a proficient in this abominable practice. To counterbalance my guilt in this, I at the same time became more constant in praying; heretofore I had only prayed occasionally; now I prayed continually when I turned in at night, and vainly imagined that I prayed enough by night to atone for the sins of the day. Believing that no other person on board prayed, I was filled with pride, concluding I had as much or more religion than the whole crew besides. The boys were employed in waiting on the officers, but in time of action a boy was quartered to each gun to carry cartridges. I was waiter to Mr. Charles Roberts, the boatswain, and was quartered at the third gun from the bow. Being ready for sea, we sailed to Boston, joined the Providence frigate, commanded by Commodore Whipple, the Boston frigate, and the Queen of France. I believe that this small squadron composed nearly the entire navy of the United States. We proceeded to sea some time in June, 1779. A considerable part of the crew of the Ranger being raw hands and the sea rough, especially in the gulf stream, many were exceedingly sick, and myself among the rest. We afforded a subject of constant ridicule to the old sailors. Our officers improved every favorable opportunity for working the ship and exercising the guns. We cruised several weeks, made the Western Islands, and at length fell in with the homeward bound Jamaica fleet, on the banks of Newfoundland. It was our practice to keep a man at the mast head constantly by day, on the look out. The moment a sail was discovered, a signal was given to our consorts, and all possible exertion was made to come up with the stranger, or discover what she was. About seven o'clock one morning, the man at the fore-topmast head cried out "a sail, a sail on the lee-bow; another there, and there." Our young officers ran up the shrouds, and with their glasses soon ascertained that more than fifty sail could be seen from the mast-head. It should here be observed, that during the months of summer, it is extremely foggy on the banks of Newfoundland.— Sometimes a ship cannot be seen at the distance of one hundred yards, and then in a few minutes you may have a clear sky and bright sun for half an hour, and you are then enveloped in the fog again. The Jamaica fleet, which consisted of about one hundred and fifty sail, some of which were armed, was convoyed by one or two line of battle ships, several frigates and sloops of war. Our little squadron was in the rear of the fleet, and we had reason to fear that some of the heaviest armed ships were there also. If I am not mistaken, the Boston frigate was not in company with us at this time. My reader may easily imagine that our minds were agitated with alternate hopes and fears. No time was to be lost. Our Commodore soon brought to one of their ships, manned and sent her off. Being to windward he edged away and spoke to our Captain. We were at this time in pursuit of a large ship. The Commodore hauled his wind again, and in the course of an hour we came up with the ship, which proved to be the Holderness, a three decker, mounting 22 guns. She struck after giving her several broadsides. Although she had more guns, and those of heavier mettle than ourselves, her crew was not sufficiently large to manage her guns, and at the same time work the ship. She was loaded with cotton, coffee, sugar, rum and alspice. While we were employed in manning her, our Commodore captured another and gave her up to us to man also. When this was accomplished it, was nearly night; we were, however, unwilling to abandon the opportunity of enriching ourselves, therefore kept along under easy sail. Some time in the night we found ourselves surrounded with ships, and supposed we were discovered. We could distinctly hear their bells, on which they frequently struck a few strokes, that their ships might not approach too near each other during the night. We were close on board one of their largest armed ships; and from the multitude of lights which had appeared, supposed that they had called to quarters. It being necessary to avoid their convoy, we fell to leeward, and in an hour lost sight of them all. The next day the sky was overcast, and at times we had a thick fog. In the afternoon the sun shone for a short time, and enabled us to see a numerous fleet a few miles to windward, in such compact order, that we thought it not best to approach them. We were however in hopes that we might pick up some single ship. We knew nothing of our consorts, but were entirely alone. Towards night we took and manned out a brig. On the third morning we gained sight of three ships, to which we gave chase, and called all hands to quarters. When they discovered us in chase, they huddled together, intending, as we supposed, to fight us; they however soon made sail and ran from us; after a short lapse of time we overhauled and took one of them, which we soon found to be a dull sailor. Another, while we were manning our prize, attempted to escape, but we soon found that we gained upon her. While in chase, a circumstance occurred which excited some alarm. Two large ships hove in sight to windward, running directly for us, under a press of sail. One of them shaped her course for the prize we had just manned. We were unwilling to give up our chase, as we had ascertained from our prize that the two other ships were laden with sugar, rum, cotton, &c, and that they were unarmed. We soon came up with the hindmost, brought her to, and ordered her to keep under our stern, while we might pursue the other, as our situation was too critical to allow us to heave to and get out our boat.

The stranger in chase of us was under English colors; we however soon ascertained by her signal, that she was the Providence frigate, on board of which was our Commodore. This joyful intelligence relieved us from all fear of the enemy, and we soon came up with our chase. In the mean time, the prize which we had taken, (but not boarded) sought to get under the protection of the Providence, mistaking that frigate for one of the English convoy, as he still kept their colors flying. Our prize, therefore, as she thought, eluded us, and hailing our Commodore, informed him, "that a Yankee cruiser had taken one of the fleet!" Very well, very well, replied the Commodore, I'll be along side of him directly. He then hauled down his English colors, hoisted the American, and ordered the ship to haul down her flag and come under his stern. This order was immediately obeyed. We now ascertained that the strange ship, which was in chase of our first prize, was another of our consorts, the Queen of France. Having manned our prizes and secured our prisoners, we all shaped our course for Boston, where we arrived some time in the last of July or beginning of August, 1779.

Source: Sherburne, Andrew. *Memoirs of Andrew Sherburne; A Pensioner of the Navy of the Revolution, Written by Himself.* Utica, NY: W. Williams, 1828, 16–23.

AFTERMATH

Andrew Sherburne continued his service in the United States Navy after this tour in 1779. He was later shipwrecked and then captured by the British. He was in the Old Mill prison in England for some time. He received a pension for his services during the Revolution, but the navy would not be his career. He later became a Baptist clergyman and pastored several churches in New England. He died in 1831.

The *Ranger* and the other ships of the United States Navy continued to fight the British Royal Navy and harass British shipping throughout the rest of the Revolution. In late 1779, the *Ranger* was ordered to Charleston, South Carolina, to help defend the city against the British siege then in progress. The city fell to the British on May 11, 1780, and the *Ranger* was captured. The ship was taken into the British Royal Navy and commissioned as the HMS *Halifax*.

ASK YOURSELF

1. Why would a young man of 14 want to go off to sea to fight the British? In what ways do his actions seem normal for a teenager, and in what ways do they seem unusual?
2. What were Andrew's primary responsibilities on the ship? Why do you think it was considered all right for a young man of 14 to carry out these duties?
3. What do you think Andrew learned while serving on the ship? Do you think that, overall, it was a good or a bad experience for him?
4. Why do you think Andrew's parents wanted him to serve on a regular naval vessel instead of a privateer? Why did they not try to convince him not to go to sea at all?

TOPICS AND ACTIVITIES TO CONSIDER

- ➷ Serving on board a ship the way Andrew Sherburne did was seen primarily as a form of apprenticeship intended to train him for a future career. Investigate how apprenticeships worked in the 18th century. Investigate why that was the primary form of job training at the time and compare that to how job training has changed.
- ➷ In the 18th century, ships had to get very close to each other in order to engage in combat because the range of their guns did not enable them to shoot very far. Investigate how naval ships have changed over the years and how that has changed naval warfare as a result. How would the engagements that Andrew described have been different had the ships involved had engines rather than sails for power?

Further Reading

Allen, Gardner W. *A Naval History of the American Revolution*. Williamstown, MA: Corner House, 1970.

Fowler, William M. Jr. *Rebels under Sail: The American Navy during the American Revolution*. New York: Scribner's, 1976.

Haworth, Stephen. *To Shining Sea: A History of the United States Navy, 1775–1991*. New York: Random House, 1991.

Miller, Nathan. *Sea of Glory: A Naval History of the American Revolution*. Annapolis: Naval Institute Press, 1974.

Mooney, James L. *Dictionary of American Naval Fighting Ships*. Washington, DC: Navy Department, Office of the Chief of Naval Operations, Naval History Division, 1959–1981.

Tuchman, Barbara. *The First Salute*. New York: Alfred A. Knopf, 1988.

44. "Hard Winter": Joseph Plumb Martin's Memoir (1779–1780)

INTRODUCTION

Bad weather has an impact on the day-to-day life of people under any circumstance, but it proved particularly difficult for armies in the field. In the 18th century, it was customary procedure for military units to cease fighting during the winter months and go into what were referred to as "winter quarters." During the American Revolution, the British army generally stayed in major cities during the winter while the CONTINENTAL ARMY stayed in smaller communities. But the Continental Army sometimes had to build structures for their winter stay. This proved particularly difficult if the army was unable to leave the field of fighting early enough to get the structures up before the winter snows hit.

The most famous winter quarters for the Continental Army were at Valley Forge, Pennsylvania, in the winter of 1777–1778. Joseph Plumb Martin of Connecticut spent the winter at Valley Forge, but he later stated that the most difficult winter for him was the one spent in New Jersey in 1779–1780. In his memoirs, he described the snowfall as well as the process of erecting structures for the soldiers to stay in during the winter.

KEEP IN MIND WHILE YOU READ

1. All units in the Continental Army would have been seeking places to stay for the winter, but units farther south would not have had as much bad weather to deal with.
2. Getting needed supplies to the soldiers proved difficult throughout the Revolution, both because of lack of funds and the difficulty of transporting goods over long distances.
3. Martin had been at Valley Forge in 1777–1778, but he describes this winter as worse than that one.

Document: Excerpt from Joseph Plumb Martin's Memoir of a Revolutionary Soldier (1779–1780)

Campaign of 1779

....We remained at and near Peekskill till some time in the month of December. The cold weather having commenced earlier than usual, we had hard combatting with hunger, cold, nakedness and hard duty, but were obliged to grapple with them all as well as we could. As the old woman said by her husband, when she baked him instead of his clothes, to kill the vermin, "You must grin and bear it."

About the middle of this month (December) we crossed the Hudson, at King's ferry, and proceeded into New-Jersey, for winter-quarters. The snow had fallen nearly a foot deep.— Now I request the reader to consider what must have been our situation at this time, naked, fatigued and starved, forced to march many a weary mile in winter, through cold and snow, to seek a situation in some (to us, unknown) wood to build us habitations to starve and suffer in. I do not know how the hearers of this recital may feel, but *I* know how I felt at the time, and I know how I yet feel at the recollection of it; but there was no remedy, we *must* go through it, and we did go through it, and I am yet alive.

Our destination was at a place in New-Jersey, called Baskinridge. It was cold and snowy, we had to march all day through the snow and at night take up our lodgings in some wood, where, after shovelling away the snow, we used to pitch three or four tents facing each other, and then join in making a fire in the centre. Sometimes we could procure an armful of buckwheat straw to lie upon, which was deemed a luxury. Provisions, as usual, took up but a small part of our time, though much of our thoughts.

We arrived on our wintering ground in the latter part of the month of December, and once more, like the wild animals, began to make preparations to build us a "city for habitation." The soldiers, when immediately going about the building of their winter huts, would always endeavour to provide themselves with such tools as were necessary for the business, (it is no concern of the reader's, as I conceive, by what means they procured their tools,) such as crosscut-saws, handsaws, **frows, augers,** &c. to expedite the erection and completion of their dwellingplaces. Do not blame them too much, gentle reader, if you should chance to make a shrewd Yankee guess how they *did* procure them; remember, they were in distress, and you know when a man is in that condition, he will not be over scrupulous how he obtains relief, so he does obtain it.

> **auger:** tool for boring holes in wood
> **frow:** steel wedge for splitting logs

We encamped near our destined place of operation and immediately commenced. It was upon the southerly declivity of a hill; the snow, as I have already observed, was more than a foot deep, and the weather none of the warmest. We had to level the ground to set out huts upon; the soil was a light loam. When digging just below the frost, which was not deep, the snow having fallen early in the season, we dug out a number of toads, that would hop off when brought to the light of day as lively as in summer time. We found by this where toads take up their winter-quarters, if we can never find where swallows take up theirs.

At this will be the last time that I shall have occasion to mention my having to build huts for our winter habitations, I will, by the reader's leave, just give a short description of the fashion and manner of erecting one of those log towns.

After the ground was marked out by the Quartermasters, much after the same manner as for pitching tents in the field, we built the huts in the following manner.—Four huts, two in front and two in the rear, then a space of six or eight feet, when four more huts were placed in the same order, and so on to the end of the regiment, with a parade in front and a street through the whole, between the front and rear, the whole length, twelve or fifteen feet wide. Next in order, in the rear of these huts the officers of the companies built theirs with their waiters in the rear of them. Next, the Field officers in the same order; every two huts, that is, one in front and one in the rear, had just their width in front indefinitely, and no more, to procure the materials for building; the officers had all in the rear. No one was allowed to transgress these bounds on any account whatever, either for building or firewood. The next thing is the erecting of the huts; they were generally about twelve by fifteen or sixteen feet square, (all uniformly of the same dimensions,) the building of them was thus; after procuring the most suitable timber for the business, it was laid up by notching them in at the four corners. When arrived at the proper heighth, about seven feet, the two end sticks which held those that served for plates were made to jut out about a foot from the sides and a straight pole made to rest on them, parallel to the plates; the gable ends were then formed by laying on pieces with straight poles on each, which served for ribs to hold the covering, drawing in gradually to the ridge pole. Now for the covering; this was done by sawing some of the larger trees into cuts about four feet in length, splitting them into bolts, and riving them into shingles, or rather staves; the covering then commenced by laying on those staves, resting the lower ends on the poles by the plates, they were laid on in two thicknesses, carefully breaking joints; these were then bound on by a straight pole with withes, then another double tier with the butts resting on this pole and bound on as before, and so on to the end of the chapter. A chimney was then built at the centre of the backside, composed of stone as high as the eves and finished with sticks and clay, if clay was to be had, if not, with mud. The last thing was to hew stuff and build us up cabins or births to sleep in, and then the buildings were fitted for the reception of *gentlemen soldiers,* with all their *rich* and *gay* furniture.

Such were the habitations we had to construct at this time. We got into them about the beginning of the year, when the weather became intensely cold. Cold weather and snow were plenty, but beef and bread were extremely scarce in the army. Let it be recollected that this was what has been termed the "hard winter," and hard it was to the poor soldiers, as will appear in the sequel. So here I will close the narrative of my campaign of 1779. And happy should I then have thought myself if that had ended the war, but I had to see a little more trouble before that period arrived.

Campaign of 1780.

The soldier defending his country's rights,
Is griev'd when that country his services slights;
But when he remonstrates and finds no relief,
No wonder his anger takes place of his grief.

The winter of 1779 and '80 was very severe; it has been denominated "the hard winter," and hard it was to the army in particular, in more respects than one. The period of the revolution has repeatedly been styled "the times that tried men's souls." I often found that those times not only tried men's souls, but their bodies too; I know they did mine, and that effectually.

Sometime in the month of January there happened a spell of remarkably cold weather; in the height of the cold, a large detachment from the army was sent off on an expedition against some fortifications held by the British on Staten Island. The detachment was commanded by Major-General John Sullivan. It was supposed by our officers that the bay before

New-York was frozen sufficiently to prevent any succours being sent to the garrisons in their works. It was therefore determined to endeavour to surprise them and get possession of their fortifications before they could obtain help. Accordingly, our troops were all conveyed in sleighs and other carriages; but the enemy got intelligence of our approach (doubtless by some tory) before our arrival on the island. When we arrived we found Johnny Bull prepared for our reception; he was always complaisant, especially when his own honour or credit was concerned; we accordingly found them all waiting for us—so that we could not surprise them, and to take their works by storm looked too hazardous; to besiege them in regular form was out of the question, as the bay was not frozen so much as we expected. There was an armed brig lying in the ice not far from the shore, she received a few shots from our fieldpieces for a morning's salutation; we then fell back a little distance and took up our abode for the night upon a bare bleak hill, in full rake of the northwest wind, with no other covering or shelter than the canopy of the heavens, and no fuel but some old rotten rails which we dug up through the snow, which was two or three feet deep; the weather was cold enough to cut a man in two.

We lay on this accommodating spot till morning when we began our retreat from the island. The British were quickly in pursuit; they attacked our rear guard and made several of them prisoners, among whom was one of my particular associates. Poor young fellow! I have never seen or heard any thing from him since. We arrived at camp after a tedious and cold march of many hours, some with frozen toes, some with frozen fingers and ears, and half starved into the bargain. Thus ended our Staten Island expedition.

Soon after this there came on several severe snowstorms. At one time it snowed the greater part of four days successively, and there fell nearly as many feet deep of snow, and here was the keystone of the arch of starvation. We were absolutely, literally starved;—I do solemnly declare that I did not put a single morsel of victuals into my mouth for four days and as many nights, except a little black birch bark which I gnawed off a stick of wood, if that can be called victuals. I saw several of the men roast their old shoes and eat them, and I was afterwards informed by one of the officer's waiters, that some of the officers killed and ate a favourite little dog that belonged to one of them.—If this was not "suffering" I request to be informed what can pass under that name; if "suffering" like this did not "try men's souls," I confess that I do not know what could. The fourth day, just at dark, we obtained a half pound of lean fresh beef and a **gill** of wheat for each man, whether we had any salt to season so delicious a morsel, I have forgotten, but I am sure we had no bread, (except the wheat,) but I will assure the reader that we had the best of sauce; that is, we had keen appetites. When the wheat was so swelled by boiling as to be beyond the danger of swelling in the stomach, it was deposited there without ceremony.

> **gill:** liquid measure roughly equal to half a pint

After this, we sometimes got a little beef, but no bread; we, however, once in a while got a little rice, but as to flour or bread, I do not recollect that I saw a morsel of either (I mean wheaten) during the winter, all the bread kind we had was Indian meal.

We continued here, starving and freezing, until, I think, some time in the month of February, when the two Connecticut Brigades were ordered to the lines near Staten Island. The small parties from the army which had been sent to the lines, were often surprised and taken by the enemy or cut to pieces by them. These circumstances, it seems, determined the Commander-in-chief to have a sufficient number of troops there to withstand the enemy even should they come in considerable force. And now a long continuance of our hardships appeared unavoidable. The first brigade took up its quarters in a village called Westfield,

QUARTERMASTERS

Supplying troops with all they need to survive in war has always been a struggle. Over the years, governments have developed different procedures to handle these needs, but most efforts have generally revolved around the development of a quartermaster system. The term *quartermaster* originated in Germany and became a commonly used term throughout Europe in the 17th century. In the United States, the Quartermaster Corps was created by the Continental Congress on June 16, 1775, shortly after they appointed George Washington commander of the Continental Army. In the early years of the Revolution, the quartermasters struggled to get needed supplies. General Nathaniel Greene became quartermaster general in 1778. Following the troubles during the winter at Valley Forge, Greene reorganized the supply system and established a depot system to ensure that supplies were more readily available for the troops. The situation improved somewhat, but supplies remained scarce at times primarily because of the difficulty of getting goods moved from place to place in the midst of war. Even today, getting supplies to troops in the field is a complicated and often difficult process that the Quartermaster Corps has to deal with on a regular basis.

and the second in another called Springfield;—we were put into the houses, with the inhabitants. A fine addition we were, doubtless, to their families, but as we were so plentifully furnished with necessaries, especially in the article of food, we could not be burdensome to them, as will soon appear.

Source: Martin, Joseph Plumb. *Memoir of a Revolutionary Soldier.* Mineola, NY: Dover Publications, 2006, pp. 93–98.

AFTERMATH

The winter of 1779–1780 was hard on the Continental Army, but the army managed to hang together and returned to the fighting when spring returned. For Joseph Plumb Martin, 1780 produced a change in his assignment. In the summer of 1780, he joined the corps of SAPPERS AND MINERS, which General GEORGE WASHINGTON had ordered created. He was promoted to sergeant at this time. The corps participated in the campaigns of 1780 and 1781, providing very important service at Yorktown where they dug the entrenchments for the Continental Army that enabled the army to lay siege to the town. Martin's corps also helped clear the field so that ALEXANDER HAMILTON's regiment could capture Redoubt #10, a key victory in convincing General CHARLES CORNWALLIS to surrender on October 19, 1781.

ASK YOURSELF

1. Why do you think the Continental Army chose to build structures for winter quarters rather than staying in towns and using already-existing buildings?
2. What is it about Martin's description of the weather that supports his view of this time as the "hard winter"?

TOPICS AND ACTIVITIES TO CONSIDER

- ➢ Investigate the reports of the various winter quarters that units of the Continental Army lived in during the Revolution. Compare and contrast the experiences from year to year and consider why Valley Forge has become the most famous of these encampments.

> Investigate the actual structures built by the Continental Army for winter quarters. Compare the reconstructions that are at Valley Forge today to the descriptions Martin gives of what his unit built. Consider what it would have been like to live in such structures.

Further Reading

Buel, Richard. *Dear Liberty: Connecticut's Mobilization for the Revolutionary War.* Middletown, CT: Wesleyan University Press, 1980.

Busch, Noel Fairchild. *Winter Quarters: George Washington and the Continental Army at Valley Forge.* New York: Liveright, 1974.

Cal, Paul L. *Connecticut Soldiers in the American Revolution: A Society's Approach to War.* Thesis, United States Military Academy, 1994.

Cox, Elbert, and Russell Baker. *Winter Encampments of the Revolution.* Washington, DC: United States Department of the Interior, National Park Service, 1941.

Martin, Joseph Plumb. *Memoir of a Revolutionary Soldier.* Mineola, NY: Dover Publications, 2006.

Raphael, Ray. *Founders: The People Who Brought You a Nation.* New York: The New Press, 2009.

Smith, Samuel Stelle. *Winter at Morristown, 1779–1780: The Darkest Hour.* Monmouth Beach, NJ: Philip Freneau Press, 1979.

Film and Television Portrayals of Martin

Aaron Carter in *Liberty's Kids,* television series, 2002–2003.

Philip Seymour Hoffman in PBS series *Liberty! The American Revolution*, television mini-series, 1997.

Rick Schroder in *The American Revolution,* television mini-series, 1994.

Morristown: Where America Survived, New Jersey Public Television and Radio, 2009.

Web Sites

History of the Quartermaster Corps: http://www.qmfound.com/history.html
Liberty! The American Revolution: http://www.pbs.org/ktca/liberty

45. IMPACT OF WAR ON THE PEOPLE: LETTER FROM NATHANIEL GREENE TO HIS WIFE, CATHERINE (JANUARY 12, 1781)

INTRODUCTION

The fighting during the Revolution produced many problems and concerns for the people who lived near the battlefields. For many, armies marching back and forth and fighting one another resulted in the destruction of property. People were forced to flee as the armies marched around the countryside trying to engage in battle. Many people lost everything they had as a result of the battle(s) in their neighborhood.

A representative description of such suffering is found in a letter from General NATHANIEL GREENE to his wife, Catherine. Greene served in the army throughout the Revolution, first in the Rhode Island militia and then in the CONTINENTAL ARMY, where he quickly rose to the rank of brigadier general. He participated in the fighting in New York and New Jersey in 1776. He served as quartermaster general from 1778 to 1780, and then took command of the Continental Army in the south following the removal of HORATIO GATES. In writing to his wife to assure her that he was okay, Greene describes the plight of a number of people who had lost most or all of their possessions because of the fighting.

KEEP IN MIND WHILE YOU READ

1. Letter writers in the military always worried about their mail being intercepted by the enemy and thus tended to guard their words carefully.
2. Mail delivery was difficult and undependable, so people took advantage of every opportunity to get a letter sent to loved ones back home.
3. It was often difficult to determine who was on which side during the American Revolution. This proved particularly true in the South where many people really wished just to be left alone and did not care very much about who ended up winning the war.

Document: Nathaniel Greene's Letter to His Wife, Catherine (January 12, 1781)

Camp on the Pedee January 12th 1781

General de Portail being released from captivity and on his way to the Northward affords me an opportunity of writing you (which I have done by every conveyance since I came to this Country.) Could I have only a single line in return, to let me know you are well, it would afford me infinite pleasure. Nothing can exceed my anxiety to know your situation, not having heard the least syllable from you since I left Philadelphia.

I have my health exceeding good, being never more hearty in my life; and could I be useful here, and know that you was well, I should not be unhappy.

You can have no idea of the distress and misery that prevails in this quarter. Hundreds of families that formerly livd in great opulence are now reduced to beggary and want. A Gentleman from Georgia was this morning with me, to get assistance to move his wife and family out of the Enemies way. They have been separated for upwards of eight months, during all which time the wife never heard from her husband, nor the husband from his wife. Her distress was so great that she has been obligd to sell all her **plate,** table linnen and even wearing apparel, to maintain her poor little children. In this situation she was tantalised by the Tories, and insulted by the british. Human misery has become a subject for sport and ridicule. With us the difference between Whig and Tory is little more than a division of sentiment; but here they persecute each other with little less than savage fury. When I compare your situation with those miserable people in this quarter, disagreeable as it may be from our long and distant separation. I cannot help feeling thankful that your cup has not a mixture of bitterness like theirs.

A Captain who is now with me and who has just got his family from near the Lines of the Enemy had his Sister murderd a few days since, and seven of her children wounded, the oldest not twelve years of age. The sufferings and distress of the Inhabitants beggars all description, and requires the liveliest imagination to conceive the cruelties and devastations which prevail. I will not pain your humanity by a further relation of the distresses which rage in this quarter; nor would I have mentioned them at all, but to convince you that you are not the most unhappy of all creation. God grant us a speedy and happy meeting, by giving to the Country peace, liberty and safety.

In your last letter, you wrote me that you had eight new **Shirts and Stocks,** and several pair of Stockings; which you intended to have brought to camp with you. As my stock is small, and the difficulty great in getting any here, I wish you to send me all you have. Please to send them in two equal divisions to the care of Mr. Pettit in Philadelphia, but dont send them, unless it is by persons who will undertake to have them safely deliverd. Mr. Pettit will take care to have them forwarded to me. I am in want of nothing of the clothing kind but shirts, stocks and stockings, these articles I am in want of and shall be more so before those you send can reach me; which cannot be less than three months. Pray be particular in giving an account of the Children; mention who are at home, and who at nursing, and the health of all. These little **anecdotes** are pleasing and afford the most agreeable family feelings. I wish to know where you reside, whether at Greenwich, Coventry or at the farm in Westerly. Where

> **anecdotes:** short entertaining reports about some event
>
> **plate:** dishes and utensils, generally made out of metal covered with silver or gold
>
> **Shirts and Stocks:** equestrian outfit—the stock is the type of tied scarf worn by formal horseback riders

CATHERINE GREENE AND ELI WHITNEY

Nathaniel Greene's wife played an important role in American history because of an event that occurred after her husband's death. When Greene died in 1786, Catherine chose to remain in Georgia rather than move back to Rhode Island. In 1792 Eli Whitney stayed at Mulberry Grove and helped out as a handyman on the plantation. At the same time, he also began building the prototype for his cotton gin that would change the American economy in amazing ways. Tradition gives Catherine Greene the credit for inspiring Whitney to build his machine. Some believe that Greene paid for the machine when Whitney built it. The cotton gin made the United States the largest producer of cotton in the world and helped cement the institution of slavery in the southern states (a factor in the coming of the Civil War in the middle of the 19th century).

is brother Bill Littlefield, and how does he spend his time? I had a letter from him some time since respecting the family interest to the Eastward; which I am not certain that I ever gave an answer to; but you will please to tell him I think he should go down to Wells (first getting a power of attorney from his father); and make enquiry respecting the situation of the lands and the sentiments and intention of the settlers, after which it will be best to consult with some good able Lawyer or Lawyers, and then take his measures.

Give my kind love to all friends and believe me to be affectionately yours
NG

Source: Letter from Nathaniel Greene to Catherine Greene, January 21, 1781. *The Papers of General Nathaniel Greene, Vol. VII: December 26, 1780–29 March 1781.* Ed. Dennis M. Conrad and Richard K. Showman. Chapel Hill: University of North Carolina Press, 1994, pp. 102–103. Used by permission of the publisher.

AFTERMATH

Greene's southern campaign proved successful in the long run and set the stage for the ultimate victory at Yorktown, a defeat which resulted in the British deciding to sue for peace. Although Greene technically lost the Battle of Guilford Courthouse because he retreated and left the British forces holding the field, the British army could not afford the losses they suffered. This battle, along with smaller conflicts in the Carolinas, led General CHARLES CORNWALLIS to withdraw the army to Virginia in the hopes of receiving reinforcements and supplies. Washington was able to corner the British at Yorktown, and the fighting in the Revolution ended when Cornwallis surrendered his army on October 19, 1781.

Following the war, Greene received Mulberry Grove, a plantation in Georgia, as thanks for his service in the South during the war. He and his family moved there in 1785. Thus, they personally witnessed much of the continued suffering that people in the South experienced even after the war had ended. Greene died in Georgia of severe sunstroke on June 19, 1786.

ASK YOURSELF

1. Greene indicated in his letter that there seemed to be more infighting between southerners than northerners during the Revolution. Why do you think that might be true?

2. Why do you think Greene thought that his wife would be interested in the description of all the suffering he saw? Do people today pay more attention to reports of tragedies than reports of good happenings?

TOPICS AND ACTIVITIES TO CONSIDER

- ☙ Wars often produce suffering for people not directly involved in the fighting. Investigate the reports of civilians and their losses in the Revolution and in later conflicts to see how they are similar and how they are different.

- ☙ Nathaniel Greene was only one of GEORGE WASHINGTON's subordinates in the Continental Army. Others included Henry Knox, Horatio Gates, and BENEDICT ARNOLD. Investigate the various generals who served under Washington, and compare and contrast their successes and failures. Consider why some succeeded while others failed.

- ☙ Nathaniel Greene was raised a QUAKER, but he had been expelled in 1773 because of his participation in military events. Investigate other military leaders who were raised as pacifists. Consider the impact that such views could have on someone in a position of authority in the military.

Further Reading

Golway, Terry. *Washington's General: Nathaniel Greene and the Triumph of the American Revolution*. New York: H. Holt, 2005.

Nosworthy, Brent. *The Anatomy of Victory: Battle Tactics, 1689–1763*. New York: Hippocrene Books, 1990.

Stegeman, John F. *Caty: A Biography of Catherine Littlefield Greene*. Providence, RI: Bicentennial Foundation, 1977.

Stephenson, Michael. *Patriot Battles: How the War of Independence Was Fought*. New York: Harper Collins, 2007.

Thane, Elswyth. *The Fighting Quaker: Nathaniel Greene*. New York: Hawthorn Books, 1972.

Thayer, Theodore. *Nathaniel Greene: Strategist of the American Revolution*. New York: Twayne Publishers, 1960.

46. The Horrors of Civil War: Descriptions of Conflicts between Patriots and Loyalists (1781)

INTRODUCTION

Throughout the American Revolution, neighbors fought neighbors as people divided over whether to support the move for independence or remain loyal to Great Britain. This division proved to be particularly evident when the war reached the South. Groups of Loyalists fought groups of Patriots in bloody engagements throughout the South in 1780 and 1781. Such fighting produced strong feelings and hatreds that lasted long after the end of the Revolution.

Part of the impact of such fighting was a desire by those on each side to seek revenge for attacks their people had suffered. Many Patriots believed that Loyalists had been particularly bloody in their attacks and sought to make them pay for what they had done. In the following selections, Moses Hall (a young infantryman from North Carolina) and William Pierce (a major from Virginia) describe their reactions to the death and destruction they had seen.

KEEP IN MIND WHILE YOU READ

1. Often, the soldiers knew some of the people who were killed in the attacks by the other side. So, the deaths were more personal.
2. Moses Hall's account is part of his pension application, written down in 1835, while William Pierce's account is part of a letter he wrote in July 1781.

Document 1: Moses Hall on a Brutal Attack against Tory Troops (1781)

The Evening after our battle with the Tories, we having a considerable number of prisoners I recollect a scene which made a lasting impression upon my mind. I was invi[ted] by some of my comrades to go and see some of the prisoners. We went to where six were standing together. Some discussion taking place, I heard some of our men cry out, "Remember Buford," and the prisoners were immediately hewed to pieces with broadswords. At first I bore the scene without any emotion, but, upon a moments reflection, I felt such horror as I never did before nor have since, and returning to my quarters and throwing myself upon my blanket I contemplated the cruelties of war until overcome and unmanned by a distressing gloom from which I was not relieved until commencing our march next morning before day by moon light. I came to Tarleton's camp which he had just abandoned leaving lively rail fires. Being on the left of the road as we marched along I discovered lying upon the ground something like the appearance of a man. Upon approaching him he proved to be a youth about sixteen who having come out to view the British through curiosity for fear he might give information to our camps, they had run him through with a bayonet and left him for dead, though able to speak he was mortally wounded. The sight of this unoffending boy butchered rather than be encumbered in the [illegible] on the march, I assume, relieved me of my distress and feelings for the slaughter of the Tories and I desired nothing so much as the opportunity of participating in their destruction.

Source: Revolutionary War Pension Applications, W10105, National Archives.

Document 2: Excerpt from Letter of William Pierce to St. George Tucker (July 20, 1781)

Such scenes of desolation, bloodshed and deliberate murder, I never was a witness to before! Wherever you turn the weeping widow and fatherless child pour out their melancholy tales to wound the feelings of humanity. The two opposite principles of whiggism and toryism have set the people of this country to cutting each other's throats, and scarce a day passes but some poor deluded tory is put to death at his door. For the want of civil government, the bands of society are totally disunited, and the people, by copying the manners of the British, have become perfectly savage. This I hope will prove a lesson to Virginia, and teach her to guard against the consequences of British influence.

Source: "Letter of William Pierce to St. George Tucker, July 20, 1781." *Magazine of American History* VII (December 1881): 434.

AFTERMATH

Atrocities between Patriots and Loyalists occurred throughout the American Revolution, creating much discord that lasted for years after the war ended. For those who experienced these events, the memories never completely faded. Both Hall and Pierce stated that they never forgot the nightmare of the savagery they experienced in the fighting in the South during the Revolution.

Moses Hall served in a variety of engagements during the Southern campaign of 1780 and 1781. Following the war, he remained in North Carolina until 1788, when he moved to Kentucky. He later moved to Indiana, which was where he was living when he applied for a pension for his service in the Revolutionary War. Hall died in 1846.

William Pierce remained in the army until the end of the war. He settled in Savannah, Georgia, where he engaged in a variety of business efforts. In 1787 he served in the

"REMEMBER BUFORD"

"Remember Buford" referred to the Battle of Waxhaws, which took place on May 29, 1780, near Lancaster, South Carolina. A group of Continentals led by Colonel Abraham Buford faced a group made up mostly of Loyalists led by Lieutenant Colonel Banastre Tarleton. Buford's men had marched from Virginia in an effort to help lift the siege of Charleston. Having heard that the city had already fallen to the British, Buford turned back home. Tarleton's men caught up with them and demanded their surrender. When Buford refused, a battle ensued. The Continentals were routed and many tried to surrender. Then Tarleton's horse was shot out from under him, and his men attacked with a vengeance, believing that the Continentals had killed their commander while pretending to surrender. When the battle ended, 113 Continentals lay dead, and 147 were wounded. As word of this battle spread, many who had been neutral joined the Patriot side because they perceived the battle to be a massacre that went beyond the accepted rules of war. "Remember Buford" and "Tarleton's Quarter!" became rallying cries for the Patriots. This event also sparked the formation of the volunteer force of "over-mountain men" that defeated the British at Kings Mountain, South Carolina, in October 1780, a victory that helped set the stage for the British withdrawal to Yorktown, Virginia.

CONTINENTAL CONGRESS from January to May and at the CONSTITUTIONAL CONVENTION during the first part of the summer of 1787. He left before the convention ended and did not sign the final document. Pierce died in 1789.

ASK YOURSELF

1. Are there differences in reactions on the part of Hall and Pierce that can be accounted for by the fact that one was an enlisted man and one was an officer?
2. Are there differences in reactions on the part of Hall and Pierce that can be accounted for by the fact that one account was written at the time of the event while the other was recorded many years later?

TOPICS AND ACTIVITIES TO CONSIDER

- In many ways, what happened in the South in 1780–1781 can be described as a civil war. Investigate other civil wars and compare stories of how the feuding groups treated the other side when they met on the battlefield.
- Much of the conflict between Patriots and Loyalists during the American Revolution revolved around what they wanted to see for their country in the future. Compare and contrast the goals and dreams expressed by various people on both sides of the fighting in the American Revolution to learn more about what they hoped for in the future.

Further Reading

Callahan, North. *Royal Raiders: The Tories of the American Revolution.* New York: Bobbs-Merrill, 1963.

Crow, Jeffrey J. *The Southern Experience in the American Revolution.* Chapel Hill: University of North Carolina Press, 1978.

Hoffman, Ronald. *An Uncivil War: The Southern Backcountry during the American Revolution.* Charlottesville: Published for the U.S. Capitol Historical Society by the University of Virginia Press, 1985.

Treacy, M. F. *Prelude to Yorktown: The Southern Campaign of Nathaniel Greene, 1780–1781.* Chapel Hill: University of North Carolina Press, 1963.

Wilson, David. *The Southern Strategy.* Columbia: University of South Carolina Press, 2005.

Film and Television

Liberty! The American Revolution, television mini-series, 1997.

The Patriot, film, 2000.

Web Site

Liberty! The American Revolution: http://www.pbs.org/ktca/liberty

Appendix 1: Biographical Sketches of Important Individuals Mentioned in the Text

Adams, Abigail (1744–1818): The daughter of a minister, Abigail Adams was the wife of John Adams and mother of John Quincy Adams, both of whom served as president of the United States. Abigail enabled her husband, John, to serve in various capacities during the American Revolution by managing the farm and taking care of the family in his absence.

Adams, James (?–1792): James Adams was a printer who began his career in Philadelphia in 1753. Born in Ireland, he learned the printing trade in Londonderry. Adams originally worked for Benjamin Franklin before going into business for himself in 1760. He moved to Wilmington, Delaware, in 1761. He tried to publish a newspaper in 1762, but without success. His business focused primarily on government and religious publications, as well as the publication of an annual almanac that proved very successful.

Adams, John (1735–1826): John Adams first came to the attention of the public in Massachusetts when he served as the defense lawyer for the soldiers charged with murder in the Boston Massacre of 1770. He later served in a variety of capacities as representative of his home state of Massachusetts and of the United States. He served on the committee charged with drafting the Declaration of Independence in 1776 and on the committee that negotiated the peace treaty with Great Britain in 1782. His final service to his country was his term as president from January 1797 to January 1801.

Arnold, Benedict (1741–1801): Originally from Connecticut, Benedict Arnold served in the Continental Army and quickly became a hero because of his service in Canada and New York. He commanded American forces in the city of Philadelphia following the withdrawal of the British army in 1778. While there, he married Margaret Shippen, the daughter of a leading Loyalist in the city. Following his court-martial and reprimand for financial irregularities, Arnold sought to surrender the fortress at West Point to the British. The plot was discovered, and Arnold fled to the British army. He led several raids in Virginia and Connecticut before fleeing to Great Britain at the end of the war. He died there in disgrace and poverty.

Beatty, Elizabeth (dates unknown): Elizabeth Beatty was the daughter of Charles Beatty, the pastor of the Presbyterian church in Neshaminy, Pennsylvania. She met her future husband, Philip Vickers Fithian, in the summer of 1770 while on a visit to Deerfield, New Jersey. They corresponded and courted on and off for the next five years. They finally wed on October 27, 1775. In less than a year, Elizabeth became a widow when Fithian died while serving as a chaplain with the Continental Army in New York.

Carter, Robert III (1727–1804): Robert Carter owned a plantation in Virginia and served as a royal councilor in the colony prior to the American Revolution, but he came to support the break from Great Britain. After the war ended, Carter concluded that human slavery was immoral. He established a program that eventually freed 452 slaves that had been attached to his estate. The process began in 1791 and continued after Carter's death in 1804.

Clewley, Lucy (1776–1857): Wife of Joseph Plumb Martin, Lucy Clewley had 10 children, 5 of whom survived infancy. The family lived in Maine.

Clinton, Sir Henry (1738–1795): Sir Henry Clinton was a British military officer who served during the Seven Years War in Germany and in a number of battles in the American Revolution. He succeeded Sir William Howe as commander in chief of the British army in North America in 1778, a position he held until his resignation in 1781. He later served as the governor of Gibraltar from 1794 until his death in 1795.

Cornwallis, Charles (1738–1805): Charles Cornwallis was a British nobleman and military officer who served in Germany during the Seven Years War and in a number of battles during the American Revolution. He was the last commander in chief of the British army in North America during the Revolution, surrendering to the Americans and the French under the command of General George Washington at Yorktown in October 1781. Cornwallis later served as the governor of India from 1786 to 1793 and again in 1805. He also served as the viceroy of Ireland from 1798 to 1801.

Cushing, William (1732–1810): William Cushing was a lawyer and jurist from Massachusetts. He served as the chief justice of the Massachusetts Supreme Court from 1777 to 1789 and as an associate justice of the U.S. Supreme Court from 1789 until his death in 1810.

Custis, John Parke (1754–1781): John Parke Custis was a Virginia planter and the stepson of George Washington. He served in the Virginia House of Delegates from 1778 until 1781. He served as a civilian aide-de-camp to Washington during the siege of Yorktown. During this service, he contracted camp fever and died shortly after Cornwallis surrendered.

Edwards, Jonathan (1703–1758): Jonathan Edwards was a Congregational clergyman who is often credited with helping to start the massive religious revival in the 18th century known as the Great Awakening. He pastored the church in Northampton, Massachusetts, from 1729 to 1750, when a dispute with the congregation led to his dismissal. He then served as a missionary to the Native Americans in Stockbridge, Massachusetts, for several years, before becoming the president of the College of New Jersey (now Princeton University). He held that post from 1757 until his death in 1758.

Fleet, Thomas (1732–1797) and John (1734–1806): Printers of the *Boston Evening-Post* from 1758 to 1775, Thomas and John Fleet tried hard to keep their newspaper impartial in the conflict with Great Britain. Their printing firm suffered greatly when the war broke out, and they never fully recovered their business. They did not revive the newspaper after the war, but their printing business continued to operate into the 19th century.

Franklin, Benjamin (1706–1790): Benjamin Franklin was a statesman, scientist, and philosopher who began his career as a printer in Boston, Massachusetts. He moved to Philadelphia, Pennsylvania, in 1723, where he published a weekly newspaper, *The Pennsylvania Gazette,* from 1730 until his retirement in 1748. He helped found groups that later developed into the American Philosophical Society and the Library Company of Philadelphia. He invented the Franklin stove, bifocal spectacles, and the lightning rod. Following his retirement, he served as the representative of several colonies to the British government in London. He also served in the Continental Congress and was appointed to the committee charged with drafting the Declaration of Independence. During the Revolution, he served as ambassador to France and helped negotiate the alliance with the French and the treaty to end the American Revolution. His final public service came as a member of the convention that met in Philadelphia in 1787 to draft what became the Constitution of the United States. The government created by this effort took effect in 1789, shortly before Franklin's death in 1790.

Franklin, William (1731–1813): The illegitimate son of Benjamin Franklin, William Franklin gained a government job through the influence of his father. He served as the royal governor of the Colony of New Jersey from 1763 to 1776. He opposed the Revolution and was arrested as a Loyalist in 1776. He went to England when the Revolution ended and lived there until his death in 1813.

Garretson, John (?–1727 or before): Englishman who wrote *The School of Manners, or Rules for Children's Behavior,* which was originally published in 1685.

Gates, Horatio (1728–1806): Horatio Gates was born in Great Britain and served in the British army in North America during the French and Indian War. He settled in Virginia in 1772 and joined the Continental Army when the American Revolution began. He commanded the victorious Continental forces at the Battle of Saratoga in 1777, a victory that led to the official entry of the French into the war on the Patriot side. Some members of the Continental Congress plotted to put Gates in Washington's place as commander in chief of the Continental Army. This effort failed, and Gates fell out of favor following the disastrous loss at the Battle of Camden, South Carolina, in 1780.

Goodwin, George (1757–1844): George Goodwin learned the printing business from Ebenezer Watson, beginning as an apprentice at the age of nine. He partnered with Watson's widow, Hannah, from 1777 to 1779 and with her second husband, Barzillai Hudson, from 1779 until 1815. The primary product of their printing business was the *Connecticut Courant* (today published as the *Hartford Courant,* the oldest continually published newspaper in the United States). Goodwin retired from the printing business in 1825.

Greene, Nathanael (1742–1786): Hailing from Rhode Island, Nathanael Greene served in the Continental Army throughout the American Revolution. He commanded troops at Trenton in 1776 and then served as quartermaster general of the army from 1778 to 1780. He succeeded Horatio Gates as commander of the southern army in 1780 and led the efforts which eventually forced the British to retreat to Yorktown, where they surrendered in October 1781.

Hall, David (1714–1772): A native of Scotland, David Hall learned the printing trade in Edinburgh and later worked in London. In 1743 he moved to Philadelphia and became a journeyman printer in the shop of Benjamin Franklin. They became partners in the business in 1748, at which point Franklin retired from the business and left its operation to Hall. In 1766 Franklin sold his half of the business to Hall, who then went into partnership with William Sellers. This partnership lasted until Hall's death in 1772.

Hamilton, Alexander (1755–1804): A native of Nevis in the West Indies, Alexander Hamilton moved to New York in 1772 where he attended King's College (now Columbia University). He served as secretary and aide-de-camp to General George Washington from 1777 to 1781. He served in the Continental Congress and the Constitutional Convention as a delegate from New York. In conjunction with John Jay and James Madison, he helped write *The Federalist Papers* in support of the proposed Constitution in 1787–1788. He later served as the first secretary of the treasury from 1789 to 1795.

His opposition to the candidacy of Aaron Burr for president in 1800 and governor of New York in 1804 helped ensure Burr's defeat. Burr, angry over Hamilton's opposition, challenged him to a duel. Hamilton was mortally wounded in the duel and died several days later.

Hancock, John (1737–1793): John Hancock was a merchant from Massachusetts who opposed the taxes and actions of Great Britain in the 1760s that led to the American Revolution in 1775. Hancock served in the Massachusetts legislature from 1769 to 1774 and in the Continental Congress as a delegate from Massachusetts from 1775 to 1780 and again in 1785 and 1786. As the president of the Continental Congress from 1775 to 1777, Hancock was the first person to sign the Declaration of Independence. He later served as governor of Massachusetts from 1780 to 1785 and again from 1787 until his death in 1793.

Howe, Sir William (1729–1814): Sir William Howe was a British general who served as commander of the British army in North America during the early years of the American Revolution. He led the British in their successful efforts to capture New York City in 1776 and occupy Philadelphia in 1777. He was replaced by Sir Henry Clinton in 1778 following the loss at Saratoga.

Hudson, Barzillai (1741–1823): Trained as a stonemason, Barzillai Hudson married his next-door neighbor, Hannah Watson, following the deaths of both their spouses. He took over her half of the printing business in partnership with George Goodwin. Hudson concentrated on the business end of the operation, leaving the actual printing to Goodwin. The business was very successful. The partnership ended in 1815 when Hudson retired.

Jay, John (1745–1829): A native of New York, John Jay served in a variety of capacities during the Revolution and afterward. He was a member of the Continental Congress for several terms during the 1770s, serving as its president from 1777 to 1778. He also served as minister to Spain in 1779 and helped negotiate the peace treaty with Great Britain in 1782. He joined with Alexander Hamilton and James Madison in writing *The Federalist Papers* to explain the proposed Constitution for governing the United States. He served as the first chief justice of the Supreme Court from 1789 to 1795. He negotiated Jay's Treaty with Great Britain in 1794–1795. This treaty was unpopular with many Americans, but it did serve to settle a number of outstanding disputes. Jay's last public service was as governor of New York from 1795 to 1801, at which time he retired from public office.

Jefferson, Thomas (1743–1826): Thomas Jefferson, a planter from Virginia, became involved in the opposition to Great Britain in 1769 and helped organize protests from that point on. In 1774 he wrote *A Summary View of the Rights of British America,* a widely read pamphlet opposing the actions of the mother country. While serving in the Continental Congress in 1776, he wrote the Declaration of Independence that was adopted on July 4. He later served as ambassador to France from 1785 to 1789, and then as the secretary of state from 1790 to 1793. His final public service was as president from 1801 to 1809. While in office, he orchestrated the purchase of the Louisiana Territory from France in 1803, and dispatched the Lewis and Clark Expedition to explore the new territory. Jefferson died at Monticello, his plantation home in western Virginia, on July 4, 1826, the 50th anniversary of the adoption of the Declaration of Independence.

Jones, John Paul (1747–1792): Originally from Scotland, John Paul Jones first served in the British merchant marine before immigrating to Virginia in 1773. He entered the Continental Navy when the Revolution began and successfully raided along the British coast in 1778 and 1779. His most famous engagement occurred on September 23, 1779, when his ship, the *Bonhomme Richard,* successfully defeated the British ship *Serapis.* Jones supposedly stated in this battle, "I have not yet begun to fight." Following the Revolution, Jones served in the Russian navy on the Black Sea from 1788 to 1789 and in Paris from 1790 until his death in 1792.

Moody, Eleazar (?–1720): Boston schoolmaster who published *The School of Good Manners* in 1715.

Pemberton, James (1723–1780): A Quaker merchant and philanthropist, James Pemberton served in the colonial assembly of Pennsylvania. He and 19 other Quakers were deported to Virginia because of their opposition to the war with Great Britain. Following the end of the Revolution, he ceased to engage in politics. He later became involved in efforts against the institution of slavery and served as president of the Pennsylvania Society for Promoting the Abolition of Slavery from 1790 until 1803.

Randolph, Edmund (1753–1813): Edmund Randolph was a lawyer and politician from Virginia who served in a variety of capacities throughout the Revolution and the early years of the United States. He served in the Continental Congress and the Constitutional Convention, proposing the famous Virginia Plan that became the basis for the Constitution. He later refused to sign the Constitution because he thought it was not republican enough, but he later supported its ratification as the best alternative available. He served as U.S. attorney general from 1789 to 1794 and as secretary of state from 1794 to 1795.

Randolph, Thomas Mann (1768–1828): A planter from Albermarle County, Virginia, Thomas Mann Randolph married Thomas Jefferson's daughter Martha, on February 23, 1790. Randolph served in both state and national politics throughout his career. He and his wife had 12 children.

Rawle, Francis (1729–1761): Only child of William and Margaret (Hodge) Rawle. Well-educated, he went on an extensive trip to Europe in 1755. He married Rebecca Warner in December 1756. He died on June 7, 1761, after he accidentally shot himself while hunting at his country seat.

Riedesel, Friedrich Adolf (1738–1800): A German nobleman, Friedrich Adolf Riedesel commanded a regiment of soldiers who fought with the British during the American Revolution. His primary service occurred at the Battle of Saratoga, where he was captured. He was imprisoned in Virginia until 1781, when he left the country and went to Canada. He returned to Europe in 1783, serving in the army until 1793 and then as commandant of the city of Braunschweig until his death in 1800.

Shoemaker, Mrs. Rebecca Rawle (1734–1819): Mother of Anna Rawle, who married Samuel Shoemaker following the death of her first husband, Francis Rawle. Because Rebecca and her family were Loyalists, she lost all the family property when it was seized during the Revolution. This included Laurel Hill, the family country home. She was able to regain Laurel Hill in 1784, following the end of the war.

Shoemaker, Samuel (?–1800): A Loyalist who was very involved in Philadelphia politics, Samuel Shoemaker served first as the city treasurer and on the board of aldermen before becoming mayor in 1769. He later served as the acting mayor of Philadelphia during the British occupation. He was declared guilty of treason by the Pennsylvania Assembly in 1778, and all his property was seized. He moved to New York following the British withdrawal.

Simpson, Thomas (ca. 1728–1784): Thomas Simpson was a native of New Hampshire and the brother-in-law of the shipbuilder John Langdon. Simpson served as first lieutenant of the *Ranger* (a ship built by Langdon) under the command of Captain John Paul Jones. Jones had Simpson arrested for disobedience, but the charges were later dropped. Simpson took command of the *Ranger* in 1778 when Jones became the commander of the *Bonhomme Richard.*

Smith, Cotton Mather (1731–1806): Cotton Mather Smith attended Yale University and graduated in 1751. He was licensed to preach in 1753. He pastored the Congregational Church in Sharon, Connecticut, from 1755 until his death in 1806. He had a good reputation for being an effective preacher and delivered more than 4,000 public discourses during his ministry.

Stiles, Ezra (1727–1795): Ezra Stiles was a clergyman from Connecticut who began his career as the pastor of the Second Congregational Church in Newport, Rhode Island. He actively served in that post from 1775 to 1776 and in absentia from 1776 to 1786. He was greatly involved in the founding of Brown University in Rhode Island in 1764 and served as professor and president of Yale University from 1778 until his death in 1795.

von Ossig, Caspar Schwenkfeld (1489–1561): Caspar Schwenkfeld von Ossig was a German theologian and preacher who led the Protestant Reformation in Silesia. He experienced a spiritual awakening in 1518. He later tried to reconcile some of the differences between the Lutherans and Roman Catholics in Germany, but his efforts proved unsuccessful. He called for religious liberty in Germany, but he became a religious fugitive when neither side would listen to his arguments. He went into hiding in 1540 and spent the rest of his life moving around to avoid arrest.

Washington, George (1732–1799): Possibly the most famous American to ever live, George Washington served as the commander in chief of the Continental Army during the American Revolution and as the first president of the United States from 1789 to 1797. He gained his first military experience as a commander during the French and Indian War. He later served in the Virginia House of Burgesses from 1759 to 1774 and in the Continental Congress from 1774 to 1775. He also presided over the Convention that met in Philadelphia in the summer of 1787 to draw up the Constitution. Washington is the only president chosen unanimously by the electoral college.

Watson, Ebenezer (1744–1777): Ebenezer Watson was a printer in Hartford, Connecticut. He originally partnered with Thomas Green, who later moved to New Haven, Connecticut, and left Watson the business in Hartford. Watson edited the *Connecticut Courant* from 1768 until his death from smallpox in 1777.

Watson, Hannah Bunce (1749–1807): Hannah Bunce Watson was the second wife of Ebenezer Watson. When he died in 1777, she took control of the printing business and continued to publish the *Connecticut Courant,* using its pages to support the war effort against the British. Hannah Watson married Barzillai Hudson on February 11, 1779, and he soon took over her share of the printing business.

APPENDIX 2: GLOSSARY OF TERMS MENTIONED IN THE TEXT

Articles of Confederation: document that established the first government of the United States. Proposed by the Continental Congress in 1777, it was finally approved by the 13 states in 1781. It remained in effect until 1789 when the new government created by the Constitution took effect.

Congregational Church: religious organization that grew out of the Puritan settlements in Massachusetts. The Congregational Church dominated Massachusetts from the mid-1600s until the early 1800s.

Constitution: document that established the permanent government of the United States. Written during the summer of 1787, it was adopted in 1788 and took effect in 1789.

Constitutional Convention: group that met from May until September 1787 in Philadelphia to write the Constitution.

Continental Army: army created by the Continental Congress in May 1776 to fight the British in the American Revolution.

Continental Congress: body that governed the United States during the conflict with Great Britain. The First Continental Congress met in Philadelphia in 1774. The Second Continental Congress met from 1775 to 1781, primarily in Philadelphia.

Cowpox: mild eruptive disease of cattle that protects against smallpox when communicated to humans through vaccination or natural inoculation.

Declaration of Independence: document adopted by the Second Continental Congress on July 4, 1776, to explain why the colonies had decided to revolt against Great Britain.

Fire Wardens: men appointed to patrol city streets at night in order to give the alarm if a fire broke out.

Great Awakening: religious revival in the American colonies that began in the 1730s and peaked in the 1740s when the evangelist George Whitefield traveled throughout the colonies, preaching to thousands.

Inflation: growth in the amount of money and credit in relation to available goods, resulting in a rise in the general price level.

Inoculation: injection of serum or vaccine to provide protection against a disease.

Loyalists: name taken by American colonists who remained loyal to Great Britain during the Revolution. The revolutionaries called them Tories.

Middle Temple: one of the four colleges in London for training lawyers in the 18th century.

Militia: army composed of citizens called out in time of emergency.

Patriots: name taken by the American colonists who revolted against Great Britain during the Revolutionary War.

Pennsylvania Society for the Abolition of Slavery: first anti-slavery society formed in America. The society was founded in Philadelphia by a group made up primarily of Quakers.

Quaker: popular name for a member of the Society of Friends, a religious organization founded in England in the 1650s. The colony of Pennsylvania was founded by William Penn in 1681 as a haven for Quakers seeking escape from persecution.

Sappers and Miners: men specially trained to dig trenches and tunnels in order to safely approach and undermine enemy defenses in wartime.

Smallpox: acute, contagious disease caused by a virus and characterized by fever and pus-filled blisters.

Spinning Jenny: early machine for spinning wool and cotton by means of many spindles.

Thirteenth Amendment: Constitutional amendment ending the institution of slavery. It was passed by Congress in January 1865 and ratified by the required number of states on December 18, 1865.

Typhoid Fever: acute infectious disease acquired by ingesting contaminated food or water, and characterized by fever and intestinal disorders.

Water Frame: spinning machine powered by a watermill.

Yellow Fever: infectious tropical disease caused by a virus transmitted by the bite of a mosquito.

BIBLIOGRAPHY

PRINTED WORKS

Akers, Charles W. *Abigail Adams: An American Woman*. Boston: Little, Brown, 1980.

Allen, Gardner W. *A Naval History of the American Revolution*. Williamstown, MA: Corner House, 1970.

Applebaum, Herbert. *Colonial Americans at Work*. Lanham, NY: University Press of America, 1996.

Atwood, Rodney. *The Hessians: Mercenaries from Hesse-Kassel in the American Revolution*. New York: Cambridge University Press, 1980.

Backman, Jules A. *Business in the American Economy, 1776–2001*. New York: New York University Press, 1976.

Bailyn, Bernard. *The Ideological Origins of the American Revolution*. Cambridge, MA: The Belknap Press of Harvard University Press, 1967.

Bailyn, Bernard, and John B. Hench, eds. *The Press and the American Revolution*. Worcester, MA: Northeastern University Press, 1980.

Becker, R. B. *Dairy Cattle Breeds: Origins and Development*. Gainesville: University of Florida Press, 1973.

Berkin, Carol. *Revolutionary Mothers: Women in the Struggle for America's Independence*. New York: Alfred A. Knopf, 2005.

Berlin, Ira, and Ronald Hoffman. *Slavery and Freedom in the Age of the American Revolution*. Charlottesville: University of Virginia Press, 1983.

Bloch, Ruth H. *Gender and Morality in Anglo-American Culture, 1650–1800*. Berkeley: University of California Press, 2003.

Bowen, Catherine Drinker. *John Adams and the American Revolution*. Boston: Little, Brown, 1950.

Bridenbaugh, Carl. *The Colonial Craftsman*. Chicago: University of Chicago Press, 1950.

Bridenbaugh, Carl. *Mitre and Sceptre: Transatlantic Faiths, Ideas, Personalities, and Politics: 1689–1775*. New York: Oxford University Press, 1962.

Brown, Jared. *The Theatre in America during the Revolution*. New York: Cambridge University Press, 1995.

Buel, Richard. *Dear Liberty: Connecticut's Mobilization for the Revolutionary War*. Middletown, CT: Wesleyan University Press, 1980.

Busch, Noel Fairchild. *Winter Quarters: George Washington and the Continental Army at Valley Forge.* New York: Liveright, 1974.

Calhoon, Robert M. *The Loyalists in Revolutionary America, 1760–1781.* New York: Harcourt Brace Jovanovich, 1973.

Callahan, North. *Royal Raiders: The Tories of the American Revolution.* New York: Bobbs-Merrill, 1963.

Calloway, Colin G. *The American Revolution in Indian Country: Crisis and Diversity in Native American Communities.* Cambridge: Cambridge University Press, 1999.

Carlson, Laurie M. *Cattle: An Informal Social History.* Chicago: Ivan R. Dee, 2001.

Carr, Jacqueline Barbara. *After the Siege: A Social History of Boston.* Boston: Northeastern University Press, 2005.

Conforti, Joseph A. *Samuel Hopkins and the New Divinity Movement: Calvinism, the Congregational Ministry, and Reform in New England between the Great Awakenings.* Grand Rapids, MI: Christian University Press, 1981.

Cooper, James F. *Tenacious of Their Liberties: The Congregationalists in Colonial Massachusetts.* New York: Oxford University Press, 1999.

Copeland, David. *Colonial American Newspapers: Character and Content.* Newark: University of Delaware Press, 1997.

Cox, Elbert, and Russell Baker. *Winter Encampments of the Revolution.* Washington, DC: United States Department of the Interior, National Park Service, 1941.

Cremin, Lawrence. *American Education: The Colonial Experience, 1607–1783.* New York: Harper & Row, 1970.

Criss, Mildred. *Jefferson's Daughter.* New York: Dodd, Mead, 1948.

Crow, Jeffrey J. *The Southern Experience in the American Revolution.* Chapel Hill: University of North Carolina Press, 1978.

Cuneo, John R. *The Battles of Saratoga: The Turning of the Tide.* New York: Macmillan, 1967.

Curry, Thomas J. *The First Freedoms: Church and State in America to the Passage of the First Amendment.* New York: Oxford University Press, 1986.

Davis, David Brion. *The Problem of Slavery in the Age of Revolution.* Ithaca, NY: Cornell University Press, 1975.

Derles, Scott, and Tony Smith. *Working Americans, 1770–1869, from the Revolutionary War to the Civil War.* Millerton, NY: Grey House Publishing, 2008.

Dunlap, William. *History of the American Theatre.* New York: Burt Franklin, 1963.

Ellet, Elizabeth Fries. *Revolutionary Women in the War for American Independence: A One-Volume Revised Edition.* Westport, CT: Greenwood Publishing Group, 1998.

Evans, Elizabeth. *Weathering the Storm: Women of the American Revolution.* New York: Paragon House, 1975.

Fea, John. *The Way of Improvement Leads Home: Philip Vickers Fithian and the Rural Enlightenment in Early America.* Philadelphia: University of Pennsylvania Press, 2008.

Fenn, Elizabeth A. *Pox Americana: The Great Smallpox Epidemic of 1775–1782.* New York: Hill and Wang, 2001.

Fleming, Thomas. *The Battle of Yorktown.* New York: American Heritage Publications, 1968.

Fortson, S. Donald. *The Presbyterian Creed: A Confessional Tradition in America, 1729–1870.* Eugene, OR: Wipf and Stock, 2009.

Fowler, William M. Jr. *Rebels under Sail: The American Navy during the American Revolution.* New York: Scribner's, 1976.

Franklin, Benjamin. *The Autobiography of Benjamin Franklin.* Ed. Leonard W. Labaree. New Haven, CT: Yale University Press, 1964.

Franklin, John Hope. *Runaway Slaves: Rebels on the Plantation.* New York: Oxford University Press, 1999.

Frothingham, Richard. *History of the Siege of Boston and the Battles of Lexington, Concord, and Bunker Hill.* New York: Da Capo Press, 1970 (1903).

Furneaux, Rupert. *The Battle of Saratoga.* New York: Stern and Day, 1971.

Gelles, Edith B. *Portia: The World of Abigail Adams.* Bloomington: Indiana University Press, 1992.

Gerb, George Winthrop. *A History of Philadelphia, 1776–1789.* Madison: University of Wisconsin Press, 1973.

Golway, Terry. *Washington's General: Nathaniel Greene and the Triumph of the American Revolution.* New York: H. Holt, 2005.

Graymont, Barbara. *The Iroquois in the American Revolution.* Syracuse, NY: Syracuse University Press, 1972.

Haworth, Stephen. *To Shining Sea: A History of the United States Navy, 1775–1991.* New York: Random House, 1991.

Heimert, Alan. *Religion and the American Mind: From the Great Awakening to the Revolution.* Cambridge, MA: Harvard University Press, 1966.

Herndon, Ruth Wallis, and John E. Murray. *Children Bound to Labor: The Pauper System in Early America.* Ithaca, NY: Cornell University Press, 2009.

Hodges, Graham Russell. *Slavery, Freedom and Culture among Early American Workers.* Armonk, NY: M. E. Sharpe, 1998.

Hoffer, Peter Charles. *Seven Fires: The Urban Infernos That Reshaped America.* New York: Public Affairs, 2006.

Hoffman, Ronald. *An Uncivil War: The Southern Backcountry during the American Revolution.* Charlottesville: Published for the U.S. Capitol Historical Society by the University of Virginia Press, 1985.

Hoffman, Ronald. *Women in the Age of the American Revolution.* Charlottesville: Published for the U.S. Capitol Historical Society by the University of Virginia Press, 1989.

Hoffman, Ronald, Mechal Sobel, and Fredrika J. Teute. *Through a Glass Darkly: Reflections on Personal Identity in Early America.* Chapel Hill: Published for the Institute of Early American History and Culture by the University of North Carolina Press, 1977.

Hume, Janice. *Obituaries in American Culture.* Jackson: University Press of Mississippi, 2000.

Hunter, Dard. *Papermaking: The History and Technique of an Ancient Craft.* New York: A. A. Knopf, 1943.

Hurt, R. Douglas. *American Agriculture: A Brief History.* Ames: Iowa State University, 2002.

Hurt, R. Douglas. *The Ohio Frontier: Crucible of the Old Northwest, 1720–1830.* Bloomington: Indiana University Press, 1996.

Hutson, James A. *Logistics of Liberty: American Services of Supply in the Revolutionary War and After.* Newark: University of Delaware Press, 1991.

Isaacson, Walter. *Benjamin Franklin: An American Life.* New York: Simon & Shuster, 2003.

Jackson, John W. *With the British Army in Philadelphia.* San Rafael, CA: Presidio Press, 1979.

Jernegan, Marcus Wilson. *Laboring and Dependent Classes in Colonial America, 1607–1783.* New York: Ungar, 1960.

Kann, Mark E. *The Gendering of American Politics: Founding Mothers, Founding Fathers, and Political Patriarchs.* Westport, CT: Praeger, 1999.

Kann, Mark E. *A Republic of Men: The American Founders, Gendered Language, and Patriarchal Politics.* New York: New York University Press, 1998.

Kaplan, Sidney, and Emma Nogrady Kaplan. *The Black Presence in the Era of the American Revolution.* Rev. ed. Amherst: University of Massachusetts Press, 1989.

Kerber, Linda K. *Women of the Republic: Intellect and Ideology in Revolutionary America.* Chapel Hill: Published for the Institute of Early American History and Culture by the University of North Carolina Press, 1980.

Kitch, Carolyn L., and Janice Hume. *Journalism in a Culture of Grief.* New York: Routledge, 2008.

Kobre, Sidney. *Development of American Journalism.* Dubuque, IA: William C. Brown Publishing Company, 1923.

Kukla, Jon. *Mr. Jefferson's Women.* New York: Alfred A. Knopf, 2007.

Kulikoff, Allan. *From British Peasants to Colonial American Farmers.* Chapel Hill: University of North Carolina Press, 2000.

Langhorne, Elizabeth. *Monticello: A Family Story.* Chapel Hill, NC: Algonquin Books, 1987.

Levin, Phyllis Lee. *Abigail Adams: A Biography.* New York: St. Martin's Press, 1987.

Londré, Felicia Hardison, and Daniel J. Watermeier. *The History of North American Theater.* New York: Continuum, 1998.

Lovejoy, David S. *Samuel Hopkins: Religion, Slavery, and the Revolution.* Philadelphia: United Church Press, 1976.

Lowell, Edward J. *The Hessians and the Other German Auxiliaries of Great Britain in the Revolutionary War.* Williamstown, MA: Corner House, 1970 (reprint 1884 ed.).

MacLeod, Duncan J. *Slavery, Race, and the American Revolution.* Cambridge: Cambridge University Press, 1975.

Malone, Dumas. *Jefferson and His Time.* 6 vols. Boston: Little, Brown, and Company, 1948–1981.

Martin, David G. *The Philadelphia Campaign, June 1777–1778.* Conshohocken, PA: Combined Books, 1993.

Martin, Joseph Plumb, *Memoir of a Revolutionary Soldier.* Mineola, NY: Dover Publications, 2006.

Mays, Dorothy A. *Women in Early America: Struggle, Survival, and Freedom in a New World.* Santa Barbara, CA: ABC-CLIO, 2004.

McCullough, David. *John Adams.* New York: Simon & Schuster, 2001.

McDonald, Forrest. *Alexander Hamilton: A Biography.* New York: W. W. Norton, 1979.

McLean, David. *Timothy Pickering and the Age of the American Revolution.* New York: Arno Press, 1982.

McNulty, Bard. *Older Than the Nation: The Story of the* Hartford Courant. Stonington, CT: Pequot Press, 1964.

Miller, Nathan. *Sea of Glory: A Naval History of the American Revolution.* Annapolis: Naval Institute Press, 1974.

Monaghan, E. Jennifer. *Learning to Read and Write in Colonial America.* Amherst: University of Massachusetts Press, 2007.

Morgan, Edmund S. *American Slavery, American Freedom.* New York: Oxford University Press, 1975.

Morgan, Edmund S. *Benjamin Franklin*. New Haven, CT: Yale University Press, 2002.

Morton, Louis. *Robert Carter of Nomini Hall, a Virginia Planter of the 18th Century*. Williamsburg, VA: Colonial Williamsburg, 1941.

Murphy, Lamar Riley. *Enter the Physician: The Transformation of Domestic Medicine, 1760–1860*. Tuscaloosa: University of Alabama Press, 1991.

Nash, Gary B. *Freedom and Revolution*. Madison: University of Wisconsin Press, 1991.

Nelson, William H. *The American Tory*. Oxford: Clarendon Press, 1961.

Nettels, Curtis Putnam. *The Emergence of a National Economy*. New York: Holt, Rinehart and Winston, 1962.

Noll, Mark A. *America's God: From Jonathan Edwards to Abraham Lincoln*. New York: Oxford University Press, 2002.

Noll, Mark A. *Christians in the American Revolution*. Washington, DC: Christian University Press, 1977.

Norton, Mary Beth. *Liberty's Daughters: The Revolutionary Experience of American Women, 1750–1800*. Boston: Little, Brown and Company, 1980.

Nosworthy, Brent. *The Anatomy of Victory: Battle Tactics, 1689–1763*. New York: Hippocrene Books, 1990.

Oswald, John Clyde. *Printing in the Americas*. New York: The Gregg Publishing Company, 1937.

Pangle, Lorraine Smith. *The Learning of Liberty: The Educational Ideas of the American Founders*. Lawrence: University Press of Kansas, 1993.

Perica, Esther. *The American Woman: Her Role during the American Revolution*. Monroe, NY: Library Research Associates, 1981.

Perkins, Edwin J. *The Economy of Colonial America*. New York: Columbia University Press, 1980.

Peterson, Merrill D. *Thomas Jefferson and the New Nation: A Biography*. New York: Oxford University Press, 1970.

Piepkorn, Arthur Carl. *Profiles in Belief: The Religious Bodies of the United States and Canada*. 4 vols. New York: Harper & Row, 1977–1979.

Pybus, Cassandra. *Epic Journeys of Freedom: Runaway Slaves of the American Revolution and Their Global Quest for Liberty*. Boston: Beacon Press, 2006.

Quarles, Benjamin. *The Negro in the American Revolution*. Chapel Hill: University of North Carolina Press, 1961.

Randall, Willard Sterne. *Alexander Hamilton: A Life*. New York: Harper Collins, 2003.

Randall, Willard Sterne. *A Little Revenge: Benjamin Franklin and His Son*. Boston, MA: Little, Brown, and Company, 1984.

Rankin, Hugh F. *The Theater in Colonial America*. Chapel Hill: University of North Carolina Press, 1960.

Raphael, Ray. *Founders: The People Who Brought You a Nation*. New York: The New Press, 2009.

Reiss, Oscar. *Medicine and the American Revolution: How Diseases and Their Treatments Affected the Colonial Army*. Jefferson, NC: McFarland and Company, 1998.

Rhoden, Nancy L. *Revolutionary Anglicanism: The Colonial Church of England Clergy during the American Revolution*. New York: New York University Press, 1999.

Roth, David Morris. *From Revolution to Constitution: Connecticut, 1763–1818*. Chester, CT: Pequot Press, 1975.

Salmon, Marylynn. *Women and the Law of Property in Early America*. Chapel Hill: University of North Carolina Press, 1986.

Samuels, Warren J., and Malcolm Rutherford. *The Emergence of a National Economy: The United States from Independence to the Civil War.* Brookfield, VT: Pickering & Chatto, 2004.

Schlebecker, John T. *Whereby We Thrive: A History of American Farming, 1607–1972.* Ames: Iowa State University Press, 1975.

Schloesser, Pauline E. *The Fair Sex: White Women and Racial Patriarchy in the Early American Republic.* New York: New York University Press, 2002.

Schouler, James. *Americans of 1776: Daily Life in Revolutionary America.* Williamstown, MA: Corner House Publishers, 1976 (1906).

Simmons, Dawn Langley. *Mr. Jefferson's Ladies.* Boston: Beacon Press, 1966.

Skemp, Sheila L. *William Franklin: Son of a Patriot, Servant of a King.* New York: Oxford University Press, 1990.

Smith, James Eugene. *One Hundred Years of Hartford's* Courant, *from Colonial Times through the Civil War.* New Haven, CT: Yale University Press, 1949.

Smith, Samuel Stelle. *Winter at Morristown, 1779–1780: The Darkest Hour.* Monmouth Beach, NJ: Philip Freneau Press, 1979.

Stegeman, John F. *Caty: A Biography of Catherine Littlefield Greene.* Providence, RI: Bicentennial Foundation, 1977.

Stephenson, Michael. *Patriot Battles: How the War of Independence Was Fought.* New York: Harper Collins, 2007.

Taylor, Alan. *The Divided Ground: Indians, Settlers, and the Northern Borderland of the American Revolution.* New York: Alfred A. Knopf, 2006.

Thane, Elswyth. *The Fighting Quaker: Nathaniel Greene.* New York: Hawthorn Books, 1972.

Thayer, Theodore. *Nathaniel Greene: Strategist of the American Revolution.* New York: Twayne Publishers, 1960.

Thomas, Isaiah. *The History of Printing in America.* Worcester, MA: Isaiah Thomas, Jr., 1810. Reprint ed. Ed. Marcus A. McCorison. Barre, MA: Imprint Society, 1970.

Toledo-Pereyra, Luis H. *A History of American Medicine from the Colonial Period to the Early 20th Century.* Lewiston, NY: Edwin Mellen Press, 2006.

Treacy, M. F. *Prelude to Yorktown: The Southern Campaign of Nathaniel Greene, 1780–1781.* Chapel Hill: University of North Carolina Press, 1963.

Tuchman, Barbara. *The First Salute.* New York: Alfred A. Knopf, 1988.

Tybus, Edward. *Colonial Craftsmen and the Beginnings of American Industry.* Baltimore, MD: Johns Hopkins University Press, 1965.

Unger, Harlow G. *John Hancock: Merchant King and American Patriot.* New York: John Wiley and Sons, 2000.

Van Every, Dale. *A Company of Heroes: The American Frontier, 1775–1783.* New York: Morrow, 1962.

Volo, Dorothy Denneen, and James M. Volo. *Daily Life during the American Revolution.* Westport, CT: Greenwood Press, 2003.

Walker, Williston. *A History of the Congregational Churches in the United States.* New York: The Christian Literature Company, 1894.

Washington, George. *Rules of Civility.* Ed Richard Brookhiser. Charlottesville: University of Virginia Press, 2003.

Weeks, Lyman Horace. *A History of Paper-Manufacturing in the United States, 1690–1916.* New York: The Lockwood Trade Journal Company, 1916.

Wilbur, C. Keith. *Home Building and Woodworking in Colonial America.* Old Saybrook, CT: Globe Pequot Press, 1992.

Wilbur, C. Keith. *Revolutionary Medicine, 1700–1800*. Chester, CT: Globe Pequot Press, 1980.

Williamson, Harold F. *The Growth of the American Economy*. New York: Prentice-Hall, 1944.

Wilson, David. *The Southern Strategy*. Columbia: University of South Carolina Press, 2005.

Withey, Lynne. *Dearest Friend: A Life of Abigail Adams*. New York: Free Press, 1981.

Wood, Gordon S. *The Americanization of Benjamin Franklin*. New York: Penguin Press, 2002.

Wrong, George M. *Canada and the American Revolution: The Disruption of the First British Empire*. New York: MacMillan Company, 1935.

Wroth, Lawrence C. *The Colonial Printer*. Portland, ME: The Southworth-Anthoensen Press, 1938.

Zilversmit, Arthur. *The First Emancipation: The Abolition of Slavery in the North*. Chicago: University of Chicago Press, 1967.

Zimmer, Anne Y. *Jonathan Boucher, Loyalist in Exile*. Detroit: Wayne State University Press, 1978.

FILM AND TELEVISION

The Adams Chronicles, television mini-series, 1976.

Alexander Hamilton, PBS, 2007.

American Experience: John and Abigail Adams, PBS, 2005.

The American Revolution, television mini-series, 1994.

Benjamin Franklin, PBS, 2002.

Benjamin Franklin, television mini-series, 1974.

Biography: Benjamin Franklin: Citizen of the World, PBS, 2006.

Biography: John and Abigail Adams, PBS, 2005.

Early American Textiles, filmstrip, Washington, DC: The Lab, 1975.

John Adams, television mini-series, 2008.

Liberty! The American Revolution, television mini-series, 1997.

Liberty's Kids, television series, 2002–2003.

Morristown: Where America Survived, New Jersey Public Television and Radio, 2009.

The Patriot, film, 2000.

Thomas Jefferson: A Film by Ken Burns, television mini-series, 1996.

WEB SITES

Abigail Adams Biography: http://www.firstladies.org/biographies/firstladies.aspx?biography=2

Adams Resources at the Massachusetts Historical Society: http:/www.masshist.org/adams

African American Experience: http://www.history.org/Almanack/people/african

African Americans and the End of Slavery in Massachusetts: http://www.masshist.org/endofslaveryAmerican Loyalists: http://www.redcoat.me.uk

The American Revolution: http://www.nps.gov/revwar

American Theatre History: http://www.theatrehistory.com/american

The Autobiography of Benjamin Franklin: http://www.earlyamerica.com/lives/franklin

Benjamin Franklin: Glimpses of the Man: http://www.pbs.org/benfranklin

Boston in 1775: http://www.Boston1775.blogspot.com

Brieg, James. "Early American Newspapering." *Colonial Williamsburg Journal:* http://www.history.org/foundation/journal/Spring03/journalism.cfm

Central Schwenkfelder Church: http://www.centralschwenkfelder.com

Clothing: http://www.history.org/history/clothing/intro/clothing.cfm

Early America Digital Library: http://www.earlyamerica.com

The Electric Benjamin Franklin: http://www.ushistory.org/franklin/index.htm

Events of the American Revolution: http://www.historyplace.com/unitedstates/revolution

George Washington's *Rules of Civility:* http://www.history.org/Almanack/life/manners/rules2.cfm

Growing a Nation: The Story of American Agriculture: http://www.agclassroom.org/gan/index.htm

The Hessians: http://www.americanrevolution.org/hessians/hessindex.html

History of the Moravian Church: http://www.moravian.org/history

History of Philadelphia: http://www.ushistory.org/philadelphia/index.html

History of the Quartermaster Corps: http://www.qmfound.com/history.html

A History of Social Dance in America: http://www.americanantiquarian.org/Exhibitions/Dance

John Adams: http://www.hbo.com/john-adams

Kriebel, Martha B. The Schwenkfelders: http://www.ucc.org/about-us/hidden-histories/the-schwenkfelders.html

Liberty! The American Revolution: http://www.pbs.org/ktca/liberty

Medicine in the Americas, 1610–1914: A Digital Library: http://www.nlm.nih.gov/hmd/americas/americashome.html

Myth and Reality in 18th-Century Agriculture or What 18th-Century Farming is Not!: http://www.history.org/history/teaching/enewsletter/volume2/april04/mythandreality.cfm

The On-Line Institute for Advanced Loyalist Studies: http://www.royalprovincial.com

Parker, Keith W. The Involvement of "The Ladies": Economic Support of Women During the American Revolution. http://www.earlyamerica.com/review/2006_summer_fall/women-revolution.html

Paterson, Richard. What Was a Hessian? http://www.ushistory.org/WASHINGTON CROSSING/history/hessian.htm

Printing Trade: http://www.history.org/Almanack/life/trades/tradehdr.cfm

Quock Walker Case: Africans in America: http://www.pbs.org/wgbh/aia/part2/2h38.html

Religion and the Founding of the American Republic: Religion and the American Revolution: http://www.loc.gov/exhibits/religion/rel03.html

Rieldel, Stefan. Edward Jenner and the History of Smallpox and Vaccination: http://www.ncbi.nlm.nih.gov/sites/ppmc/articles/PMC1200696

Rural Trades: http://www.history.org/Almanack/life/trades/tradehdr.cfm

Schwenkfelder Library and Heritage Center: http://www.schwenkfelder.com

Thomas Jefferson Digital Archives: http://etext.virginia.edu/jefferson

The Thomas Jefferson Papers at the Library of Congress: http://memory.loc.gov/ammem/collections/jefferson_papers

Thomas Jefferson's Monticello: http://www.monticello.orgTimothy Pickering as Quartermaster General: http://www.qmfound.com/COL_Timothy_Pickering.htm

Timothy Pickering as Secretary of State: http://history.state.gov/departmenthistory/people/ pickering-timothy

Trades of Milliners and Weavers: http://www.history.org/Almanack/life/trades/tradehdr.cfm

United Empire Loyalists' Association of Canada: http://www.uelac.org

Washburn, Wilcomb E. Indians and the American Revolution: http://www.americanrevo lution.org/ind1.html

INDEX